REMAKING MEN

Jung, Spirituality and Social Change

David J. Tacey

London and New York

First published 1997
by Routledge
11 New Fetter Lane, London EC4P 4EE

Simultaneously published in the USA and Canada
by Routledge
29 West 35th Street, New York, NY 10001

Typeset in Times by Routledge
Printed and bound in Great Britain by
Clays Ltd, St Ives PLC

British Library Cataloguing in Publication Data
A catalogue record for this book is available from the British
Library

Library of Congress Cataloguing in Publication Data
A catalogue record for this book has been requested

ISBN 0–415–14240–7 (hbk)
ISBN 0–415–14241–5 (pbk)

REMAKING MEN

Masculinity is discussed by contemporary authors either in socio-political terms or in popular writing that concentrates on Jungian mythopoetics and spirituality. The outward-looking, sociological standpoint ignores the spiritual view; the inward-looking spiritual tradition disregards historical context and the conditioning of society.

In *Remaking Men: Jung, Spirituality and Social Change*, David Tacey achieves a new synthesis of these two traditions, examining his own and other men's experience with both spiritual and political insight. He is critical of the way popular, conservative discourse on masculinity has appropriated and distorted Jungian psychology, and believes that political, antisexist and historical considerations should be brought into discussions about the inner world.

From this radical standpoint, Tacey addresses such topics as father-absence, homoerotic desire and the dilemmas of feminine men – the autobiographical element adding sensibility to his scholarly and engaging discourse. This is a captivating treatment of masculinity that will break new ground for the men's movement.

David J. Tacey teaches Jungian and Psychoanalytic Studies at La Trobe University, Melbourne, where he is also Senior Lecturer in Literature. He is the author of *Patrick White: Fiction and the Unconscious* (1988), *Edge of the Sacred: Transformation in Australia* (1995), and numerous essays and articles on Jungian thought, cultural studies and men's issues.

CONTENTS

counter spiritual sweetness; refusing the popular idealisation of the archetypal father; the death of God: the
religious dimension of father-absence; the Hamlet
complex and beyond: to thine own self be true

the symbolic realm of the mother-image; liberation in a
new key; modern men, the dragon fight, and domestic
violence; fusion with the mother, separation, and return;
the mother-bond, spirituality, and change: a personal
account; the popular discourses about soft men;
protesting too much: from wimps to warriors; oppositional mythopoetics: Bly and Hillman; Robert Bly,
tribal elder; return to the mother as a path of development

time-honoured sexism and initiatory process; 'going
primitive' and the popular idealisation of manhood; the
fathering capacity and negative capability; the authority
of spirit and political authority; toward a spiritual
renaissance; sexuality and adolescence; cynicism, brilliance, and depression; substance-abuse, drugs, alcohol;
risk-taking and suicide; rites of war: a traditional initiation backfires in Vietnam; men (obsessively) at work: the
search for validation; clubs, gangs, buddies; initiation
into what? growing up in a moral and cultural vacuum

psychical bisexuality and the unconscious; political
reality and psychic reality; homophobic mateship;
homoerotic desire in adolescent rites of passage; dreams
of same-sex love and father–son reunion; homophobia
in so-called 'consciousness-raising' men's groups; the
analyst's response to homoerotic material; the heterosexual analysand's response; body, psyche, father

PREFACE

Men and women reflecting on the nature of masculinity is one of the most popular subjects of recent years, and yet I believe there is still more to be said about this topic. In the burgeoning literature on masculinity, there is a widening gulf between the 'critical' writings which seek to destabilise patriarchal masculinity in the name of feminist or politically progressive causes, and the 'popular' writings which seek to promote a new–old masculinity in the name of spirituality, mythopoetics, and Jungian psychology. As a critically-minded academic who is also a Jungian, as a politically-conscious thinker who is also steeped in mythopoetics, I have attempted a book which strives to get these separate traditions talking to each other. I am interested in new fusions such as progressive mythopoetics, self-critical spirituality, and politically-informed Jungianism. The rifts in our culture between spirituality and politics, therapy and society, inner and outer, continually haunt me, and conversations must begin across these rifts and divides.

There must be a growing number of people who are concerned about the fanciful, escapist, and often reactionary nature of the Jung-influenced men's movement. This popular tradition seems to be caught up in a fatuous optimism about the inner world (a kind of spiritual 'cargo cult'), and in conservative and simplistic appropriations of Jungian theory. On the other hand, many students and readers are disappointed by the spiritual hollowness and chronic pessimism of the contemporary academic discourses on masculinity. These discourses ignore or denigrate Jung and his theory of archetypes, and appear incapable of responding to the spiritual and emotional dimensions of men's experience. It is time to bring depth and surface, emotional life and sociopolitical awareness together in a lively discourse that attempts to look inside and outside at the same time.

Some readers may feel that I am misrepresenting the contemporary men's movement by focusing only upon two of its more prominent strands: the profeminist position and Jungian mythopoetics. I realise that the movement per se is much broader and more complex than this – some writers have identified up to a dozen or more different and socially active strands. At times I do refer to other ideological positions, including gay liberation, Marxian radicalism, humanist role-theory liberation, sociobiological conservatives, and the men's rights lobby, but my concern is not to map the entire field, but to focus on the conflict between feminist awareness and masculine mythopoetics. I attempt to compare and contrast these positions, in the hope of creating a synthesis in which these contrary views are held together in dynamic, if at times precarious, balance.

A basic argument of this book is that the feminine archetypal principle requires urgent attention in our hypermasculine culture. This means that we require not only a new politics in the social sphere, but also a new feminine psychology in the in-dwelling soul. For me, part of this psychological reorientation has involved overthrowing old habits of scholarly practice. When I first began to write this book in the early 1990s, I started with the so-called objective pose and the impersonal approach, which is standard in patriarchal scholarship. But as I began to explore the emotional and experiential dimensions of the male psyche, my own emotions and experiences arose as well, and I could no longer bracket out my subjectivity from the scholarly study of contemporary masculinity. In a sense, my own rebellious feminine had interrupted and overturned my conscious masculinist project. After three decades of second-wave feminism(s), we know that the impersonal stance has been a patriarchal construction all along, and that scholarship that now includes the personal standpoint as part of its content is a more authentic and honest kind of scholarship.

The inward soul teaches us that the 'personal is political', that the personal matters. But this has to be handled with tact and poise. It is not that the personal-subjective element can suddenly swamp the intellectual framework, so that we encourage a kind of relentless confessional. It is simply that a personal, experiential element is introduced to complement and transform the intellectual structure, so that the project is kept honest. The fact that I am not a clinician and do not have recourse to the case materials of clients has also forced me to draw on my own experience when story and flesh were needed to adorn the bones of theory. I cannot pose here as a therapist of other people's wounds. This book partly records my own experiences as a client in therapy, and later as both 'therapist' and 'client' in my own self-therapy. This work presents and critiques my psychospiritual development – and I hope that it is a critique and not merely an indulgence of my 'personal growth'. The dynamic interaction of intellect and heart means that the intellect can still critically evaluate what the heart puts forward out of its own passionate and still largely unknown depths.

Throughout this book I draw freely from my experiences as an analysand in the care of Jungian analyst James Hillman. Chapter 5, in particular, is based almost entirely on the homoerotic theme that arose during our analytic sessions. In the United States during the early 1980s, James Hillman provided me with a positive example of how to live a plural life; how to be intellectual, enquiring, and forceful, yet also open to the 'thought of the heart' and the 'logos of the soul'. The paradoxical state of the 'thinking heart' has become foundational to my own life and academic practice, thanks in no small degree to Hillman's analytical involvement. I acknowledge the Harkness Foundation of New York, for its generous funding of my two-year post-doctoral fellowship with Hillman.

At La Trobe University in Melbourne, I am currently Senior Lecturer in Literature and Head of a Freud/Jung programme in Psychocultural Studies. Over the last ten years, I have taught courses on Jung, Hillman, and Samuels in the School of English and Faculty of Humanities. In 1996 I began teaching a specialist graduate course, 'Remaking Men', and I would like to thank my students for their involvement and contributions.

In 1991 I conducted a forum for men only called 'The Post-Patriarchal Male Psyche', and I acknowledge the contributions of the male participants, even if some confessed that they had been pushed to the forum by their female partners! I am especially indebted to Felicity Sloman and Michael Carr-Gregg of the Royal Melbourne Children's Hospital (Centre for Adolescent Health), for encouraging me to present public lectures and seminars on teenage spiritual development, risk-taking, and rites of passage. I am also grateful to: Peter Condliff of the Royal Melbourne Institute of Technology (Social Work), for sponsoring my short course

'Masculinity, Patriarchy, and Psychoanalysis' in 1991; to Merringu Men's Centre, Canberra, for arranging the seminar 'The Male Psyche and Society' in 1993; and to Australian Medical Publications for inviting me to speak on 'The Psychology of Adolescence' in 1994. The media have been interested in my ideas on masculinity from the early 1990s, and I would like to acknowledge the input of numerous journalists from radio (the ABC National network), television (SBS and ABC networks), and newspapers (*Sydney Morning Herald* and *The Age*). Nothing focuses the mind more than a good interview with an intuitive journalist, and these interviews have contributed to the public accessibility of my writings.

I am indebted to Sharon Gregory-Tacey and Ana Gregory-Tacey for inspiration and support. Numerous individuals have made valuable contributions to the content of this work, either in personal discussions, correspondence, critical feedback, or editorial work. These include Ian Austen, Renos Papadopoulos, Andrew Samuels, Peter Tatham, and Edwina Welham in the UK; and John Beebe, Robert Bly, Alfred Collins, William Doty, Robert Hopcke, Harold Schechter, and James Wyly in the USA. In Australia I would like to thank Sue Austin, David Bathgate, Giles Clark, Bob Connell, Trish Dutton, Robert Farrell, Andrew Fuller, Peter Fullerton, Robert Hall, Jack Heath, Andre de Koning, Michael Leunig, Roman Mankowski, Michele Stephen, and Robert Ware. I am grateful to Bob Pease of RMIT for inviting me to read his doctoral thesis, 'Becoming Profeminist: Reforming Men's Subjectivities and Practices' (1996), which brought me up to date in sociological, profeminist and postmodern literatures on masculinities.

In the course of preparing this book, work-in-progress was published in various journals and publications, as follows: an early review-essay on masculinity research was published as 'How New is the New Male?', *Australian Society* (Melbourne), Vol. 10, No. 16, June 1991, pp. 33–35; parts of Chapters 1 and 2 were published as 'Lost Sons and God-Talk', *The San Francisco Jung Institute Library Journal*, Vol. 13, No. 3, October 1994, pp. 5–27; sections of Chapter 3 appeared as 'Attacking Patriarchy, Redeeming Masculinity', *The San Francisco Jung Institute Library Journal*, Vol. 10, No. 1, March 1991, pp. 25–41, and an Australian version was published as 'Reconstructing Masculinity: A Post-Jungian Response to Contemporary Men's Issues', *Meanjin* (University of Melbourne), Vol. 49, No. 4, Summer 1990, pp. 781–792; a further part of Chapter 3 appeared as 'Incest, Society, and Transformation: An Australian

Perspective', *Psychological Perspectives* (Los Angeles), Issue 23, November 1990, pp. 16–31; a brief section of Chapter 4 was published as 'The Rites and Wrongs of Passage: Drugs, Gangs, Suicides, Gurus', *Psychotherapy in Australia* (Melbourne), Vol. 1, No. 4, August 1995, pp. 5–12; an earlier version of Chapter 5 appeared as, 'Homoeroticism and Homophobia in Heterosexual Male Initiation', in Robert H. Hopcke, Karin Lofthus Carrington and Scott Wirth (eds) *Same-Sex Love And the Path to Wholeness*, Boston and London: Shambhala, 1993, pp. 246–263. I am grateful to the editors of these Australian and American publications for their careful editing of my material, which has been incorporated in the present book.

David J. Tacey
Faculty of Humanities
La Trobe University
Melbourne, Australia

Will men change without being forced to? Or will men change as part of a larger social change?

Shere Hite[1]

Only by going into the place where the corruption of power and energy is at its worst do we reclaim that power and use it to heal ourselves.

Alix Pirani[2]

We are cured when we are no longer only masculine in psyche, no matter whether we are male or female in biology. Analysis cannot constellate this cure until it, too, is no longer masculine in psychology. The end of analysis coincides with the acceptance of femininity.

James Hillman[3]

In maintaining a privileged position in the patriarchy, men cooperate in an ironic subjugation of themselves.

Tom Absher[4]

POLEMICAL INTRODUCTION
Jungian thought and the post-patriarchal psyche

THE RISING FEMININE

Remaking Men is concerned with change and transformation in masculinity, society, spirituality, and Jungian psychology. This book is probably best placed in an ongoing tradition of writings that sees the feminine archetypal principle rising in our time.[1] The feminine in men and women alike is emerging with new potency, displacing the old patriarchal forms in psyche and society, and demanding an entirely new understanding of social structure, personal identity, and human relationships. I am not just talking about the social impact of political feminism, I am talking about a colossal psycho-spiritual shift in the collective Western psyche, of which political feminism is one major element. Masculinity must not be eroded or washed away by the rising tide of the feminine, but instead 'remade', reconstructed, and allowed to become the intelligent and self-critical partner of the new feminine reformation. The present book is written in a revolutionary spirit, but it will not please all revolutionaries because it argues for balance and integration rather than for the eclipse of masculinity by femininity.

THE DEVOURING FATHER AND JUNGIAN CONSERVATISM

It seems to me that some desperate compensatory mechanism has been triggered in the Western psyche, and that there is an element of real urgency about the return of the feminine. The progressive spirit in society is pushing us toward an 'androgynous' psychological condition, undoubtedly because the unchecked masculine has ruled for so long, and its excesses and desecrations are now painfully

1

apparent to any alert person. We best advance the spirit of the time by admitting the feminine into our lives and hearts, into our social structures and political institutions. But patriarchy is notoriously resistant to change, and in Greek mythology it is well represented by the figure of Chronos-Saturn, the recalcitrant and static ogre who devours his own offspring lest they pose a threat to his hegemonic rule.[2] Direct combat may not be the answer; instead we must, like Zeus acting on Rhea's plan, outwit the tyrant and trick him into releasing all the diverse and plural life-forms – the lost femininities and 'alternative' masculinities – that he has systematically devoured. We are now engaged in a race against time. (And in more than one sense: Greek *chronos* = time.) Will we oppose the Western tyrant before it devours everything? Will we win back feeling, intuition, and soul before patriarchal 'progress' leads us into an irreversible spiritual wasteland? Will we be able to protect the environmental ecology, the biosphere and the very fabric of life on earth, from the ravages of the 'consumer' society? Chronos-Saturn will go on its consuming course, swallowing the feminine and converting all masculinities into a likeness of itself, unless we break the cycle of power, conquest and domination.

Jungian studies in the problem of contemporary masculinity are hardly new. Ever since Robert Bly's *Iron John: A Book About Men*[3] burst upon the international scene, we have witnessed a veritable avalanche of Jungian or pseudo-Jungian texts which attempt to 'solve' the crisis of masculinity. But although this new tradition of 'mythopoetic' writing about men is often insightful, and always alert to the critical situation of contemporary masculinity, I find it largely unsatisfactory. To me, this new tradition is basically reactionary, conservative, and backward-looking. It asks how men can recover their former balance, not how they can discover a new, post-patriarchal equilibrium. It assumes that men must reconnect with masculine archetypes, and it invents terms like the 'Deep Male' and the 'Inner Warrior' to remythologise this new pact with masculinity. But the 'therapeutic' fix-it mentality is in danger of losing sight of the biggest cultural issue of our time: patriarchal masculinity *must* be challenged and displaced by the rising feminine. If men are 'cured' of the crisis, and if Saturn is returned to rule, then we are actually in worse shape, collectively, than ever before. Patriarchy is not merely some abstract entity 'out there'; it has provided the deepest emotional foundations for the construction of traditional masculinity. Men must be allowed to feel the pain of the disintegration of their former props and supports, and the collapse of patriarchy must be genuinely registered in every individual heart. We have too much therapy that wants to numb the pain, heal the wounds, 'initiate' men into outmoded patriarchal constructs, bridge the (necessary) distance that separates sons from fathers. Because of all this 'helpful' therapy and mythopoetic cushioning – Connell calls it 'masculinity therapy', where broken masculinity is dropped off for repair[4] – we are in danger of employing depth psychology to outwit the psyche, and to stifle its important transformations.

In this book I want to build on what Andrew Samuels has already started, namely, a repossession of Jungian theory for progressive, rather than regressive, social and political causes.[5] In the 1970s and 1980s, James Hillman was also working on this progressive project: deconstructing the strong Western ego, deepening psychological pain to its mythological sources, rather than opposing pain with saccharine cures, illusory promises, or fantasies of mandalic 'wholeness'.[6] There is already an important tradition of Jungian writing on masculinity that is politically progressive and intellectually adventurous,[7] but these writings are virtually drowned out by the simplistic and popular Jungian blockbusters. The question we have to pose is this: is Jungian theory to be used to encourage change, or to escape from change? It has long seemed to me that Jung, like Freud, Heidegger, or Nietzsche, can be used either to move ahead with the times or to betray the *zeitgeist* in a nostalgic recovery of the past. In psychoanalytic tradition, we have a Freudian 'Right' and a Freudian 'Left': the first read Freud as a wily and cunning arch-conservative, exploring the unconscious only to recover the norms of a patriarchal society, while the second see the Great Man as a psychological and political revolutionary, a founder of a psychosocial critique that must inevitably change the world.[8] Because of the illusory 'stability' and purported 'timelessness' of the archetypes, Jung has proved attractive to the conservative opponents of change, and the revolutionary possibilities of Jungian theory have been denied.

FATUOUS OPTIMISM AND TRICKS WITH ARCHETYPES

The theory of archetypes is often wheeled out by 'concerned' humanists and therapists who have seen enough social change – and clinical casualties of change – and who want to turn the cultural clock back fifty or even a hundred years, to protect men from the

3

chaos and suffering of modern times. Jungian archetypes are viewed, quite wrongly, as fixed and stable elements embedded in an unchanging eternal mind. Just when the foundations of patriarchy are shaking, and when the potentials for real change are greatest, some Jungians (qualified analysts, as well as others) churn out best-selling texts which promise stable 'archetypes' (read 'stereotypes') of gendered identity:

> As students of human mythology, and as Jungians, we believe there is good news for men. . . . It is our experience that deep within every male are blueprints, what we can also call 'hard wiring', for the calm and positive mature masculine.[9]

In a time of patriarchal disintegration, the external 'positive masculine' forms and figures are not to be found, but we need have no fear, for the 'good news' is that the unconscious, and its so-called 'hard wiring' (a 'real man's' phrase, designed to win the confidence of male readers) will look after us. Although, in this 'time with no father',[10] our own human fathers and father-figures 'may not live up to [our] expectations',[11] there is an ideal, all-nurturing, all-loving Father to be found within ourselves.[12] In popular Jungianism there is a hopelessly unrealistic view of psychological experience. This literature is peddling illusions, and exploiting people's capacities to follow psychological advice. The patriarch-king, Saturn, may be impotent, and his Judeo-Christian counterpart, the jealous Father God (who will have no other Gods before him), may be dead, but new-age messianic Jungianism can promise a new kind of omnipotent Father, and a new version of 'good news for modern man'. The old God took care of us from his vantage point in the heavens, but the new God is down below, imaged as a kind of bearded benevolence in the unconscious.

Popular Jungianism has degenerated into a new-age fantasy system, where everything we lack in society or personal experience is provided by the ever-reliable (and never rusting) 'hard wiring' of the unconscious. Robert Bly, witnessing men turning 'soft' through their contact with the feminine, enjoins men to toughen up by going 'down' into the unconscious and reawakening the so-called Hairy Wildman. Robert Moore and Douglas Gillette, noting that the stereotypical models for men are disintegrating and losing credibility, use the theory of archetypes to convince men that the reliable old models, King, Warrior, Magician, Lover, can be found again in the deep unconscious. Handbooks and manuals (again designed to attract the 'practical' male reader) are produced to lead men into a step-by-step recovery of the broken patriarchal models.[13] Guy Corneau and Alfred Collins, aware of the painful gap between fathers and sons, between old patriarch and rebellious youth, invent new archetypes such as 'Fatherson', and conjure up other Jungian magical tricks, to will all gaps and ruptures away.[14] Gregory Vogt insists that the Lost Son can, if he wants to, return to the bosom of the Great Father.[15] With the power of archetypes, reality can be refashioned, reshaped, to suit the desires of any fantasy agenda.

CONTRARY MOVEMENTS: EMBRACING THE FATHER AND KILLING THE PATRIARCH

According to Robert Bly and the mythopoetic circle, 'What Men Really Want'[16] is to become one with the father and to be 'initiated' into the father's world. They speak about this 'initiation' as the fulfilment of desire, an almost intoxicating sense of belonging and deep reparation. But I read this cheap psychology as anti-psychological; it does not give men what they want at all, but merely caters to their regressive longing for an infantile and unconscious patriarchal paradise, replete with infantile idealisations of the father that any Freudian would immediately recognise. In times of epochal change and transformation, the sons must not simply repeat the traditional pattern and become part of the father's tribe. The sons must strike out anew, rebuild the world and refashion its politics, and the most creative sons of all must 'father' themselves, not simply engage in a conventional 'Return to Father', which only succeeds in propping up the ailing patriarchy. This is a lonely path, a courageous path, and it requires above all that men make a commitment to the creative spirit of the present and the dream of the future, not just to the spirit of the past.

The Jung-influenced popular men's movement would have all men discover that they are 'really' just their own fathers in a new generational form. 'Gee whiz,' say the new graduates of Iron John initiation camps, 'I am simply a younger version of my own Dad'. Then they can go back to sleep, back to patriarchal unconsciousness, feeling considerably better now as 'initiated' men, less stressful, less lonely, and ecstatically linked with dear old Dad. In this way, tyrannical Saturn has triumphed; he has replicated himself again, thus ensuring his continued sovereignty. At the other end of the spectrum, men engaged in the contrary discourse of what is called profeminist men's studies plot ways to overthrow the patriarchy, defeat the father's authority, and render impotent the Devouring Father of our culture. This primarily academic discourse, based in feminism, marxism, and revolutionary fervour, seeks to liberate men by killing off the father.[17] For this intellectual tradition, no father equals freedom; whereas for the mythopoetic tribe, no father equals unbearable isolation and a psychological inferno.

BEYOND IRON JOHN AND OEDIPUS: FINDING A NEW RELATIONSHIP TO THE FEMININE

I have things in common with both traditions, but I am not an advocate of either tradition. My opposition to 'mythopoetics' is already clear: it mistakes nostalgia for creative inspiration, it engages in false idealisations of the father, and its gaze is obsessively personal, inward, and backward – and very often homophobic as well. On the other hand, I find academic men's studies tinged with Oedipal colourings. There is too much emphasis on direct confrontation, 'revolutionary violence', and on *murdering* the father, rather than on tricking him or displacing his authority. In the mythic pattern I am interested in, Saturn is not assassinated, but simply 'stripped of his authority' 'by Zeus's force and deceitful cunning'.[18] Too many academic radicals want to kill the father – and what then? When the father is killed, we find that we unconsciously return to mother, to infantilism, satiety and self-destruction in the false paradise of the maternal source. The 'defence of the feminine' in much so-called profeminist men's studies is actually an unconscious idealisation of the mother and an identification with her archetypal world. In some profeminist writings, the penis is linked with rape, manhood is synonymous with violence, maleness is a violation of an innately feminine nature, and indeed masculinity itself is no more than an abominable fiction or construct that 'progressive' politics must attempt to destroy. The Oedipus complex is no real solution to the crisis of masculinity, because masculinity must never be fused with the mother. If such a fusion occurs, masculinity falls into the unconscious, and then we can expect compensatory eruptions and explosions of primal, and probably fascistic, masculinity. Ironically, the radical killing of the father could bring on a social-political regression more terrifying than any 'backlash' idealisation of the masculine.

The Iron John tradition is virtually All-Phallus, while the

contrary antimasculinist discourse is No-Phallus. Why can't we have the phallus without appalling idealisations or guilt-ridden demonisations? We must unpack and disassemble patriarchy, while at the same time developing new meanings and metaphors for masculinity, which must never be constructed as the 'enemy' of men or women. I earnestly believe that we need to find a 'third way', or a 'middle path' between the extremes of patriarchal nostalgia (Iron John) and matriarchal identification (Oedipus). The *zeitgeist* urges us to defend the feminine, but the development of masculinity forces us to differentiate ourselves from the mother. The answer to this dilemma can be found, I think, in the masculine commitment to the feminine soul, or *anima*. After liberating himself from the maternal unconscious, the classic hero finds that he must subordinate himself to a higher form of the feminine, to the inspiratrice, beloved, or Lady Soul. This is the task that I believe contemporary men are called to carry out today.

The postmodern or post-patriarchal hero does not have to throw in the quest and go back to mother, but every would-be contemporary hero must make a genuine commitment to the feminine soul, as the ultimate cure for male narcissism and infantilism. Too much academic discourse on masculinity sees the call to the feminine through the lens of the Oedipus complex, as a guilty self-sacrifice or mutilation of consciousness (in the myth, a tearing out of our own eyes). This is a literalistic, morbid, and destructive reading of the feminine spirit of the time. In my view, men must continue to differentiate themselves from the maternal unconscious, just so that the feminine archetypes can be properly served and attended by a sensitive and invigorated consciousness. Paradoxically, the feminine spirit of our time demands that the masculine be *further* developed so that a higher consciousness can realise the enormity of the challenge of integrated (masculine and feminine) awareness. In this book, I argue continually for a paradoxical, nonliteral awareness of the problems of contemporary masculinity. It is through paradox, and the constant consideration of contrary points of view, that we discover the middle way out of our cultural dilemmas.

SPIRITUALITY AND POLITICS: ETERNITY AND TIME

According to William Blake, 'Eternity is in love with the productions of time'.[19] If this were only true in our own time! The people in our day who are 'in love' with eternity move toward Jungian

7

archetypes, myths, spirituality, religions. That is to say, they move *out* of time and into archetypal or mythic space. They move to the outer perimeters of the known world, near the distant realms of outer space and what are called in astrology the 'slow-moving planets'. This remote world is beautiful and enchanting, but nothing much appears to happen: asteroids only pass here every 600 years. People who get attracted to eternity need to be steered back into time, else reality itself disintegrates in a kind of cosmic fog. As Jung would put it, 'reality has to be protected against an archaic, "eternal" and ubiquitous dream state',[20] and the world of the ego bolstered in face of the enchantment of the collective unconscious.

If we left the management of the political world to the seekers of eternal wisdom, hardly any progress in social structure and lived experience would be achieved, because society constantly pales in comparison to the hypnotic attraction of the slow moving cosmic wheels. Spirituality has an innate tendency to want to escape from the bounds of the real, but if spirituality is to be authentic and socially transformative, this innate tendency has to be arrested and spirituality must be politicised and linked with the social and historical process. From an intellectual perspective, any human experience is the product of its culture, so that a universalising spiritual discourse lacks credibility if it fails to engage the field of social reality. If the popular, Jung-influenced spiritual discourses are not firmly grounded in the real, they can readily, and perhaps rightly, be dismissed by hostile critics as so much froth and bubble, having little or no political consequence.

A case in point is the work of well-known Jungian populariser Robert Johnson. In some ways, Johnson is an admirable spiritual writer: accessible, poetic, suggestive, profound. His works resonate in the mind long after they have been read. He has discovered popular and commercial success by mixing a simple, direct prose with a strangely incantatory language and a universalising, didactic voice. But Johnson is so enamoured of the timelessness of the archetypes that he writes as if politics, social structure, and the historical process did not exist. His 'depth' and profundity carry him away from reality to a mythic realm where time is measured in bundles of 800 years or more. Hence Johnson can tell us that the twelfth-century version of the Grail myth holds the 'spiritual prescription for our own time'.[21] With alarming naïveté, Johnson writes about He, She, and We as if gendered experience had not changed since the time of King Arthur and the Knights of the

Round Table.[22] Johnson's view is that the Man is essentially the provider, quester, hero, and 'active partner'; whereas Woman is essentially nourisher, home-bound, domestic, and static.

I have sat in a crowded lecture hall and watched many spiritual seekers become entranced by Johnson's droning mythopoetics, while a number of more politically alert listeners became visibly disturbed and downright angry at his social blindness and lack of political awareness. Watching these opposite responses in the room is like witnessing my own contradictory response to mythopoetics: one part of me amazed, another part appalled. But when we listen closely to Johnson's conservative vision and strangely rigid view of gendered experience, we realise that he is indeed functioning on geological time, and that he is simply giving a glamorous, mythopoetic twist to utterly outmoded and stereotypical gendered patterns. He has a way of making the banal and ordinary appear miraculous by adorning conventional attitudes with the mantle of myth. The problem with gazing constantly at the slow-moving planets is that we eventually get drawn into their mystic depths, and become oblivious to the changes, disruptions, and revolutions that are patently obvious to everyone else.

The opposite problems attend much radical, academic discourse. Here, life is lived on the fast-moving surface. Progressive intellectuals sometimes anticipate huge social changes from a national convention, or expect a three-day leading-edge conference to change the world. They write books with titles like *Slow Motion* or *Backlash*, complaining about the rate of change.[23] Why isn't change happening faster? A considerable amount of feminist scholarship has resigned itself to a defeatist pessimism, convinced that 'men's behaviour is ultimately unchanging and inevitably coercive'.[24] The political feminist gaze looks at traditional masculinity, and sees only the static and destructive figure of Chronos-Saturn, and it knows that we are running out of time. Nevertheless, change is taking place and, as Lynne Segal has written, 'Men can and do change'.[25] There is hope, after all, that men can get out of Saturn's gravitational field long enough to allow substantial change to take place in both psyche and society.

The problem with surface-level intellectual discourse is that it fails to see the extent to which the archetypes or 'slow-moving planets' influence our lived experience. Much sociology of masculinity and gender theory strikes me as hopelessly inadequate; it calls for change and demands instantaneous release from stereotypes without even beginning to reckon with the powerful archetypes that regulate our lives, all the more powerful for not being seen by the intellectuals. Little wonder this facile sociology gets frustrated with the subjects it tackles, because it is made to see how hopeless its own methods are for accessing the core issues and getting to the root problems. It is astonishing how often we are told that masculinity is merely a construct of society, one that can be exploded simply if we stop believing in it. This is social positivism and extraverted awareness gone mad, completely unaware of its own limitations and arrogantly believing in the premises of its own social theory. How can theories of the human world dispense with or ignore the massive contributions of both Freud and Jung? Unless a depth dimension is taken into account, political and social science will remain frustrated and frustrating, a testimony only to the machinations of the hubristic intellect.

For their part, the Jungians – especially the popular Jungians – have an enormous amount to learn as well. The 'depths' they are so attracted to are not artificially removed from the 'surfaces'. The archetypes reach into time and form the very basis of the historical process. According to Jung, archetypes can never be known in themselves, but are always known only through the 'archetypal images' which are part of the fabric of history, time, and society. The conventional separation between surface and depth is therefore entirely false, as depth and surface are really two ways of looking at the one reality. Whether we are attracted to archetypal background or sociopolitical foreground is more a matter of personal taste and psychological type, than it is of the nature of reality. I agree fully with James Hillman and Andrew Samuels that the Jungian understanding of the 'inner world' has to be radically revisioned.[26] For Hillman, the constant privileging of the 'inner' has made the therapy-loving generations into political duds.[27] Samuels argues insightfully that the inner life is not hermetically sealed off from culture or society, but our psyche is a 'political psyche', intimately part of, and a major player in, the world of political events. If 'eternity is in love with the productions of time', then the newly emerging holistic paradigm must learn to bring archaic background and social foreground together, which means that spirituality and politics have to start talking to each other.

THE DANGEROUS SENTIMENTALISATION OF 'MEN'S FEELINGS'

Another dualism that must be subverted is that which separates reason from the heart. In contemporary men's experience, this is a particularly pressing problem. Especially at midlife, men who suddenly discover the feeling heart are liable to decide that the 'head' is Saturnian, static, bad, and that the fluid life of the heart must be the only source of truth. Men who set out on a spiritual path frequently become anti-intellectual, aggressively opposed to 'theory' and committed to a cult of 'experience'. The intellect and life of the mind are sometimes felt to be part of the 'false self' that the male quester is leaving behind in order to achieve 'authenticity'. A cult of feeling has arisen in the popular discourses about men, and this cult has been actively encouraged by some new-style therapists who believe that only they can guide men to feel what is inside them, only they can give men 'permission' to locate and identify their feelings. The first commandment in the new cult of feeling is: thou shalt be saved by feeling. There is a truly salvational tone to the new-style cult, and a kind of childlike joy and wonder can arise in men who have suddenly made contact with their long-repressed feeling life.

There is not much that we can do about this, because this undifferentiated feeling is simply where many men are 'at' at the moment. After the long dryness that was (still is) patriarchal supremacist conditioning, we are currently involved in a 'wet' phase of Western male experience. Nevertheless, we can hardly expect others to wholly swallow these large doses of sentiment, and men must not expect that all audiences will be receptive to their cathartic expressions. Unfortunately, in a society in which many men are over-educated and caught up in the head, 'men's liberation' has an annoying habit of representing itself as the throwing out or 'transcendence' of the mind.

The intoxicated feeling that often arises from men in therapy and/or awareness groups is difficult to direct or educate, and attempts to test this feeling against reality can result in bitter recrimination and hurt. However, the initial euphoria is self-limiting, because after the ecstatic release come feelings of resentment and aggression. Men suddenly feel angered by a patriarchal system that has taught them to repress their feelings, and that represented feeling and emotion as feminine weakness. Men

11

suddenly feel cheated by life, angered by their fathers who provided the repressive model, distraught by the awareness that no affective or feeling ties bind them to their fathers, and anxious to seek reparation and redress. Real or surrogate fathers are sought out, and feelings pour forth in a way that no-one could have anticipated. The rigidly controlled male is suddenly a bleeding heart, which alternately produces ecstasy, depression, and rage.

Very quickly, this male rage can be marshalled into backlash political activities against women, feminism, and social progress. Men's so-called 'awareness groups' can readily turn into misogynist cliques if this newly released anger is not integrated and properly understood. I have witnessed this process in my own involvement in a men's liberation meeting. In the early 1990s, a local men's group was greatly interested in Robert Bly, Jung, mythological archetypes, and 'the male spirit'. More recently, this same group has shifted gear, and I am astonished to find that those men who were sensitising themselves to poetry and fairytale are now talking about 'men's rights' and 'equality for men', are promoting Warren Farrell's *The Myth of Male Power*,[28] and are hitting out at what they call 'feminist propaganda' in local newspapers and government offices. At a public meeting in 1993, the mental atmosphere was so claustrophobic and intolerant of the feminist challenge to men that I was forced to walk out of the meeting, causing a scene on my way out. I felt confused, hurt, and disappointed, but also much the wiser about the darkness in men's hearts and the grassroots development of fascist feeling.

When energy and emotion are released in repressive males, what emerges from the unconscious is by no means all goodness and light. There is a great upwelling of what Jung calls the shadow, and what religions call evil, and if this darkness is not accepted, recognised for what it is, and transformed by a cosmology or religion large enough to contain it, the darkness will simply spill over into the world, and all sorts of external figures and forces, especially women, will be blamed for male misery and anguish.

Men who conduct very superficial journeys of self-discovery, or who cannot be bothered facing the darkness inside them, will be particularly prone to negative projections and a 'paranoid' view of the external social world. Some of the popular philosophies and new-age therapies readily available today have no room for darkness or evil. Instead, they have a completely delusional 'light-and-positive' view of human nature, and the men who get caught up in these inferior systems have very little chance of dealing with the shadow or of integrating their own darkness. Men's liberation is going to have to deal squarely and honestly with the reality of the psyche, and, in demanding individuation and personal growth, many men are going to get far more than they bargained for. If individuation, or confrontation with the unconscious, is courted, men will have to face whatever actually does emerge from the unconscious – whether or not it fits in with men's movement 'spiritual' ideology or popular expectations and tastes.

THERAPY CULTURE AND ACADEMIC CULTURE: MEN'S PAIN AND MEN'S POWER

The wetness of contemporary men's experience is repugnant to many dry intellectuals, who do not like crying, moist feelings, bleeding hearts, confessionals, or soul-searching. Academic men's studies and the popular men's movement, however, do have more in common than either would perhaps care to realise. Both groups inhabit a post-patriarchal world, and while therapy culture *feels* the legacy of an outworn patriarchy in the empty heart and suffering soul, academic culture *thinks* about how to overthrow the remaining structures of political patriarchy. Both cultures will have to come together in a future radicalising discourse.

Although they look at each other with some alarm and disdain, therapy and academic cultures have grasped opposite ends of the same historical situation. Therapy culture assumes that patriarchy as an identity support structure is dead, and it sets about inculcating a 'survival mentality' that will help individual men in the task of rebuilding their lives. However, therapy culture fails to see that political patriarchy is still very much alive, and that, although men may feel themselves to be disenfranchised and emotionally adrift, they are still in charge of social authority. There is a dangerous split here between the internal psychic reality (where we are all made to feel 'inferior' and powerless) and the external reality (where Chronos-Saturn continues to rule).

Academic culture grasps very well the continued hegemonic power of men, but is blind to the fact that many men are already suffering, as it were in advance (and ahead of the feminist schedule), the emotional fallout of the disintegration of patriarchy as a psychological and identity-forming reality. Academic culture cannot see what the crying men are getting at: their tears are viewed

13

as crocodile tears, indulgent sensitive new-age tears, which have no validity and merely mask the reality that men still hold the power. 'Oh dear,' said one feminist commentator to Warren Farrell, 'are the power-boys having a bit of a cry?'[29]

We live in a complex time where we have to come to terms with the paradox of men's power and men's pain. In my life as an academic, I talk the language of men's power on a daily basis. In my second life as a public speaker and participant in the therapy culture, I see men's pain everywhere and feel a great deal of it myself. Both sides of contemporary men's experience are real, and both have to be taken into account. We are not dealing here with a contradiction, but with a paradox, and only if the paradox is not understood is the link between pain and power lost. I would say that the ability to sustain this paradox, and the tension between power and pain, is what constitutes full psychological health in a post-patriarchal world.

The problem with the popular emphasis on 'men's healing' is that it forgets why men are wounded in the first place. As a participant in some therapeutic forums, I found myself leaning more and more toward the academic perspective, asking critical questions about male identity, feeling stifled by the 'good vibes' approach, and wanting to present arguments for the necessary destructuring of masculine identity. I began to realise that, although the popular forums purportedly stood for 'men's pain', they actually want to outwit that pain, get around it, transcend or get rid of it. The leader of a men's forum told me that his primary objective was to make men feel happy again about being men. 'Isn't that what we are all aiming for?', he asked, wondering why I would not join forces with him in a united movement. I made it clear that such sunny clichés were not what inspired me to become involved in contemporary men's experience.

The popular healing or therapy discourses urgently need an injection of the academic perspective, for this alone brings the feminist, cultural, and social perspectives, the 'big picture' in which individual experiences acquire larger meaning and historical significance. Before we remake masculinity we must unmake it, and understand why it had to fall apart. In our remaking efforts, we must become self-critical and be careful to distinguish between new and old masculinities, to differentiate the new self-esteem from the old masculinist arrogance, to separate the new happiness from the old complacency, to tell the difference between human rights and patriarchal privileges. These lessons are far from having been learned, and that is why every leader of popular men's forums owes it to himself and to his followers to become acquainted with academic, profeminist men's studies, and to read seriously in these areas. Instead of using Robert Bly's *Iron John* as a textbook, or Sam Keen's *Fire in the Belly*, team leaders should look at Lynne Segal's *Slow Motion*, or Kenneth Clatterbaugh's *Contemporary Perspectives on Masculinity*.[30]

I think that if men knew more about why they are suffering, if they understood better the cultural, political and historical reasons for their disorientation, the effects of this increase in knowledge could only be positive. The personal mess is not then so terribly personal, and creative insight, rather than guilt-feelings, could be better mobilised. Jung puts it very well:

> if the connection between the personal problem and the larger contemporary events is discerned and understood, it brings release from the loneliness of the purely personal, and the subjective problem is magnified into a general question of our society. In this way the personal problem acquires a dignity it lacked hitherto.[31]

Ironically, for contemporary men to gain the larger, contextual view that Jung recommends, they need to read feminist and feminist-inspired writings, and not the popular Jungian material that wards off the social-political world.

What has alarmed me over the last ten years is the deep splitting that turns the power–pain paradox into an overt and warring contradiction. Dogmatism and extremism tend to attach to those who see one side of the paradox and not the other. Those who see only men's pain rapidly become sanctimonious, nostalgic, 'wet', and fundamentalist. Those who see only men's power become intolerant, moralistic, punishing, and guilt-ridden. It is fairly typical to see one perspective at a time, but when a single perspective hardens into an ideology then I believe we have lost touch with the truth.

We must, I believe, muddle away at getting both perspectives in our minds at the one time. Men's pain and men's power, spirituality and politics, feeling and reason: the claims of both sides must always be examined, balanced, and placed against each other. This is my own 'dialectical' mode used throughout this book. At one moment I will emphasise mythopoetics and archetypes, at another moment I will be concerned with politics and social process. I realise that this Janus-faced approach can appear confusing. In my course on 'Remaking Men' some of my Jungian students wondered why I was spending so much time on the sociology and politics of masculinity. On the other hand, some sociologists place me in the same camp as Robert Bly and the Jungian conservatives, simply because I am fascinated by the archetypal background to the problem of masculinity. These problems with typing and categorising are bound to emerge as we struggle to break new ground, to develop a spirituality of men's experience that is politically aware, and a gender politics that is alert to psychodynamics and the archetypal background.

1

ARCHETYPES, GODS, MEN AND WOMEN

All the true things must change and only that which changes remains true.

Jung[1]

POPULAR DISTORTIONS OF JUNGIAN THEORY

The advocates of popularised Jungian theory, and the hypercritical opponents of Jung, appear to agree on one thing: that contact with primordial archetypes produces conformity, gender rigidity, and social-political conservatism. For the popular discourses, this is a cause for celebration and joy, since we are restored to our archetypal 'origins' and rediscover how we were 'meant' to be. For the progressive intellectuals, this spells political disaster, and an achievement of personal stability at the cost of social progress. How, they ask, are we ever to get beyond hegemonic power structures and rigid gender categories if Jungians keep reinventing the past and, moreover, representing such backward thinking as 'therapy'? Even Kenneth Clatterbaugh, who provides a fairly balanced and even-handed account of the Jung-influenced spiritual men's movement, remains decidedly ambivalent about the value of archetypal theory. He writes that, if Jungian work puts the seal of spiritual approval upon conventional and oppressive forms, how can Jungian work support or promote change?[2]

My own view is that the popular Jungians distort Jung's message, and that the anti-Jungian intellectuals, in turn, read this popular distortion as 'classical' Jung. Unfortunately, this comedy of errors, in which unreal ideas about archetypes get circulated and reinforced, is what characterises much popular and academic discourse about Jungian theory at the end of the twentieth century. It is a

17

rather bleak scenario, but Jung himself is not exempt from all moral responsibility, as I will go on to explain shortly.

For popular Jungianism, truth, knowledge and spiritual direction are all 'down there', in a treasure chest of eternal wisdom. A certain infantilism is evident in the hapless and desperate stance of a 'lost' modern consciousness that renounces responsibility and gives itself over to the direction of primordial archetypal figures. We slink back to the treasure trove of the collective unconscious, like prodigal sons and daughters, prepared to recover the ancient ways of human experience. We idealise the archetypes as all-knowing parental or ancestral figures, and the 'advice' that we receive from these reified oracular presences is usually fairly predictable: 'abandon your wayward paths and return to the tried and true Way of tradition'. In other words, the 'archetypes' sound remarkably like social stereo-types, and the voice of wisdom is basically inseparable from the voice of the Freudian superego. If we start worshipping the superego in times of social instability and gender fluidity, it is little wonder that we end up with profoundly reactionary solutions to our social problems. In so much 'wisdom writing' in the Jungian vein, whether we turn to *Iron John* or *Women Who Run With the Wolves*, the therapeutic advice is the same: give up the 'errors' of conscious-ness and return to the 'truth' of the ancestors. 'To find the Wild Woman, it is necessary for women to return to their instinctive lives, their deepest knowing. Let us . . . shed any false coats we have been given. Don the true coat of powerful instinct and knowing.'[3]

To me, this reading of psychological experience is illusory. Why must archetypes always be presented in this idealising fashion? Why is society always represented as a 'false coat' and denigrated in favour of the 'truth' of primordial instinct? If all the answers are buried in the ancient past, what is the point of the present and the future? Why the imbalance of power, and why represent the ego as a passive figure to be freely manipulated by invisible instinctual forces?

This romantic philosophy, which always seems to me to run very close to fascist ideology, engages in a deliberate and systematic infantilisation of Jungian theory. As I read Jung, the primary, undifferentiated, 'ancestral' archetypes are to be resisted, and even defeated – certainly not surrendered to in the manner advocated by popular Jungianism. The Great Mother, the Spirit Father, or the Ancestral Archetypes, are presented by Jung as 'dragons' to be battled with and heroically resisted by the developing ego

18

consciousness. The notion that we abandon our stance in consciousness and society, and 'don the true coat' of primordial archetypes, is
actually Jung-in-reverse. Jung spent much of his intellectual energy
warning against an unconscious or infantile return to an identification with the archetypal figures.[4] For Jung, a loss of social
awareness and egoic identity in favour of a new identification with
archetypes is tantamount to psychological regression and psychosis.
'For weak-minded persons', he writes, 'the danger of yielding to this
temptation [identification with the collective psyche] is very great'.
The puny mortal, lost and disoriented in the world, gives way to
'the nostalgia for the source', and 'blots out all memory in its
embrace'.[5] In a terrible irony, popular sentiment reads regression as
Jungian individuation, and mistakes psychological infantilism for
spiritual progress. It is little wonder that creative thinkers, encountering this popular misreading of archetypal theory, dismiss the
entire Jung tradition as claptrap.

Jung insists that individuation is above all a *dialogue* with the
unconscious psyche. The ego needs to maintain its essential connection with social reality as it attempts to 'have it out' with the
unconscious forces. As the ego makes its 'descent' for the sake of
renewal, it must resist the 'inertia' of the unconscious, and the
forces that would paralyse it, and maintain its human integrity at all
costs. A tell-tale sign of failure is the tendency to inflate one's significance, so that we suddenly claim to be a 'Wild Man' or a 'Wild
Woman', and not the complex and confused ordinary mortals
whom we in fact are. Naturally the writings which encourage these
inflations and identifications become best-sellers, and in many
recent cases of Jungian work, the temptation of commercial success
wins out over psychological truth. It is fatal for the ego to fuse with
any one of the archetypes, and those who encourage such fusions
must be counted as the enemies of humanity.

The clear-minded Jungian thinker and the responsible analyst do
not encourage a mass stampede back to the pristine sources of
wisdom. Rather, the ego must be encouraged to accept its own relative confusion and complexity, as well as the burden of its own
individuality and personal isolation. When we make contact with
the unconscious, and so become privy to some of the collective
secrets of the ages, we must compensate for this 'dialogue with the
Gods' by increased amounts of humour and humility: two of the
best antidotes to spiritual arrogance and inflation. The new-age
Jungian gurus of our time – to adapt Jung's own words in a

different context – not only 'accept [this] inflation, but now exalt [it] into a system'.[6] Popular Jungianism systematically confuses spiritual enlightenment with infantile fixation – an ironic situation, since the popular gurus rarely mention Freud (if they do so, it is only to attack him), and the Freudian realism and capacity for suspicion in Jung's own work is lost, forgotten, or ignored. Few wish to be reminded of the fact that Jung was, during the early, formative years of his work, a Freudian. The 'return of the repressed' in Jungianism will be synonymous with a new and higher regard for the psychoanalytic elements in archetypal psychology. In some ways, we all suffer massively from the Freud/Jung split: Jungian psychology loses itself in fatuous optimism and empty-headed romanticism, whereas an appalling pessimism and a kind of 'grey realism' continues to cloud the Freudian tradition.

ARCHETYPES, TIME, AND RELATIVITY

The romantic idea that the archetypes are fixed in an eternal dream space, and that these stable entities can be accessed by anyone at any time and in any place, has to be contrasted with Jung's idea that the archetypes are, 'in themselves', unknowable and beyond human experience. Jung insisted that the essential nature of the archetype is a metaphysical question. At its core, he argued, it is invisible, empty and without content. As the archetype enters time and space it acquires content and substance, and at this point it becomes an 'archetypal image'. All we can know, Jung said, are the archetypal images, never the archetypes themselves.[7] Thus, archetypal images may have universalist or Platonic cores or nuclei, but they are profoundly determined by historical and cultural factors, and by the contingencies of time and space.

Hence the popular Jungian notion that the 'trickster' or 'magician' figure, for instance, must be the same across cultures and societies, is misleading. There is no such thing as a fixed archetypal figure, since by definition the archetypal figures are caught up in, and subject to, the flux of temporal and historical conditions. However, the sentimental mind does not want to hear about such complexity or relativity. It wants things to be safe and sure, and the 'archetypes' must conform to a naive understanding. Because this is what a certain kind of popular mind wants, some Jungian writers construct manuals and textbooks that list the Gods and Goddesses as if they were frozen in time, and immune to cultural difference and relativity. Jean Shinoda Bolen confidently asserts at the beginning of her book, *Goddesses in Everywoman*: 'Archetypes exist outside of time. ... The Greek Goddesses are images of women that have lived in the human imagination for over three thousand years'.[8] This is nonsensical, but of course it sells books and turns those who risk these pronouncements into instant gurus. Bolen's books, *Goddesses in Everywoman* and *Gods in Everyman*,[9] are bestsellers precisely because they take intellectual short-cuts, and falsify Jung and his theory of archetypes. The idea that the Gods and Goddesses of Mount Olympus have been living in some suspended animation for thousands of years, and can today be drawn out of this mythic space and brought to life in the same condition in which they existed for ancient Greeks is simply a piece of science fiction. This would make an excellent story-line for *Star Trek*, but a hopeless work of intellectual theory. While the invisible core-nuclei remain the same, the archetypal figures are hugely conditioned by culture, and cannot be efficiently transported across time and societies. Bolen invites her readers to 'look up' this or that archetype, in the promise of figuring out who and what they are, and in the hope of getting to know themselves better. Invariably, readers fantasise themselves into the shape of some noble and exotic form, creating more mental junk and psychobabble that serves merely to alienate them from the true archetypal ground of their being.

In effect, popular Jungianism attempts to turn the archetypes, the seething currents of psychic change and transformative energy, into reliable, predictable, secure, and familiar 'building blocks' of lived experience. Bly's 'Wild Man' and Estes's 'Wild Woman' look incredibly tame after they have gone through the mythopoetic mill and become very 'conscious' modern clichés. A parallel with theoretical physics suggests itself. The popular image of the archetype can be compared with the premodern Newtonian understanding of matter as fixed foundations or building blocks. However, the archetype is actually closer to the postmodern notions of subatomic quantum physics, which place emphasis on unpredictability, movement, process, self-transformation. Also, in quantum physics the subjective factor is vital: how we look at matter determines in part how it will be perceived. The archetypes are invisible, unformed sources of light and radiance; a veritable 'Heraclitian fire' which has nothing cosy, secure or comfortable about it. It is only the social engineering and manipulation of archetypes that produces stereotypes, those entirely predictable and usually conservative

21

constructs of psychosocial reality. Direct encounter with archetypal nuclei can lead to new life or death, transformation or explosion. In the popular mind, the archetype is confused with the stereotype, a confusion which has resulted in the unfair dismissal and discrediting of Jungian theory.

SOUL, GODS AND HUMAN IDENTITY

In the popular domain, there is a widespread notion that the ancient Gods can provide models of identity and sexuality for boys and men, while the Goddesses provide such models for women and girls. The origins of this notion are obvious: the Gods are felt to be masculine archetypal essences that have a bearing on males, while the Goddesses represent feminine styles appropriate for women. However, this simple equation is mistaken, mainly because the Gods and Goddesses represent metaphorical possibilities within the human psyche, and cannot be neatly parcelled out to this or that gender. The masculinity of the Gods and the femininity of the Goddesses must not be equated with the maleness of men and the femaleness of women. To make such an equation is to engage in concrete or literal thinking, to read the mythical deities as men and women rather than as immortal archetypal beings.

I have frequently encountered the view that in personal disorientation or crisis, one simply has to make contact with a mythical figure which is of the same sex as oneself, and one can be assured of renewal, increased strength, and personal meaning. This is a convenient fiction which may actually work for some people and may be demonstrably true in certain circumstances. However, despite obvious differences between men and women in bodily structure and social conditioning, I do not believe that men have one kind of soul and women another. Archetypal energies flow through the psyche of whatever sex: archetypes do not obey the gendered distinctions and barriers that may be important in the social and political sphere. As James Hillman has said, 'an archetype as such cannot be attributed to or located within the psyche of either sex'.[10]

In ancient times, the polymorphous nature of the soul was honoured and respected. There was no simple determinism that linked the gender of the God with the gender of human beings. The Great Goddess Athena commanded followers and devotees from the entire community. Dionysus was a male God, but his disciples were mostly women. The cults of Aphrodite involved both men and women. Similarly, men and women worshipped at the shrines of Poseidon or Zeus; men and women prayed to Hestia, invoked Apollo or Hermes, or sought guidance from Hecate. The soul is androgynous, perhaps because it is not entirely or quite human, connecting us to a deep, profound, fluid level of psyche where contradictory forces continually interact, where fixed positions are dissolved, and where one trait or attribute often changes into another.

The popular fusion of archetype and gender is, at bottom, a symptom of the nervousness of our time, an attempt to create a fixed world order amid the chaos of contemporary experience. It is also a fundamental and determined resistance to the bisexuality or androgyneity of the soul. The soul, as both Freud and Jung knew, is structurally bisexual, but many of us cannot cope with that and want to cling to the apparent solidity of a single psychosexual identity. Our indwelling souls are bisexual, but we want to belong only to one sex. A woman might announce, after reading *Goddesses in Everywoman*, 'I find my mythic pattern best reflected in Artemis-Diana'; a man might claim, after studying *Iron John*, that he finds his deepest nature to be embodied in the figure of the Warrior-Hero. Yet a depth psychological analysis of the same people might reveal that the woman is actually governed by a Zeus or Jupiter complex, and the man is actually the son-lover of the Great Goddess. These people would serve their spiritual growth better by acknowledging and honouring these transgendered archetypal identities. We must learn to serve and follow whatever it is in the psyche that wants to appear. But we should not underestimate the importance of our all-too-human fear of internal complexity and bisexuality. In contemporary times, fear of the opposite sex has reappeared as a psychospiritual phobia to the bisexual nature of the indwelling soul.

While it seems that the soul is androgynous, and that our archetypal options are many and diverse, it is also apparent that the limited human self that experiences the archetypal field remains profoundly gendered. We are not the Gods and Goddesses; 'we', as experiencing subjects, are bound by time, space, and the body. The subjective ego-self that experiences the objective God-self is incarnated as a specific gender. Thus, we do not, or most certainly should not, describe ourselves as *being* Athena, Artemis, or Hermes, but rather as the 'son' of Athena or the 'daughter' of Hermes. This is not only an appropriate recognition of our incarnated selfhood, but also an appropriate recognition of our humility before the Gods.

Our experience of gender remains a deep paradox and a mystery: the range of what we can inwardly connect with is not bound by gender, but the gendered subject experiences this plural range within the confines of incarnated selfhood.

It is useful for men and women to conceptualise and mythologise their gendered experience of the archetypes. It is important that men and women write about, discuss and share in groups and meetings their common psychological and spiritual experience with respect to the great universal forces. The idea of 'women's business' and 'men's business' builds gender solidarity, social awareness, facilitates networking, and helps us recover a sense of community. But the sense of community cannot, in the final analysis, end with our gender. If we are to transcend a divisive or separatist sense of community we have to realise that, while our gendered experience of the Gods is legitimate, it is also relativised by the fact that the opposite sex has direct access to the same archetypal figures whom we consider to be intimately 'ours'. Moreover, a real danger inherent in the mythologisation of one's own gender is that there is a natural tendency to demonise the opposite gender. This process took place in the early days of the women's movement, and it is occurring today as the men's movement establishes itself. If one gender becomes god-like or imbued with the aura of spiritual reality, then the other gender, by way of archetypal compensation, assumes a demonic kind of appearance. The same kinds of processes result from other forms of recollectivisation, such as racism, nationalism, and so on. If the group to which one belongs is elevated and revered, then other groups will automatically be deemed 'other', outside the magic circle, or not-self. For these and other reasons, I do not believe that Jungian psychology should be exploited by divisive groups, whose agendas are, as Patricia Berry saw, to make a 'dogma of gender'.[11]

The new tradition of 'Goddess spirituality' has enabled women to empower themselves emotionally and politically by fusing their identity with the mythic source of the archetypal feminine. But from the viewpoint of the androgynous soul, the exclusive identification of women with the archetypal feminine is a fallacy – but one that has served a progressive political purpose. David Wilde has made an interesting point about differences between political ambitions and depth psychological concerns. 'One-sidedness is a risk the politically orientated may sometimes have to take in order to achieve their goal, but the psychologically orientated should eschew

24

it like the plague.'[12] What is 'politically correct' may not be psychologically or spiritually correct. Always we must have a double vision in mind: the concrete human and political experience of the archetypal realm, and the fluid, metaphorical, transgendered nature of that same world.

The feminist Mary Daly said that androgyny is for a different age, not for our own.[13] First, women have to become equal to men, femininity must be valued the same as masculinity, and then, perhaps much later, we can learn about androgyny. She is right, of course, to realise that the idea of androgyny subverts the theoretical basis of political activism and the fight for social justice. But if androgyny is archetypal, and if it wants to assert itself in our time, then it will do so, regardless of its collision course with the political feelings of the day. In this regard, I recall a key moment at a feminist conference on women and drugs at Melbourne University,[14] when Jungian analyst Linda Leonard[15] was asked to expound on the basic differences between men and women. She was almost booed off the stage when she said that, from her own clinical experience of the unconscious, there seemed to her very little intrinsic difference between the psyches or souls of the sexes. Several women in the audience, desperate to assert their *difference* from men and patriarchy, tried to make her look a fool for not having learned the basic tenets of political feminism. It was a memorable moment where psyche and politics clashed. Both sides of the argument were right, however. Linda Leonard was justified in adopting an androgynous position with regard to the psyche, and the women interrogating her were politically justified in demanding a separate and discrete social identity.

JUNG'S MURKY WATERS AND SEXIST CATEGORIES

The popular writings that wilfully fuse archetype and gender claim Jung as their psychological source and authority. Here we enter very murky waters indeed. Jung spoke about masculinity and femininity in two different contexts. On the one hand, masculine and feminine are abstract universal archetypes found in both men and women. In this context, masculine and feminine are present in the psyche of whatever sex, in much the same way that all astrological and planetary influences (including masculine Mars and feminine Venus) are present in the astrological chart or horoscope of every individual, regardless of sex. The late alchemical Jung, for instance, generally

25

assumes that the archetypal masculine (Sol) and the archetypal feminine (Luna) are currents or forces running through the universal human psyche.

But where Jung reveals himself to be most vulnerable and problematic is in his frequent tendency to *assign* archetypes to a particular gender. In fact, Jung makes a general habit of fusing an archetypal figure or principle with the sexes. In 1927 he wrote: 'Woman's psychology is founded on the principle of Eros, the great binder and loosener, whereas from ancient times the ruling principle ascribed to man is Logos'.[16] Eros is equated with feeling, relatedness, love; while Logos is concerned with reason, spirit, differentiation. For Jung, since this apparent fusion of gender and archetype has been encouraged 'from ancient times', this provides the moral authority for continuing and supporting it. Depressingly, Jung was making the same pronouncements a quarter of a century later, in 1951:

> Woman's consciousness is characterized more by the connective quality of Eros than by the discrimination and cognition associated with Logos. In men, Eros, the function of relationship, is usually less developed than Logos. In women, on the other hand, Eros is an expression of their true nature.[17]

In the unconscious, however, the situation is reversed. Jung says that the anima is the feminine soul found in men, which compensates the Logos-orientation in consciousness. So too in women he designated an animus or masculine spirit, which compensates the Eros of the conscious mind.

This neat but very algebraic and sexist model was first exploded by James Hillman in the late 1960s and early 1970s. It was Hillman who pointed out that Jung did not follow the logic of his own argument. One cannot claim that archetypes are universal, then assert that they are found in one gender but not in another. Archetypes are either original predispositions in the human psyche, or they are not. In *The Myth of Analysis*, Hillman said it was ridiculous to assume that all women are governed by Eros, all men by Logos. Similarly, it is bizarre to suggest that only men have animas or souls, and only women have spirits or animuses. If we are going to talk about soul (anima) or spirit (animus), then we have to drop Jung's cramped model and assume that all archetypes are present in both men and women at all times. Hillman wrote: 'the *archetype* of the anima cannot be limited to the special psychology of men, since the

26

archetypes transcend both men and women and their biological differences and social roles'.[18]

Jung obviously read the psychological situation of his own time in archetypal, rather than sociopolitical, terms. He explored the relatively stable, conventional, even stilted Swiss-German society of his day and said: these are the 'archetypes' at work in it, therefore, this is how men and women are, have always been, and must always be. Jung's model is predicated on the doubtful assumption that men are always conventionally 'masculine' and have feminine souls, and women are always 'feminine' with masculinity in the unconscious. Jung's conservatism is amply demonstrated in the famous remark in his 1927 essay 'Women in Europe': 'A man should live as a man and a woman as a woman'.[19] This kind of statement simply could not be made today, because it begs too many questions, and relies on social expectations that have since been erased. As Anthony Storr commented: 'Jung, true to his generation, believed that the sexes were strongly differentiated psychologically as well as physically'.[20]

If women are the carriers of Eros, then suddenly we arrive at the injunction that women 'should' or 'ought to' carry this archetypal principle. But why *must* they carry it? Feminist authors and commentators say, quite rightly: to please men, to embody for them and to represent to them the feminine values and attitudes that they have not had time or interest to develop in their one-sidedly masculine search for identity. Author David Wilde puts this point of view (or prejudice) neatly when he asserts (without irony): 'when *women* start denying the feminine principle which we men need so desperately to understand better and value more, then we are in dire trouble'.[21] It suits men best to keep their women 'feminine', and what better way to keep them in order than to argue that it is for their own psychological health that they should strive toward conventional femininity. It is little wonder that many early feminists instinctively saw Jung as their natural opponent, for he was trying to put in stone what they were attempting to unravel and make fluid. Jung seemed to be giving psychological and even divine sanction to social stereotypes. Not only society, but nature, psyche, and even the Gods have designated woman's proper role. As Andrew Samuels has written, 'the door is opened for the pernicious use of Jung's theory of opposites to reinforce the patriarchy'.[22]

Jung wrote:

In women . . . Eros is an expression of their true nature, while

27

their Logos is often only a regrettable accident. No matter
how friendly and obliging a woman's Eros may be, no logic on
earth can shake her if she is ridden by the animus. Often the
man has the feeling – and he is not altogether wrong – that
only seduction or a beating or rape would have the necessary
power of persuasion.[23]

This is sexist, prejudicial, and harshly judgemental. Since this statement appeared late in his career, it is not as if we can excuse this on
the grounds that it represents the views of 'early Jung'. Women who
are inherently intellectual, with a dominance of Logos, are said to
be *dominated* by Logos, or worse, animus-ridden. They are doing
themselves and their 'nature' harm by trying to be intellectual, and
should really leave the hard thinking to men, who are better at it.
They would be better off cooking or gardening, or serving men with
their 'differentiated' function of relationship. Similarly, men who
are naturally governed by feeling, intuition, and Eros, and judged to
be atypical, are looked on with some suspicion, and are felt not to
be the full quid. Such men are said to be living as inferior women,
burdened by a mother-complex, or have identified themselves with
their mother's Eros. 'With them the question becomes one of
personal vanity and touchiness, as if they were females.'[24] All sorts
of psychic equations are invented to explain why men and women
are not enacting conventional behaviour and why they have strayed
from the straight and narrow.

At first, it may appear strange that the first generation of
Jungian women analysts strongly encouraged the identification of
women with Eros and the so-called feminine principle. The works of
Marie-Louise von Franz, Esther Harding, Barbara Hannah, Toni
Wolf, Emma Jung, Jolande Jacobi, and the early school of female
analysts see nothing oppressive or reductive in the patriarchal equation: woman equals Eros.[25] This is because the secret payoff for
such narrow categorisation is actually a form of psychic inflation.
Eros is an archetypal principle, a grand cosmic force, and in encouraging his circle of women to identify with Eros, Jung was inviting
them to step outside their limited humanness and to become
archetypal. Women were secretly to view themselves as living incar-
nations of the Goddess, and this, I believe, accounts for the strongly
cultic atmosphere around Jung and his society of women in Zurich.
One would have to concur with Mary Daly's grim assessment that
'it is possible for women to promote Jung's garbled gospel without

awareness of betraying their own sex and even in the belief that they are furthering the feminist cause'.[26]

It would take a later generation of Jungian (or post-Jungian) women to see through the pleasurable drug of inflation, and to realise that the categories Jung had allowed for women were limited and oppressive. It is a very long way, for instance, from the hymn to femininity and the Moon Goddess in Esther Harding's *The Way of All Women* and *Women's Mysteries* to the astute political awareness of Naomi Goldenberg's *The Changing of the Gods* or Patricia Berry's polemical essay, 'The Dogma of Gender'.[27] By the 1970s, feminist sensibility had caught up with the female analysts and writers who rightly would no longer tolerate the patriarchal climate of Jung's theories of gender.

There is sometimes confusion and misunderstanding here: defenders of Jung, such as Anna Belford Ulanov, claim that 'Eros' is a mighty and wonderful force, equal in value and power to the masculine Logos – therefore, she argues, what are these women complaining about? Don't they see that the archetype assigned to women is great and wonderful, not in the least demeaning?[28] This protest is well meant, but it misses the point. The issue for feminist women is not whether or not Eros is a mighty force, but whether or not women must conform to any preordained structure or principle, especially one that is put to them by men. D. H. Lawrence was correct in realising that 'the real trouble with women is that they must always go on trying to adapt themselves to men's theories of women'.[29] It does not matter how much the followers of Jung heap praises upon the principle of Eros, because feminists will continue to regard this as an oppressive classification, rather than as a releasing or elevating strategy.

SORTING OUT THE POST-JUNGIAN LEGACY

In one sense it was radical for Jung to postulate in the 1920s and 1930s that men had a feminine side and women a masculine side.[30] This announcement must have shocked many at the time, and no doubt it helped to liberate others, such as artists, poets, and free-thinkers. But Jung's concept of the androgynous aspect of the psyche was severely limited by his conventional understanding of gender roles and identity. A man can acknowledge the feminine psychic component, but he has to remain and *must* remain recognisably masculine. This conventional expectation is something of a bottom line in classical Jungian theory, which tends toward a normative-conservative world-view. The anima and animus are unconscious compensatory figures, and Jung is saying, in effect, that they had better remain unconscious too, and not imbalance or disturb the strictly gendered consciousness. 'If one lives out the opposite sex in oneself one is living in one's own background, and one's real individuality suffers.'[31] Although Jungian thought makes strong gestures toward archetypal androgyny or structural bisexuality, it seems that for Jung, theory is one thing, and practice quite another.

There is an internal conflict between Jung's conservative conditioning and his radical psychological discoveries. After all, Jung believed that the unconscious must be made conscious. We know from our own psychological experience that 'integration' of an archetypal content rarely or never takes place without significant disruption to the conscious mind and its established norms. Although Jung made considerable moral demands on his clients, the idea of a sterile or antiseptic 'integration' of an unconscious content – where the ego remains cool, balanced, and puritanically detached from whatever is emerging – is a philosophical abstraction and a remote possibility. In actual experience this never happens. The anima drives a man mad with desire, with unattainable or exotic femininity, long before anything resembling 'integration' takes place. If, as I believe, men are being forced to encounter the archetypal feminine as never before, then we can anticipate a general and universal disruption of the male stereotype, and its replacement by any number of roles, categories, or personae. In the sixty or seventy years since Jung's pronouncements on gender, the social stereotypes that Jung took for granted have been debunked, unconscious contents are demanding more attention, and patriarchy itself has been challenged. Therefore what 'Jung thought' about gender can no longer be considered unconditional, and the post-Jungians must move *beyond* Jung in order to redeem his theories.[32]

There are feminine men and masculine women, and society has begun to tolerate and even expect these new sexual personae. What 'compensates' the conscious lives of these new men and women may be the opposite of what Jung envisaged. A strong masculine spirit may compensate the new feminine man, and a feminine soul may compensate the masculine woman. This may account for the apparently dramatic rise in homosexuality and lesbianism in our society.

Our task is not to think about ways of reversing this process and of re-establishing the conventional heterosexual norm, but rather to accept the changes as they take place and to shift our theoretical and moral positions accordingly. The truly modern therapist instinctively knows this, and realises that his or her task is not to churn out a more conventional citizen but to obey the dictates of the patient's psyche. If this means moving in a more androgynous direction outside the normal images of society, then so be it. The processes of the soul, rather than the norms of society, have become the new locus and source of moral authority.

If we take away the patriarchal encrustations from around Jung's ideas, the androgynous and compensatory model of the psyche is still useful and can serve our new needs and guide our postmodern development. In a sense, this is what post-Jungian theory since James Hillman has done: removed the patriarchal assumptions and conservative biases of Jung's psychology, adopting his androgynous understanding of the psyche without his moral imperatives and without what feminist theologian Mary Daly called 'Jung's androcratic animus–anima balancing act'.[33] Post-Jungians have dropped the expectation that men must be basically masculine and women basically feminine, and there seems to be little anxiety any more about whether the patient is obeying the archetypal principle that supposedly governs his or her gender. The goal of post-Jungian therapy is not to engineer a balancing act that always favours the social norm, but to arrive at a sense of self which is alert to contradictions, tensions, and to the plurality of the psychic field.

The Jungian world seems riven with conflicts about the issue of gender. Gareth Hill reports that a recent conference on masculinity and femininity at Ghost Ranch in New Mexico 'produced one of the most acrimonious debates some participants had ever experienced at a Jungian gathering'.[34] In his introduction to Jung's *Aspects of the Masculine*, John Beebe points out that Jung's early tendency to link archetype and gender 'has led to premature dogmatizing by some Jungian analysts as to the essential psychological character of men and of women and a storm of protest by other analysts, who have argued rightly for the complexity of individual experience'.[35] Some analysts want to separate archetype from gender, while others want to keep the original understanding that fixed archetypes govern men and women. Gareth Hill, for instance, wants to distinguish archetypal masculinity and femininity from the idea of maleness and femaleness, and he feels that Jungians should speak a more precise language:

> In Neumann's writings, as in Jung's, 'masculine' and 'feminine' are constantly used in two senses that become confused with one another: as inherent, gender-linked traits and as nongender-linked archetypal principles and patterns. It is saddening that many Jungians still tend to perpetuate this confusion by speaking of the feminine as if it is the special province of women, or speaking of women's psychology as 'feminine psychology' or men's psychology as 'masculine psychology'.[36]

Eugene Monick, however, insists on a more traditional approach:

> Males and females are significantly different anatomically and biologically. It is my assumption that from these differences certain distinctions have evolved into the psychological characteristics of masculinity and femininity. The characteristics are gender-specific since their basis is biological: they are instinctual and archetypal. Their presence within the psychologies of individual male and female persons, however, quite clearly crosses over the gender line.[37]

Monick's position is the more typical 'classical' Jungian view today: the differences are there, based in the body, instincts, and genes; however, as far as the psyche is concerned, simple differences give way to symbolic complexities. This classical view still carries with it a good deal of baggage concerning what *kinds* of archetypal constellations and balancing acts are 'appropriate' or 'correct' for the different sexes.

While a few creative souls dream Jung's work onward into the future, a great many public and high-profile Jungians exploit the murky or muddled elements of Jungian theory to their own popular and commercial ends. What takes place in the popular works already mentioned in this chapter, and in the Introduction, is a series of dangerous fusions and confusions. Archetype is fused with gender to produce a new Jungian fundamentalism; archetype is fused with the individual person to manufacture inflationary fantasies; and archetype is confused with stereotype to produce a guilt-ridden and superego-driven politics of conformity. This new gender fundamentalism is upbeat and wildly enthusiastic. Like a religious fundamentalism, it *knows* what is right for us and caters directly to our fears and anxieties. In a time of rapid change and uncertainty, our weaker natures are magnetically attracted to 'healers' and 'prophets' who are absolutely certain about human behaviour and psychology.

The mass-market Jungian writing is almost entirely from the United States, although this work is marketed internationally with great success. There is a distinctly cultic sensibility to this new tradition, which produces recipes, schematic programmes and firm models for our gendered identity and psychosexual development. The mythopoetic writing has 'fans', disciples, and followers, but not critical readers. While I disagree with Richard Noll's thesis that Jungian psychology proper is a charismatic cult, one can certainly see the importance of his critique when we look at its more inferior varieties.[38] When reification and concrete thinking take over, then the Jungian enterprise is finished as far as its intellectual credibility is concerned.

Andrew Samuels is acutely alert to the damage being done to Jungian psychology by the popular fundamentalists. Samuels is alarmed at how the reactionary side of the Jungian world has been allowed to dominate for so long, and he is particularly critical of the package-deal approach to male identity promoted by Robert Bly. Samuels decries the fact that American Jungian analysts have not tackled Bly or criticised his reactionary project, but instead some have actually chimed in to the agenda he has set. Even James Hillman, whose early and major work encouraged diversity, fluidity, and a challenge to conventional notions of gender, appears to have succumbed to Robert Bly's dogmatic project (this will be further explored in Chapter 3). Samuels argues that 'The way in which Jungian psychology has been hijacked by the mythopoetic movement is a disaster that stifles its progressive potentials.' He writes, obviously with analysts James Hillman and Robert Moore in mind, 'some analysts have not only been hijacked, but are also in the grip of what is called [after the famous kidnapping case] the "Stockholm Syndrome"' – namely, the peculiar propensity to become like, and to model oneself upon, those who have taken us captive.[39]

But what has taken Jungian psychology captive is not so much Robert Bly, Robert Moore, or Pinkola Estes, but a new fundamentalism that appears to be sweeping the world at all levels of cultural and political life. Jungian psychology is simply one strand in a reactionary push that wants to restore an old law and bring back an old moral order. In times of collective disorientation, such as at the end of psychological and political patriarchy, a large majority of people seem to go weak at the knees and cannot stand the strain of the new. Symbolic thinking is too difficult, too hard, and we want instant gratification of our wishes; hence the inner world is constructed as a firm and safe world that gives us whatever we need. Metaphor and fluidity give way to security and 'hard wiring', and emphasis on the feminine gives way to 'wildness' and 'Iron John'. The question remains: will Jungianism free itself from this terrible affliction, especially when rigid thinking is so strongly encouraged by commercialism and popular demand? The important thing is to keep on confronting, challenging, and contradicting the vulgar versions of Jungian thought, and to rescue the spirit of Jung from infantilism and regression. This means that more analysts should be prepared to go public about their disagreements, and not simply complain privately about the state of Jung studies while the commercial fundamentalists completely dominate the public stage.

RESCUING THE FEMININE PRINCIPLE

Whenever I lecture on the subject of gender, I am invariably asked: why talk about 'masculine' and 'feminine' principles at all if this discourse gets us into so much strife? If we are talking about transgendered currents that run through our psychological lives, why can't we find other, less confusing terms to designate these universal energies? Surely, this reasoning goes, we can scotch these sex-linked archaisms in favour of less tyrannical and less constricting notions of human character and possibility. Immediately, the educated mind turns to alternative concepts such as Yin and Yang, Receptive and Active, Dark and Light, or else it sifts through various philosophical traditions, finding more palatable and less hackneyed correlates to masculinity and femininity. In his essay 'Beyond the Feminine Principle', Andrew Samuels asks 'Why can't we just talk of *Weltanschauungen* or just of hemispheres?' In this essay, he appears to be advocating an abandonment of, or at least a relaxation of, the use of universal psychological principles in Jungian therapy. As a clinician, Samuels is alert to the dangers posed by 'the feminine principle' when women attempt to shape their lives, and to limit their lives, in accordance with it.

I take these points seriously, but the popular abuse of the

archetypal principles is no reason for disposing of them altogether. This is rather like saying that because dictators and hegemonic leaders have employed religious ideas in service of repressive regimes, we had better bury religious ideas for fear of what trouble they might cause in the future. If we repress the unseen archetypal world in the name of social progress, we only achieve an illiteracy about archetypal matters, not human advancement. I am inclined to be suspicious when we attempt to get rid of something archetypal because it does not accord with contemporary taste. Here I tend to defend the mythopoetic dimension, believing that reasoning based on ideological premises is likely to please the intellect but to confound the wisdom of the heart. The soul would rather that we dig deeper into the soil we already have, rather than import a new pile of earth because we dislike the smell of the old.

So my own response to this problem is to say that although masculine and feminine principles are indeed confusing, they are what we have to work with. Masculine and feminine are not only a cause for intellectual confusion and embarrassment, but also, strangely, a source of spiritual power. The psyche continues to use male and female, man and woman, as symbols of the polar opposites that move through the personality. We continue to dream in the archaic and concrete language of ancient symbols, and we cannot rail against the psyche for using sexist or stereotypical language. The point is that masculinity and femininity have to be constantly raised from the literal level to the metaphorical level, where they can be dealt with in philosophical and psychological ways. In our interpretations, we need to translate the language of fantasies and dreams into more abstract terms, but we must not lose touch with this primal ground of gendered fantasy. We do not dream about Yin and Yang, or about brain hemispheres. Our dreams are peopled with inner men and inner women, and if we shift into completely abstract discourse we will be in danger of losing contact with the fertile ground of richly symbolic psychic experience.

In persisting with the language of masculinity and femininity, we stay in touch with passion and desire. Whoever heard of brain hemispheres having sexual intercourse, or Yin and Yang making love? The psyche loves sexuality and Eros, and we would deprive it of its central passion if we were to jettison sex-linked categories in favour of more intellectual ones. Jung correctly saw in the sexual couplings of our dreams an alchemical exchange and interaction, a coming together of disparate and contradictory parts of the soul, a union of like with unalike. Masculine and feminine remain crucial because they force us into the realm of sexuality, they keep ideation and instinct linked, and so, for all the baggage they necessarily carry, we cannot and must not desert them.

We must also employ a 'binocular' vision when talking about the feminine principle. It seems that when Jungians get hold of this term, they use it to refer to an inward, feeling-based, psychic reality, and this concern blinds us to the repression of the feminine in the social-political world. As Samuels has said, 'much Jungian discourse on the "feminine" seems directed away from political and social action', so that 'dwelling upon interiority and feeling becomes an end in itself'.[40] Sociologist Bob Connell has similar objections to the 'feminine principle'. Connell argues that the theory of masculine and feminine principles,

> yields an interpretation of feminism not as resistance to the oppression of women, but as the reassertion of the archetypal feminine. In past history it is not men who have dominated women, so much as the masculine that has dominated the feminine. One can see why Jungian theory has become central to the current backlash among formerly progressive men. For this approach immediately yields the idea that modern feminism is tilting the balance too far the other way, and suppressing the masculine.[41]

Although it is true that Jungian thought has been exploited by reactionary forces, this is not to be blamed on the idea of the feminine principle. We can ill afford to debunk the feminine principle simply because it is interpreted by an introverted psychology to point to interior realities. The idea of the feminine principle should not make us play off the inner against the outer, since this principle actually makes us see how extensive and profound the repression of the feminine is in Western culture. The idea of the archetypal principle should not depoliticise this repression, but reveal it to be more far-reaching and systemic than even ideological feminism could imagine. Archetypes should widen, not narrow, our perspectives, and they should radicalise, not normalise, our views about gender. If Jungians see one side, and sociologists the other, this is merely because we have yet to develop methods for handling the enormity of archetypal problems. It is our own limitations and prejudices that blind us to the total view, which will show us, eventually, that the split between spirituality and politics is our own cultural invention, and that archetypal transformations require us to respond in complex and paradoxical ways to the big issues of the time.

2

THE FATHER'S ABSENCE
AND DEVOURING PRESENCE

'Father' and 'son' are not only a succession in time, but various ways
of incarnating the ancestral archetype.

James Hillman[1]

In times of social revolution and dramatic change, the archetypal
father becomes problematical and problem-stricken. The archetypal
father symbolises the old world order, established tradition, and the
moral edifice constructed by that tradition. In times when the
unconscious is trying to push for a new order or a different kind of
consciousness, the old father is experienced as weak, anachronistic,
or failing. In traditional fairytales that reflect such a change in
consciousness, we sometimes meet an ailing king or sick ruler who
must be cured of his malady lest the entire land and its people fall
into ruin and decline.[2] The fact that the king is sick, wounded or
dying indicates that consciousness has lost touch with the vital
forces of the unconscious, and that society itself is separated from
the self-renewing capacities of nature. The ruler-king must be
allowed to enter deeply into his illness or woundedness so that a
proper revitalisation can take place. Sometimes the king must die or
pass into oblivion so that a new consciousness can be born.

THE DECAYING PATRIARCH

It is a rare father figure indeed who cheerfully greets his own demise
and offers himself to the new in a spirit of self-sacrifice. The old
father usually clings desperately to whatever power he has left,
giving orders and commandments from his throne even as his health
and moral authority continue to be undermined. The forces that

would bring healing – usually of a feminine or non-heroic character – are so utterly alien to the ruling consciousness that it is not in a position to welcome these forces for what they are, or for the rebirth they can bring. The father would sooner die than have to lose face and pride by lowering his colours to that which he considers to be inferior to him.

But the 'once upon a time' world of the classic fairytale has become today's actual sociopolitical reality. We call the ailing king 'patriarchy', and many of us have long recognised that it is in dire need of transformation. Our ruling consciousness, grounded as it is in the old father or senex archetype, resists change and clings to the past. Moreover, the contemporary patriarch is clever and well-informed: he 'knows' that the feminine can bring healing and that it has enormous power through its deep association with the *zeitgeist* or spirit of the time. Old Father Time, Chronos-Saturn, knows that *his* time is up, but he will do anything to prolong his rulership. Our patriarchal institutions today seem to attempt a tokenistic 'integration of the feminine', most often simply by 'adding women' to the existing patriarchal structures. I live and work in a university system that believes it is moving with the times by 'adding women' to an otherwise unchanging and unchallenged masculine formula. It often seems to me that the patriarchal institutions have no intention of changing; rather, women often become the sacrificial victims to patriarchy's reinvention of itself. The patriarchy rewards new women enlisted in its service for replicating and reproducing its own values and ideologies.[3] In this way, Western society is embroiled in a parody of archetypal process. We engage in what looks like revolutionary change, while actually maintaining the status quo.

It goes without saying that, as patriarchy moves into decline, we mostly see the horrible face of the archetypal father. 'The king is sick' means today that the patriarchal fathers of society are sick. I have met many men and women who can hardly imagine a good, positive, or enabling father figure. All they see is the conniving wretchedness of the ancient tyrant. We see this archetypal figure at its decadent, corrupt and deceitful worst. Our century has been littered with demonic or negative fathers, whether we refer to corrupt politicians, false messiahs, Führers, madmen masquerading as gurus, crooks passing as entrepreneurs. In the death-phase of the ruling senex, the 'rotten' aspect of the power-hungry senex comes to the fore, as this archetype enters the phase that compares with the alchemical condition of *putrefactio*. As Yeats put it, at the end of the Christian-patriarchal era, 'The best lack all conviction, while the worst/Are full of passionate intensity'.[4] The creative aspect of the father has been eclipsed, and during this eclipse a demonic parody of the father arises.

The fact that more men and women are saying that they have experienced inadequate, or abusive, or dysfunctional fathering is therefore archetypally conditioned by the time and to some extent an historical inevitability. For instance, throughout the world at the moment the Christian community is shocked and demoralised by the sordid revelations concerning the 'reframing' of some priests and clergy as paedophiles, abusers, sodomites, and sexual criminals. But it is not just the churches that are being exposed in this way; all the professions are discovering dirt, guilt, and filth in their ranks. No matter what institution we put our nose into these days, there is always the faint or strong whiff of corruption in the corridors. The *putrefactio* really does mean that the patriarchy stinks. The father-king is rotting and being robbed of his glamour and former majesty by the revelation of atrocious and corrupt elements. His once-sublime rule is now being exposed as a tyrannical dictatorship, and being responded to with disgust and distaste.

THE ADVERSARIAL POSITION

When the archetypal father is corrupt, we find that the progressives in society will turn against him and adopt an aggressive stance. This is hardly a recent phenomenon, since in every culture and in every period of history where 'change' occurs, the old father must be deposed. Those who feel inspired by the new, and who sense that there is a better world ahead, a world worth supporting and fighting for, will find the old father oppressive and will try to hasten his downfall and demise. These are our radicals, visionaries, intellectuals, and social reformers. For them, the old king is actually a bloody tyrant with teeth and a fascist boot, a Devouring Father who 'swallows' life and the future by refusing to allow the new to be born. This 'new' consists not only of psychic and social elements formerly repressed or squashed under the old regime, but above all a higher form of social justice and equality. At least, the archetypal fantasy of each successive age or generation is that it is fairer, more humane and enlightened than the cultural order that it is replacing.

In Greek mythology, still our best source of imagery for archetypal processes, we find the figures of Uranos, and Chronos-

Saturn, those monstrous giants (memorably painted by Goya) who literally eat their offspring and who therefore had to be deposed, unseated, or castrated by the forces of progress. When the tyrannical father rules psyche or society, progressives will see and find 'monstrous' forms and injustices around them, injustices that call forth a radical, proactive response. Reformers will feel morally impelled to make those injustices known to all, and to 'expose' the monstrous elements in society. For example, political radicals today will be sickened by the monstrousness of patriarchal capitalism and consumerist excess, which they will feel authorised to attack and overthrow. Feminists see the destructive presence of the cruel, tyrannical father and the famous 'dead hand of patriarchy', which they will feel obliged to defeat and overwhelm wherever possible. Social and legal workers will want to see the old moral order brought to public account and reckoning, and justly humiliated if necessary. These are all important and potent fantasies; sometimes they are overzealous and inappropriately applied, and sometimes they are motivated by revenge and the desire to find a scapegoat for human evil. But these fantasies are what keep the wheels of civilisation turning, making people ever-hopeful of a brighter and more prosperous future. Even if actual change leads to an economic or political downturn, the notion that monstrousness can be overthrown and repressions lifted is a guiding and enabling moral vision.

POLITICAL REALITY AS A PSYCHOSOCIAL FIELD

Conservative-minded people who are not motivated by these future-oriented values and visions will feel that the radicals are 'overdoing it', 'becoming too extreme', 'getting carried away', etc., simply because they are not seeing the same psychosocial field. As an intellectual with humble, working-class origins, I have moved continually between the high cultural elite where the senex is perceived as a dangerous tyrant, and the ordinary community where the senex is either not perceived at all, or is felt to be a basically benevolent figure who works slowly but surely to our eventual betterment. The current political head of my state of Victoria, Jeff Kennett, is viewed as an oppressive dictator by most intellectuals, but as a hard-working and dedicated economic reformer by the wider community. The common folk may perceive that the 'system' is self-interested and sometimes dishonest, but they generally believe it is supportive of the common good. Some radicals will say that the masses have become complacent and have been 'duped' by the patriarchy. But certainly the working class, as I have experienced it in Australia, is anything other than a revolutionary proletariat, eager to seize control when the revolutionary intellectuals show them how to go about it.

The common folk will claim that the radicals are suffering from acute bouts of paranoia and need to relax into a more affirmative and positive attitude. As a radical, left-wing student of the 1970s, I used to send members of my family books and articles about the destructiveness of the patriarchy. After a couple of years, I received a letter which asked me to please stop sending this material, because it was upsetting the family and it made our Christmas gatherings unpleasant occasions. I had to admit to myself then that one person's liberational mission was another person's source of irritation and disturbance. In the 1960s and 1970s, it was assumed that students *saw* the negative father, that his movements and traces were clearly discernible. In those radical years, when every student seemed to be governed by the *puer aeternus* or spirit of rebellion, the negative father was strongly constellated and his presence was palpable and noted by many. It was always astonishing to me to then return to my uneducated family community to find that most people doubted the validity of the apparition – it had little more status than UFO sightings or visions of angels.

Today, the majority of my university students are not seeing the negative senex in the way that I saw him in my own student days. University lecturers nowadays have a hard time convincing conservative students that the Devouring Father exists, that there is a battle to be waged, and that we must act now to bring the future to birth. Obviously, there are periods of history when particular archetypal figures loom large, and then they go back into hiding or recede into the background.

THE ENDURING PRESENCE OF FATHER-ABSENCE

Ironically, while social revolutionaries experience the archetypal father as a cruel and ruthless presence, many others in the community are making the opposite kind of protest: the father is negative because he is absent, ineffectual, or impotent. This rapidly growing public awareness of the father's crippling or disabling absence has taken the anti-patriarchal revolutionaries by surprise, and they are at a loss to know what to do about it. The discourse of radicalism is fixed in the recognition that the father, despite his ailments and corruptions, is still firmly seated on the throne of social power. If large numbers are beginning to say that the throne is vacant, that there is no tyrant seated there, then the revolutionaries are suddenly made to look anachronistic and out of touch with social reality. Are they engaged in an authentic battle, or are they merely shadow-boxing? The fact that many intellectuals are still fighting for a Marxist-Leninist cause that the general public perceive as being lost with the demise of international Marxism, adds considerable weight to the sense of anachronism or staged radicalism.

One way to deal with this apparent dilemma – does the father destroy by his presence or by his absence? – is to say that, while the negative senex today makes a continued grab for sociopolitical control, inwardly and spiritually he has already lost his power. At a depth psychological level, the ruler-king is bankrupt, and many people know it and can feel it. The widespread phenomenon of the Absent Father, is, I believe, largely derived from the loss and disappearance of authentic 'father-energy' at an archetypal level. Everywhere around us people discuss, feel, suffer and mourn the loss of the father. In countless men's groups and gatherings across several continents, men are saying that they feel deserted and neglected by their fathers, not just their sires, but all others – surrogate fathers, mentors, social and political leaders, Führers, gurus, analysts, uncles and wise friends. James Hollis writes: 'Not only are the personal fathers missing; the Old Men, with their tribal wisdom, are dead, lost to corporate board rooms, or adrift in the materialist culture'.[5] In *Finding our Fathers*, Sam Osherson quotes an American survey in which only one in five males reported that their relationship with their fathers was satisfactory.[6] Men are saying that they cannot properly grow up or become mature men, because the guiding hand or support of a patriarchal figure is not present at any level of their psychic experience. These are remarkable allegations, and it is certainly important that we take them seriously.

For some time, I adopted the view that the personal fathers were entirely to blame. Fathers were always missing, not present when sons, daughters, and women needed them. Or they were physically present but emotionally absent; they were 'around about', but their presence was not helpful or effective. Later, I took a different tack: the 'absence' of the archetypal father made personal fathers everywhere

43

appear absent, even when they were present. However, this position subsequently seemed too extreme, suggesting that most of us are suffering from a shared delusion. At the moment, I adopt a modified version of this second view, believing that we are involved in an experience of the father where internal and external levels synchronistically reflect the same transpersonal image of absence, loss, or ineffectuality. I cannot deny the fact that human fathers seem absent and are experienced as hollow, but I can qualify that perception by saying that it is archetypally conditioned.

Most modern library computer systems now have a category known as 'father-absence', which library users can look up to discover dozens of titles relating to the 'absent father'. In these lists, we find sociological, political, cultural, psychological, and sociobiological responses to the problem. Sociology and psychology writings tell us that the father is not around for his children, since he is consumed by patriarchy and hardly has any self left over to share with his family. These writings point to fundamental differences between premodern and postmodern times.[7] In earlier times, fathers worked with their sons in shared careers, trades and businesses, thus helping to transform their sons into men, into active agents of patriarchal structures. Fathers passed on their own skills, or they handed over their land- or work-tradition to the son, who was thereby admitted into manhood by an acceptance of social responsibility, and by an internalisation of the work-ethic. Today, fathers have been forced by changing social conditions to relinquish this task and have been disenfranchised as initiators of their sons. Fathers no longer stand before youths as symbols of cultural stability, urging sons to put childish things behind them and to enter a new world of life-transforming values. We are also informed that many of today's fathers are actually immature 'sons' who have been unable to embrace manhood in a creative way. As James Hollis argues, 'fathers cannot transmit what they have not acquired themselves'.[8]

These standard sociopolitical protests, personal complaints, and familiar descriptions of the contemporary father figure are true enough. All I wish to emphasise is that these descriptions need to be complemented by a deeper archetypal awareness, a recognition that the father of our culture is missing. When the Great Father is missing, all human fathers appear ineffectual.

NEGOTIATING THE FUTURE: OPPOSING THE FATHER AND REDEEMING HIS SPIRIT

If the contemporary gap between fathers and sons is not merely an ordinary 'generation gap', but an archetypal gap between the old world and the new, a patriarchal style and a post-patriarchal style, then we do well to heed the wisdom of the gap and to understand its grim but very real meaning. Contemporary men, or those men who genuinely suffer the consequences of the time, find themselves profoundly isolated from the past and alienated from their own masculine heritage. They are made to suffer an historical disjunction in their personal lives. We should note that this awareness must override our humanistic and 'therapeutic' response, which is to paper over the gap between father and son and to effect a 'healing' reconciliation. More on this in a moment.

We must also realise that, despite the gap and the necessary disjunction between world-views and styles, the son is simply the father's life all over again, or that same life in a different historical context. The son may be required to reject the style and consciousness of the father, but the psychic life or 'spirit' of the father must be continued. This is a deeply paradoxical realisation, and it is always extremely difficult to talk about psychic reality in everyday language, because our language is so linear, and we can only say one thing at a time. Perhaps this is why poetry is the true language of the soul. James Hillman comes close to the complexity of the situation when he says that the son does not need to *kill* the father, but rather he needs to 'redeem the father'. The essential task, he writes, is 'to redeem the father by surpassing him'.[9] The father's life is profoundly changed in the being of the son, not by extinguishing that life, but by linking it with the progressive forces of the present, and thus by bringing it into line with the future. In the language of fairytale, the king dies to be replaced by a young prince who is simultaneously the past and the future. He contains within himself the life of the king, but he also embodies in his person the promise of future generations. The prince, or new king, must deal with the pressing realities of the time; he must make some genuine attempt to come to grips with the time-spirit. If he does not make this adjustment, his is a bogus authority and he must perforce be deposed by a more worthy successor. If the new generation lacks courage, it will be 'devoured' by the tyrannical father archetype and must suffer the same fate as the old ruler-king.

So we have before us two separate but related tasks: claiming the new, and redeeming the old. Each requires different methods, styles, and hermeneutics. The first demands what Paul Ricoeur calls the 'hermeneutics of suspicion'. By viewing the past with a healthy dose of irreverence or suspicion, we free ourselves from its terrible burden and can move ahead with confidence and a truly forward-looking orientation. Contemporary intellectuals in the humanities and social sciences trade on the hermeneutics of suspicion to such an extent that one could say they have become addicted to it. There is so much suspicion, doubt, questioning and criticism that knowledge has virtually become synonymous these days with demystification, demythologising and deconstruction. All the 'de' words tell us that suspicion is operating, and that the traditional patriarchal canon is being disassembled and the patriarch of tradition is being *de*bunked. This can be a lot of fun, even exhilarating, but taken to its extreme it results in a life-deadening nihilism, in which the living spirit of the past has been abandoned and the essence of the father has been betrayed. As such, the new cannot really be born at all, because it requires the spirit of tradition to ignite the flame and keep it burning.

The other task, redeeming the old, demands what Ricoeur calls the 'hermeneutics of affirmation'. Here we have to affirm the heritage of the past by ensuring that the present and the future contain at their core the spirit of traditional culture. That is to say, there is a primary concern here for such august verities as integrity and truth. Here we no longer look for disjunction, severance, bold or brash statements about the superiority of the new. In affirming the past we diminish the hype and exaggerated claims of the new, and instead of gloss or glamour we look for depth and authenticity as the ruling values and standards. This view affirms that there is 'nothing new under the sun', and that life is best conducted when this sobering attitude is fully realised. Then we overcome the crippling modern sense of alienation, for we awaken to our profound continuity with the past, with the fathers of tradition, and with the struggle of the ages. The great danger of this task is that it forgets why the new *must be different* and how it must maintain its distinct identity even while drawing vigorously upon the past. This task frequently lapses into a kind of ineffectual sentimentalism, where attachments to the past become cloying and fetishistic. In its extreme form, the new is frowned upon and the continual salutations to the past drive the innovators and modernists mad with rage.

We are talking here of course about puer and senex again; the spirit of revolution, fast, pacy, brilliant, brash, and the spirit of evolution, slow, gradual, faithful, entrenched. The new and rising generation has to use the elements and styles of both archetypal figures. It requires the puer or young son to cheekily denounce the old and bring on the new. And it requires the 'father' in the son to recognise the traditional essence at the heart of the new, thus ensuring that the new is not cheap and worthless. In redeeming the father, both styles and mechanisms must come into play. In the current debates about men's issues, we find that either one or the other style is usually in the ascendant. We have still to discover a public men's movement that honours both styles at once, that has the guts to oppose and the courage to embrace.

THE KILLING DISCOURSES: PROFEMINIST MEN'S STUDIES AND THE ATTACKING OF PATRIARCHY

My colleagues in the university system and elsewhere who work on gender issues from a political and liberational perspective are keenly involved in killing off the old in order to bring on the new. They work tirelessly to this end, and in many ways I feel they deserve more recognition than they get, because they are attempting a work of liberation in the true classical style. Too often, casual onlookers will think of them as ratty and paranoid, professional stirrers and fighters who, like the hired gunmen in the Wild West, kill for a living. Wherever the patriarchy raises its ugly head, a gender studies scholar will be there with a fast gun, to shoot it down.

In classical mythology, there were no guns, only sickles and scythes. Like the young Chronos, who was guided by Gaia, the maternal principle, the new profeminist liberators hold the sickle in their hands, poised ready to cut off the balls of the tyrannical and devouring ogre. After castrating Ouranos, Chronos-Saturn is then able to seize control, but famously he then grows up to become a tyrant himself. From the spilt blood of the tyrannical Ouranos emerges the beauty of the new and also, as Freud knew so well, the guilt at having deposed the old. This is wonderfully symbolised in this same myth, for from the spilt blood and severed phallus of Ouranos arises Aphrodite (or beauty), a pristine Goddess of the future, who emerges sublimely from frothy seas (the Greek *aphros* = white foam). Yet, long before the wonderful Aphrodite is born, the excised manhood of the old tyrant gives birth to the Erinyes, who can be psychologised as guilt feelings, which accompany the emergence of the new.

Is this the myth that academic men's studies is enacting? I think not, because we find precious little Aphrodite, not much awareness of beauty, and very few guilt feelings in the vigorously antipatriarchal and profeminist writings about men. It could be that the myth of the next generation of Greek Gods reveals more about its archetypal style. Chronos, or Father Time, grows into the likeness of his father, devouring his own offspring, lest they challenge his supremacy. Moreover, Chronos had been warned by his own father that he was fated to be overthrown by a powerful son. 'He was therefore continually on his guard, and swallowed his children.' Rhea, his wife, was stricken by 'an insupportable grief', and when she was about to give birth to Zeus, whom she felt would be 'the future father of gods and men', she devised a plan to trick the terrible father. She offered the devourer 'a great stone wrapped in swaddling-clothes' and Zeus grew up to become a strong and handsome opponent of his father.[10] According to Apollodorus, the mature Zeus punished his father by forcing him to take 'a draught that made him vomit up the stone and with it the gods, his own children, whom he had swallowed'.[11] Kerenyi reports that by this world-transforming act, 'Zeus liberated not only his own brothers and sisters, but also those of his father, whom Ouranos still held in fetters'.[12]

I think that contemporary men's studies must in some respects be following this ancient mythic pattern, although modern radicals do not like to believe that they are recreating anything 'ancient'. In psychological terms, the devouring Chronos is preventing other styles of masculinity (his sons Zeus, Poseidon, Hades) and other feminine forms (his daughters Hestia, Demeter, Hera) from coming to birth. The fact that Chronos consumes the new indicates that a single archetypal complex has seized control, and everything in psyche and society is subsumed by his one dictatorial style. This is precisely what the new men's studies is about: releasing suppressed or devoured styles of masculinity and femininity from the all-devouring hegemonic complex that is called patriarchy. The book titles alone tell us that we must move *Beyond Patriarchy*, that we must dissolve the stereotype (*Unwrapping Masculinity*), refuse the patriarchal style (*Refusing to Be a Man*), and we must develop a sense of multiple and diverse styles of masculinity (*The Making of Masculinities*).[13] The title, *Men Freeing Men: Exploding the Myth of the Traditional Male*,[14] indicates that we are in the archetypal arena of Zeus the liberator, who both 'frees' Gods and men, and 'explodes' the supremacy of the old patriarchal form.

In *Beyond Patriarchy*, Michael Kaufman calls for the complete subjugation of patriarchy. All of us, he argues, are caught up in the tyranny of this single, overbearing archetypal form. The patriarchal style, he writes, without making reference to Goya's Saturn, is synonymous with violence, aggression, power, and control, and requires 'a suppression of a whole range of human needs, aims, feelings, and forms of expression' to ensure its upkeep and continuation.[15] Kaufman imagines he is describing a sociopolitical construct, but isn't this a perfect description of Ouranos or of Chronos-Saturn? Doesn't this God 'feed upon' a whole range of human forms to satisfy its raging appetite? The mythic dimension does not make the sociopolitical critique any less real; on the contrary, it gives that critique an archetypal basis, making it more powerful than before.

But what happens in too much academic men's studies is that a kind of mythological slippage occurs. We start off in a Zeus-like liberational pattern, where the father is tricked into releasing all the forms and figures he has devoured, and suddenly we enter a different kind of mythic territory, where the emphasis is upon *killing* the father. When 'killing' dominates our political vision, we readily get caught up in the Oedipus complex: attacking the father so that we might marry the mother. Unseating the father or opposing his oppressive authority is a creative act, but *killing the father* leads to Oedipal regression and incestuous coupling with the maternal source. If radical men do not confine or discipline their rage against tradition, they (we) will regress to a more destructive mythologem, the one that Freud felt was always 'waiting' to be released in the psychic structure of every male. Perhaps we could say that the more 'primitive' our rage against the father, the more likely it will be that regressive Oedipal impulses will be aroused. Radical men must not allow themselves to be carried away by rage against the father, lest they merely lead us into an Oedipal destiny, where men and Western culture alike can expect to find blindness (unconsciousness), sorrow, misfortune, and death. Before I join a 'men's liberation' circle, I for one want to be sure that we are not simply enlisting in the Oedipus club.

After Oedipus kills Laius and marries Jocasta, we are warned that

> the Erinnyes were waiting. A terrible epidemic ravaged the land, decimating the population, and at the same time an incredible drought brought with it famine. When consulted, the oracle of Delphi replied that these scourges would not cease until the Thebans had driven the still unknown murderer of Laius out of the country.[16]

If we kill the father merely to marry the mother, we have engaged in an act of regression and symbolic incest that will not liberate the world but destroy it. When caught in the Oedipal mode, we do not move beyond the father after killing him, but we move back into a chaotic, pre-patriarchal age where the father's order is absent and consciousness is ruined. There is a very real possibility that well-intended men's studies will simply be caught up in this kind of cultural regression.

'Politically correct' men's studies have a tendency to get stuck in the killing mode. This is hugely ironic, because these studies purport to be against violence, opposed to male aggression and patriarchal destruction, yet the very thing they are attacking seems to dominate their own style. The destructiveness of the senex perpetuates itself in the rebellious sons, where it manifests itself as a lethal intellectual style. Some profeminist men's groups become incredibly critical and negative, always attacking male character and personality, as if every man were a terrible rapist or mankind a one-eyed Cyclops. Indeed, the more radical proponents of the new men's studies seem to be indulging their hatred of *all* styles of masculinity, as well as their dread of their own phallic manhood. An emotionalised form of thinking in men's studies fails to differentiate between the good and the bad in masculinity, and views maleness itself as synonymous with evil and wrongdoing.

In 'Toward a New Sociology of Masculinity', Bob Connell and others address the problem of grossly reductive and negative images of masculinity:

> Some accounts of masculinity . . . face a characteristic danger in trying to hold to feminist insights about men, for a powerful current in feminism, focusing on sexual exploitation and violence, sees masculinity as more or less unrelieved villainy and all men as agents of the patriarchy in more or less

the same degree. Accepting such a view leads to a highly schematized view of gender relations, and leads men in particular into a paralyzing politics of guilt. This has gripped the 'left wing' of men's sexual politics since the mid 1970s.[17]

The 'politics of guilt' places us again in the precinct of Oedipus. If the father, patriarchy, and masculinity are attacked for primarily Oedipal reasons, the men's liberation movement will be swamped and devoured by its own guilt feelings (the Erinnyes). Such guilt overtakes the personality when it regresses to the maternal source. For Freud, this guilt is interpreted personalistically in terms of the son's incestuous longing for cohabitation with the mother. The son's libido is paralysed by its attachment to the fantasy of incest, which immediately constellates prohibition, paralysis, and the 'incest taboo' by way of a counter-response.[18] For Jung, however, this process can best be understood in a symbolic way. The 'mother' represents the matrix of the unconscious, and 'killing the father' means, in Jungian terms, that the personality is now in danger of regressing to an archaic, preconscious or infantile state. Such regression constellates overpowering guilt, not because of literal incest, but because this symbolic incest runs counter to life and consciousness itself. We are guilty because we have contravened our destiny, betrayed the father, and renounced (at least temporarily) the game of life.[19]

According to Jung and Neumann, Oedipus's act of 'putting out his own eyes' is a self-violation which is also a symbolic self-castration. His incestuous union with the mother (at once literal and symbolic) has corrupted his sexuality, so that the 'natural man' has been defiled. In most profeminist discourses, the phallus too is dirty, corrupt; an organ of shame and guilt. The male phallus 'causes' men to be more violent than women, 'forcing' them into aggressive activities, and is a symbol of woman's oppression and defilement. In radical feminist literatures, the phallus is that which transgresses, violates, attacks, penetrates, enters where it is not wanted; in fact it becomes a symbol of rape and corruption. This kind of extremist discourse, which seems to point to psychic disturbance rather than political revolution, indicates to me that the antipatriarchal cause has been attacked by the Erinnyes. Progressive discourses must oppose the father but not kill him, and they must 'shrink the phallus'[20] but not mutilate it. If our radical activity gets caught in the killing and mutilating mode, society will not move forward at all, because we become paralysed by negative archetypal forces. The extremist radical of our time is too often 'swallowed as he castrates, unable to bring real change'.[21]

THE NOSTALGIA FOR PERMANENCE: SPIRITUAL UNION WITH THE FATHER

On the other side of the cultural divide, my colleagues in the spiritual men's movement understand full well the importance of the fathering spirit. As discussed, they are alert to the *suffering* caused by the absent father. They are able to see that when the father is absent, the son himself will not be allowed to enter his own mature masculinity. As Robert Bly has said, the father is a kind of doorway through which the son must pass, and if the doorway cannot be found, or is closed for some historical and/or personal reason, then the son suffers the condition of ongoing and chronic immaturity, living life as an Oedipal man, effeminate, incapacitated by guilt, and alienated from his own masculinity.

The spiritual men's movement realises, correctly, that the dissolution of patriarchy does not make men 'free' to be who they like, but takes away a crucial archetypal foundation in the experience of masculinity. Despite the idealism of political rebels, the dissolution of patriarchy will not bring on a new golden age, but will necessarily leave many men in an emotional and psychological quandary. Already today, numerous men in the mainstream are showing signs of deep and angry confusion about identity, sexuality, gender role, direction, purpose – and this situation is bound to get worse. Not all of these men can go on journeys of individuation; many are not equipped to do so, and many more do not have the time or money for the essential self-reflection, meditation and questioning that individuation demands. The spiritual men's movement reckons that when collective masculine structures break down, chaos and disruption will ensue for the vast majority. Although the political men's movement is anti-elitist and against hierarchies, the spiritual movement is, in a very conservative sense, 'democratic' in its emphasis upon the common man's plight and its insistence that individual men need collective support. Patriarchy is not simply some artificial sociopolitical structure 'out there', but is also an archetypal structure inside the psyche, a structure which ensures social stability, emotional security and smooth passage into manhood. Men who find themselves involved in the mythopoetic movement set themselves these tasks: to transcend the alienation from the personal father, either directly or through surrogate fathering and mentoring; to recover respect and trust in men and masculinity; and to seek initiation into a post-Oedipal state of maturity.

These are, from a personal, emotional and 'therapeutic' position, noteworthy and commendable objectives. So-called 'uninitiated' men have quickly figured out what manhood is, how to achieve it, and why it is desirable. In case they forget, there is a huge and ever-growing literature to remind them of every step along the Masculine Way.

However, where does this rush for security and stability take us? Over recent years, I have become critical of the spiritual men's movement because it loses sight of political realities. It has to be pointed out that the gap that so many men are keen to bridge, or deny, is itself archetypally sanctioned. It is not just an unfortunate crack in our personal lives, but a deep fault line in history. What about the deathly and demonic face of the patriarchy? What about the feminine *zeitgeist*? What about the urgent need for a new, post-patriarchal consciousness? All too often, the spiritual movement ends up in conservative politics, reactionary attitudes, and a restoration of 1950s values. I think Susan Faludi is correct to list the spiritual men's movement as an important public force in the contemporary backlash against feminism.[22]

If men want only to lick their wounds because of rifts between themselves and their fathers, if they mourn the prestige of the masculinist tradition, if they would rather that patriarchy had not been wounded in the first place, then naturally feminists and social critics are going to launch stinging attacks on their politics. The baffled and 'embattled' nature of the responses of some men to these attacks shows just how dissociated 'personal feeling' and 'political reality' have become in our culture. Men do not yet understand that the personal *is* political, and that deep and intimate feelings have social causes and political consequences. We do not realise that we suffer history in our individual lives, and that cultural change does not just happen outside, in the streets, or to other people, but takes place in our own experience and at considerable personal cost.

The new spiritual writing is written out of men's pain, a pain that carries its own legitimation and that clearly cannot be contradicted. Alfred Collins writes movingly about his own alienation from the father:

I recall with pain that Dad seemed disappointed in me and seemed not to understand me. We withdrew from one another, and our 'Fatherson' entered a phase of opposition and strife from which it did not emerge before his death.[23]

Guy Corneau writes about men's experience with the same note of high anxiety and desperation:

My father left me alone, refusing to recognize me; my arguments were worthless and always would be. I could try, but I was not a man. If only he could have known how hard I was trying to reach him, how much I needed him![24]

It has become very fashionable for writers to declare their own anguished separation from the father, and to use that separation as psychological authority for exploring the 'wounded male spirit'. In the patriarchal past, a 'real man' would not bother with emotions or feelings at all: he would just get on with his masculine achievements. In post-patriarchal times, the announcement of one's alienation from the father and of one's unfulfilled need for the father, or father surrogates, is an obligatory statement of one's bona fides, an expected qualification before one can be accepted as a serious contributor to the debates about contemporary men's experience.

The pain speaks of father-absence, and the pain cries out to be healed. The 'healing' is the presence of the father, and the continuity of father and son, or, politically, patriarchy. At best, this literature advocates an 'enlightened patriarchy', where the extremes and problems of the past are acknowledged, and where it is hoped that in future the patriarchy will be more caring and concerned. And so we find today a virtual subculture of writings that all testify to the near-ecstasy and personal relief of connecting with patriarchal archetypes: *Like Father, Like Son: Healing the Father–Son Wound in Men's Lives*; *Absent Fathers, Lost Sons*; *At My Father's Wedding*; and *Return to Father*.[25] These works suffer from a disease called anti-intellectualism. The authors have decided that they will write from the gut and their emotions, and will not bother about 'head stuff' concerning feminism, rupture, history, alienation. In writing from the gut, we get blasted with an emotional longing that is alarmingly primal, fierce, and unschooled.

In his book *Fatherson*, Alfred Collins argues that fathers and sons are intimately related at a psychological level, and that an archetype called 'fatherson' can be accessed by the son to bring

54

about healing. This is a classic case, it seems to me, of what Nietzsche called 'word-magic', whereby a new word, in this case a power word which is also elevated to the status of archetype, is invented to perform certain kinds of magic and to undercut the pain of reality. A primitive nominalism or word-magic can be found in much of the recent Jungian literature, where new terms, archetypes and concepts are invented to make us feel better about the messes we are in. To some extent, this is an example of psychology being used against the psyche.

In 'fatherson', two words become one, and the result is not just another word but a manifesto. The word is meant by Collins to carry the thesis that father and son, as Kohutian self-objects for each other, define a single emotional field, but the argument relies too heavily on the simple and assertive neologism. What we find in this theory, as pleasant-sounding as it is, is a 'denial of rupture' (Lacan) between new men and the old patriarchal order. Collins asserts the inevitability and even the sanctity of Patriarchy and Kingship, arguing that he finds deep emotional support and security from his own manly bond with these archetypally-santioned institutions.

The spiritual men's movement has clearly grasped one aspect of the contemporary archetypal dilemma, the need to achieve a deep connectedness with the father, but the necessary detachment or separation from the *traditional* father and *conventional* patriarchy has been conveniently overlooked. The healing emphasis of men's therapy culture has healed a wound that is a necessary creative source, a place of tension and change, and the wound from which the future will spring. A new authentic masculinity obviously cannot merely be 'more of the same'. What kind of healing is it that denies the possibilities of the future? Here we detect the Chronos complex: a new generation of masculinity, separated from the traditional kind, itself grows steadily into the likeness of the original model. What would be the point of millions of therapeutic sessions and millions of suffering clients, if all we can manage is a 'regressive restoration' of anachronistic masculinity?

The crisis we are facing is clearly philosophical and paradigmatic. How do we bring on the new? How do we 'redeem the father by surpassing him'? When the son discovers his inner longing to reconnect with the father, must the recognition of this longing always lead to the loss of the independent position of sonship and to a regressive return to patriarchy? Ruptures are creative, ruptures can work toward good, but what we find today is an inability to tolerate rupture and a flaming passion for unity.

USING IRONY, HUMOUR, AND FREUD TO COUNTER SPIRITUAL SWEETNESS

One way to undercut the contemporary sentimental and nostalgic fusions with the father is to introduce more irony and criticism – more intellectual life – into the debates. The set formula has the Lost Son on a spiritual journey to find the Absent Father. But just how *absent* is this father? Do we, for instance, unconsciously inflame the adult longing for the father by exaggerating his absence in childhood? Is the contemporary love affair with the father simply our poor attempt to counter our Oedipal guilt and extricate ourselves from Oedipal isolation?

Some years ago, when I was trying to see if I had any place in the spiritual men's movement, I spoilt the atmosphere at a consciousness-raising meeting by questioning the new myth of the absent father. I suppose this was my attempt to see if the group could bear the salty sting of the intellect, to see if there was room for anything other than caring concern and niceness. I said that we all freely accept that our fathers were absent in our childhood, but I very much doubted that this was actually the case. In one sense, this myth results from the fulfilment of our childhood Oedipal longings. 'Oedipus?' said one of the outspoken Lost Boys, 'Why bring him into it? We are men of the 1990s, and our experience is unique.' Perhaps it is unique, I said, but perhaps it is a re-run of a universal male pattern. When sons are seeking the mother's attentions and set themselves up as rivals of the father, their deepest wish is that the father would go away. Perhaps this wish becomes *all too true* as we observe the father pulling away from the Oedipal triangle and allowing the son his desired closeness to the mother.

I told the group, who by this stage were rendered speechless by my heresy, that I would be among the first to admit my own covert complicity to the experience of father-absence. I gave my father the clear message that I did not want him around, since I wanted to bask alone in the company of my mother. Dad was bitter about this at first, and made several attempts to correct the situation: he frequently complained that I was rejecting him, criticising my mother for turning me into a mumma's boy and a cissy. From when I was about 8 years of age, he would sometimes nostalgically recall the 'good old days', when I was, as he put it, 'Daddy's friend and helper'. In very early childhood, I followed him around most of the time, taking on his interests, modelling myself on his example, and, during school holidays, going with him to work where I attempted to be his mascot and assistant. After that I turned him into a rival and attempted to undermine his authority. Don't most boys do this?

It seems to be incredibly hypocritical to subvert the father during this developmental phase, and then to complain, years later at men's groups and in therapy rooms, that the father was absent for us. Men are shedding crocodile tears in the men's movement. The men who, as teenagers in the 1960s and 1970s, attacked social and political fathers, and often felt embarrassed about or ignored their 'conventional' 1940s and 1950s dads, are now railing against the distance that separates them from the patriarchal order. Personal fathers became sickened and disheartened by our undermining tactics and radical styles (they hated the long hair, torn jeans, Jimi Hendrix and marijuana), and gradually they withdrew into work, team-sport, and beer. I have discussed this, somewhat shyly, with my own father, who said, 'Well, you've come good at last – and you've cut your bloody hair'. But many years of covertly systematic rejection had worn him down, and naturally he retreated into a shell of silence.

Guy Corneau writes about the 'hereditary silence that has been passed down from generation to generation, a silence that denies every teenage boy's need for recognition'.[26] This is certainly as true here in Australia as in Corneau's native Canada. And, although Corneau concedes, 'I feel I'm as responsible for it as he is', this insight is not elaborated, and throughout his book the blame squarely falls on the father – or on the older generation of fathers and their inability to deal with matters of the heart. Corneau writes, without any apparent irony: 'I sat there *in my mother's chair*, waiting for my father to speak. I felt timid, tongue-tied; I was begging for confirmation of my manhood' (emphasis added).[27] The snag in the men's movement is that sensitive new-age guys are not really 'sensitive' enough to see how they might have conspired to produce this situation. Boys sit in judgement on the father from their mother's chairs – i.e. from the standpoint of the mother-complex, from where they wound and emotionally castrate the father. Having undermined and castrated Dad, they then *castigate* him for not providing the masculine reinforcement and the phallic reassurance that they need. Wake up all you guys who claim that father's absence is denying your entrance into manhood: this is a modern fantasy which must be seen through before psychological growth can occur. The splitting, projecting and persecutory fantasies of modern men will not heal the wounds, but will simply reinforce their fate as the lost generation, the generation that could not grow up.

REFUSING THE POPULAR IDEALISATION OF THE ARCHETYPAL FATHER

Whenever the 'simple' and 'kindly' old man appears, it is advisable for heuristic and other reasons to scrutinize the context with some care . . . the old man has a wicked aspect too.

Jung[28]

Another way to counter the regressive return to patriarchy is to challenge the contemporary popular idealisation of the father figure. We can partly understand the spiritual movement's idealisations in terms of an unconscious compensatory movement away from painful reality. If Dad was absent when I needed him, and ineffectual and evasive when present, then an expectation of an ideal father arises by way of compensation. Surely the powerful influence of psychotherapy upon our culture has a part to play in this 'cargo cult' mentality. After all, therapy provides us with the idea of a necessary regression to a painful past, and the notion that a magical 'transference' can come into play to provide a healing counterweight to the 'negative' experience of one's childhood experience of the parent. If we add to this psychoanalytic expectation the Jungian notion that archetypes are well-springs of healing energy, then we arrive at the popular belief that an internal father will come to our aid and lift us out of depression and isolation into an experience of wholeness.

A real tendency in contemporary spiritual writings is to point the finger of blame at the real father and to idealise the internal father. It is widely assumed, especially in self-help books for men, that an internal potential to become a father is present in every man, that this inward figure is an archetypal Seer or Wise Old Man, and that we can turn to this visionary figure for renewal. This notion is wildly idealistic, though perhaps it serves to keep many wounded and isolated men in life and in the battle for psychological survival. I do not intend to explode this new myth entirely, because I believe there are real healing potentials in the psyche, and that these can come almost miraculously to our aid, especially when we are in a desperate or critical condition. It is true that the father archetype can be activated in the psyche of the son, and that this archetype spans a very wide variety of psychological styles, from the authoritarian style of Zeus-Jupiter, through to the prophetic and visionary styles personified in such figures as Merlin and Tiresias.

But when we initially engage with the *internal* father image, Merlin or the Wiseman-Seer is not the figure whom we encounter first! Most strongly constellated in the psyche is the same kind of father figure whom we have dealt with in life. If our personal father was perceived as a sulky, sullen, silent, sardonic, stoical, senex figure, then that figure does not disappear when we leave Dad's orbit, but becomes a part of internal psychological reality. For men who encountered in childhood negative experiences of the father, the internal figure is usually stamped with exactly the same face. This is one of the first things that clients in analysis are forced to deal with. The very father figures whom they have hated or fought in society, family and life are revealed as aspects of their own unconscious character. This is a moral challenge which appears to scare some people away from psychoanalysis altogether. It is easier to imagine that the negative fathers are outside one's own psychic domain and encapsulated in ineffectual personal fathers, or in destructive and power-driven political leaders or world figures.

The new self-help literature which creates an idealised picture of the father-within-the-son is dangerously misleading. One example is the enticing remarks printed on the back cover of Guy Corneau's *Absent Fathers, Lost Sons*:

> For men today, regaining the essential 'second birth' into manhood lies in gaining the ability to be a father to themselves – not only as a means of healing psychological pain, but as a necessary step in the process of becoming whole.
>
> (Corneau 1991)

In similar vein, Alfred Collins writes: 'a wise father sits enthroned in the back of a young iconoclast's mind'.[29] In contemporary Jungian discourse, there is a real tendency to equate the senex or father with the archetype of the Self. The prevailing view is that the inner father will heal psychological pain and create wisdom and wholeness. The inner father is a God-father, an old, smiling, bearded presence who works ceaselessly for the health and development of his fragile, battered, alienated sons. Anti-Jungians find plenty of evidence here for the idea that 'archetypes' are simply infantile delusional ideas designed to fill in the gaps left by unsatisfactory life experience of the parental figure. The great beneficent father in the sky has reappeared as a delusional presence in the psyche of suffering contemporary men.

Some years ago I submitted an essay to an American Jungian journal. The manuscript editor decided that the term 'senex' was too difficult and academic-sounding, and so translated all my specialist terms into what was called 'ordinary language'. To my amazement, I found that 'senex' had been changed in every instance to 'Wise Old Man'. I got on the telephone and fax to point out that this was unacceptable. This was not merely an editorial change, but a confusing mistranslation of my meaning. We settled on the term 'father' as the more acceptable translation, though I pointed out that 'father' reminds too many readers of their Dad, whereas the formality of the Latin 'senex' establishes more fully the archetypal context. This little episode alerted me to the general and widespread idealisation of the father archetype. In America especially, archetypes are always in danger of being deprived of their shadows, which is why, I think, the American analyst James Hillman is always emphasising the shadow aspect of everything.

The father complex does not exist to serve my personal well-being. No genuine Jungian would ever believe such a silly idea. Like any other complex, this one basically serves itself, and we often have to work hard to extricate ourselves from the grip of his one-sidedness and obsessive control, before his purpose in 'maturing' us can be realised. It may be that a naive, pseudo-Jungian belief in the self-regulating function of the psyche has prevented us from understanding that the psyche is, after all, the source of disease and disorder, and not simply the source of constant healing. In *Jung and the Post-Jungians*, Samuels argues that 'it is important to protect the idea of the self-regulating psyche from panglossian excesses, in which everything is seen as being for the best or as part of some giant benevolent plan'.[30] The optimistic attitude toward psychic life that is promoted by popular Jungianism is sometimes a real obstacle to a full appreciation of psychological reality. With a new literature and ethos now devoted to the image of the idealised father, the negative internal father-imago gets lost. But despite the best intentions of the son, the negative father will be around some-where, usually where we least expect it.

The spiritual men's movement notoriously fails to see that the demonic face of the patriarchy is part of the wider nature of its same idealised archetype. Spiritual writers sometimes claim to be alert to the dangers of patriarchy, and then go on to argue that patriarchy does not represent a 'true' style of 'mature' masculinity.[31] But this is disingenuous; we all know that Ouranos and Chronos-Saturn are aggressive oppressors, and that these Gods are not simply naughty boys, but are the oldest and most 'mature' of all the masculine deities. The devouring, crushing aspect of the archetypal father is a central part of its character, and if we fail to give it due recognition we are more likely to fall victim to it. Some time ago, Hillman warned us that the senex archetype 'does not permit the ego to select from it the sweeter parts'.[32] If we are conscious of the evil capacity of the father we will all live in a saner and more tolerable society.

Recently, Hillman has argued insightfully that the negative father acts as a kind of 'negative incentive' to individual development and the realisation of one's own separateness:

> The destructive father destroys the idealized image of himself. He smashes the son's idolatry. Whenever, wherever we idealize the father, we remain in sonship, in the false security of a good ideal. A good model, whether kind analyst, wise guru, generous teacher, honest chief, holds these virtues of kindness, wisdom, generosity, and honesty fixed in another, projected outside. Then, instead of initiation, imitation. Then the son remains tied to the person of the idealized figure.[33]

The negative father 'smashes the son's idolatry' – and the idola-trous men's movement needs to read more of the literature of the political men's movement to discover how it can liberate itself from imprisoning idolatry. Hillman's useful formula is that the killer father 'kills idealization'. When the idealisation is undermined, the son is cut loose, independent of the father, and hence more able to assume fatherhood himself. Hillman therefore argues that,

> The cry to be fathered so common in psychological practice, as well as the resentment against the cruel or insufficient father so common in feminism . . . fail to recognize that [the father's] shadow traits against which one so protests are precisely those that initiate fathering.[34]

61

THE DEATH OF GOD: THE RELIGIOUS DIMENSION OF FATHER-ABSENCE

I have been arguing all along that archetypal and cultural aspects of father-absence impact upon our human experience of fathers. Now it is time to look at the religious dimension, and what we can learn from the felt 'absence' of our Father in Heaven. Hillman wrote:

> When the father is absent, we fall more readily into the arms of the mother. And indeed the father is missing; God is dead. . . . The missing father is not your or my personal father. He is the absent father of our culture, the viable senex who provides not daily bread but spirit through meaning and order. The missing father is the dead God who offered a focus for spiritual things.[35]

The 'higher dimension' of the father archetype, which would include logos, spirit, wisdom, pneuma, is missing in our rabidly materialistic culture. Nietzsche was the first to cry that 'God is dead' in the modern world, and he was quick to add in this same discourse that 'we have killed him'.[36] The idea of a Father God is a crucial element in the souls of men and women, and it is little wonder that many men have fallen victim to a kind of vulgar and inferior longing for Him.

The loss of the Heavenly Father is not only due to our materialism but also to fundamental shifts at the archetypal level. The uprising feminine, or the Goddess, has got heaven out of balance, and has (necessarily) nudged the Father off his royal throne. At least, this is one simple description of complex metaphysical events that in themselves completely defy description. It seems very hard to find the Heavenly Father today. We can find Ouranos long enough to get the sickle to his balls, or Chronos-Saturn long enough to get him to drink a brew that will throw up the swallowed and repressed masculinities. But the Heavenly Father appears to be out of our reach, or too high up.

With Christ we can cry, 'My God, my God, why hast thou forsaken me?' (Matthew 27: 46). But today's cry to the *deus absconditus* is not properly understood in its religious context. Instead, it is Dad who withholds his love, or the fathers of society who do not care, or the patriarchy which is not doing its duty, or 'mateship' which is not including me. The spiritual foundation of the absent father escapes our attention. Could this mean that the spiritual men's movement is not 'spiritual' enough? Nietzsche's 'God is dead' also means that *we are dead* to this crucial archetype; we are not alive to its capacity to shape our psychological lives. We have to learn to see the resonances, echoes, and subtle influences of Judeo-Christianity upon our contemporary experience. The spiritual men's movement seems conveniently to repress our Jewish-Christian background, and in popular Jungianism there is a rush to ancient pagan and shamanic systems but very little interest in our own religious heritage.

Christ's cries of abandonment were also heard within the earlier Jewish tradition, at a time of cultural renewal and transformation:

> My God, my God, why hast thou forsaken me? why art thou so far from helping me, from the words of my groaning? O my God, I cry by day, but thou dost not answer; and by night, but find no rest.
>
> (Psalms 22. 1–2)

Modern men at emotional weekend retreats imagine they are the first to utter these words, but such sentiments are basic to times of transition and unrest. However, today the uttering of 'groaning' words and cries of alienation can become a kind of cult habit, or a repetitive and self-indulgent style. This suggests to me that when the religious dimension of our experience is repressed or ignored, it reappears in inferior 'religiosity' and popular cultism.

The mythopoetic men's movement has quickly developed a cultic atmosphere, with core beliefs, a set of dogmas, mana-charged gurus and leaders, and devotion demanded of the followers. We should be particularly suspicious of its articles of faith, which include: our fathers are absent; we need to be initiated and redeemed by older men with power; the movement will release us from the unbearable burden of selfhood; we cannot access heart or feelings except through this male community; and the movement builds a brotherhood that helps compensate for the absent personal father. Most big cities now have local leaders who claim to have had actual contact with the movement's charismatic founders (Bly, Moore, Meade, Lee, Farrell), and thus, through a kind of apostolic succession, minor players in the movement claim spiritual authority in their respective communities. As Samuels has noted, 'Without realizing it, the movement aspires to becoming a kind of religion – a desire that is inflated and dangerous'.[37]

Inflation is evident in much that takes place in the men's movement. We have already discussed the fantastic idealisation of masculinity itself, which arises cleansed of the past, falsely separated

63

from 'ugly' patriarchy and hyper-masculinity, and floating heaven-ward on a cloud of incense. The refusal to link 'new masculinity' with patriarchy, violence, exploitation, competition, rape of the earth, and so on, indicates that this secular cult cannot come to terms with its own shadow or its history. If some of our spiritual energy could be returned to genuinely religious pursuits, I think we would be freed from ugly and fetishistic attachments to religious substitutes. It would be healthier for everyone if we could recover access to Our Father Who Art in Heaven, rather than have the graven images and human idols of the 'spiritual' men's movement. But today, I suspect, we can only regain access to the Father God if we first meet and deal directly with the feminine forces which have displaced him. The way to the Father is not through a regressive return to the masculine mystique, but through a new experience of the sacred feminine.

THE HAMLET COMPLEX AND BEYOND: TO THINE OWN SELF BE TRUE

> The new is prefigured from the beginning in the old and the king is himself both senex and puer.
>
> Hillman[38]

The dilemma of contemporary masculinity is neatly and powerfully portrayed by Shakespeare's *Hamlet*. The uncanny contemporary relevance of Shakespeare is due to the fact that he worked timeless archetypal themes into his dramas, themes that are invariably repeated in different social contexts and human situations. Prince Hamlet is forced to swear to the spirit of his dead father, the old King Hamlet, that he will depose the current king, who rules without moral authority or the force of truth. The current king, Claudius, is actually a usurper, murderer and adulterer. Because the ruling principle in the land is corrupt, the entire kingdom is in grave moral danger: 'something is rotten in the state of Denmark'.[39] Hamlet must restore moral order and spiritual justice to the land by exposing the usurper and claiming his own rightful succession to the throne.

In today's sociopolitical terms, the corrupt ruler-king is hege-monic patriarchy, which is ruthless, imbalanced and unlawful. It is, like King Claudius, a corrupt rulership parading as the Law. We live under the illusion of justice and appropriate leadership, but those of us who, like Hamlet and Horatio, are awakened by the spirit of truth, are made keenly alert to the injustices and corruptions that abound. This awareness places enormous responsibility upon us, a responsibility that we immediately recognise, but find formidable:

> The time is out of joint. O, cursed spite
> That ever I was born to set it right!
>
> (1. 5: 188–189)

The false, tyrant king must be routed, and by this act the spirit of the archetypal father is redeemed. Moreover, this drama is simultaneously psychological and political, located in the individual psyche of Hamlet and in the nation state of Denmark. Hamlet himself must overthrow the present order, and then he must take upon himself the role of just ruler and rightful king. The spirit of the father is redeemed by the liberating achievements of the son, who then becomes the new father. The creative son who has the guts to act is in fact the embodiment of the father's spirit. Jung writes: 'So, from the Father, comes the Son, as the Father's thought of his own being'.[40]

What makes *Hamlet* especially modern, however, is the protagonist's famous procrastination, or inability to act. In Jungian terms, we might call this the frustration of archetypal intent.[41] The archetypal imperatives are made clear, and the son must overcome the corrupt senex in order to redeem the state, but how exactly do we achieve this redemption? How to deal with the corrupt father and how to redeem the father's spirit? There is a gap between theory and life, and while the archetypal theorem sounds simple, modern life is complex and complicated.

Hamlet himself is tortuously divided.[42] How can he overthrow the present king, who is the reigning monarch, his own uncle, and his mother's husband? Hamlet begins to doubt the authenticity of the ghostly apparition and its awful command. How can he know that the 'spirit' of the father is an authentic spirit? What if it is some dreaded demon of night, urging him to draw upon himself a terrible fate as murderer of a king? Hamlet assumes, of course, that in order to 'revenge' his father's death (1. 5: 25), he must perforce *kill* Claudius. As we have seen, *killing* the father immediately invokes the spectre of Oedipus, and a hundred years ago Freud and Ernest Jones perceptively elicited the Oedipal complications in Shakespeare's great tragedy. Killing his own uncle is an act of parricide, and Hamlet is frozen in inaction because this murder of a father figure would automatically release the infantile fantasies involving a regressive return to the mother. According to Freud, the incest taboo and prohibition is what stops Hamlet in his tracks, generating a psychological and emotional paralysis.[43]

Hamlet and Oedipus should make it clear to us that killing the father is not the way forward. Although the negative senex is himself a killer (Claudius, Ouranos, Chronos), to turn his own killing upon himself is to fall into his own mythic pattern, and to become paralysed by an incapacitating Oedipal regression. Contemporary radicalism, with its repetitive symbolic parricide, its constitutional opposition to tradition, and its panicky desire for the new, is today stuck in this mythic pattern, and apparently can find no way out. My own disenchantment with the political left, after a decade or more of involvement, arose from a loss of interest in a perpetual adversarial code of conduct, a code that did not allow enough of the past to be affirmed. The father in me got tired of the rebellious son having all the say. We must not condemn ourselves to eternal sonship and rebelliousness, and end up murdering what is authentic and just in the fathering spirit. We have to learn to develop new styles of rebellion and creativity, styles involving trickery rather than assassination, Hermes rather than Oedipus, redemption rather than murder. As the archetypal Son of the Father, Christ's mission is singularly impressive and paradigmatic: 'Think not that I came to destroy the law or the prophets: I come not to destroy, but to fulfil' (Matthew 5: 17). Christ did not destroy Judaism, but he fulfilled the prophets by moving beyond them. Our vision must be teleological and forward-looking, and our emphasis must be upon how we can redeem our culture by incarnating the spirit of progress.

If we cannot overturn corruption and redeem the spirit of the father, then society and all players on the human stage will be destroyed by destiny gone wrong. Ophelia and Polonius are destroyed by Hamlet's poisonous indecisiveness, and later Laertes, the Queen, and Hamlet himself are subdued by the tragic course of events. The redemption of the father's spirit, and the renewal of the senex through the agency of the puer, must be carried out if they are willed by fate. At the end of the play, the archetypal pattern has been negatively 'fulfilled', as the corrupt king is subdued in the chaos, and as the young Fortinbras, Prince of Norway, enters to claim the fallen nation. But the stage is strewn with corpses, and Hamlet is not alive to experience the redemption of his father's spirit or of his nation state.

For young men today, a chronic repetition of the fight with the tyrannical father is a form of neurosis, but so too is the wimp's way of avoiding the fight altogether. The decision of some 'spiritual' men to refuse the battle and to become one with the father in ecstatic union ('if you can't beat him, join him'), is an existential betrayal and a form of intellectual suicide. The mythopoetic men's movement is unattractive to thinking men precisely because the puer's creative mission is not realised but extinguished in the banality of patriarchal tradition. The tensionless or 'happy' state of the mythopoetic man who suddenly fuses with the archetypal father is a fool's paradise. I feel an almost physical revulsion for some individuals in the men's movement who beam confidence and self-satisfaction from their symbolic marriage with the father.

The way out of this dilemma, the way to masculine redemption, involves integrity, commitment, and risk:

This above all: to thine own self be true,
And it must follow, as the night the day,
Thou canst not then be false to any man.

(1. 3: 78)

Ironically, this wisdom comes from the foolish and utterly conventional Polonius, a sign of the moral reversals and complexities in a corrupt and shoddy world. Men must risk their own separateness, and draw strength and creativity from the wound that cuts them off from the past. Battles must be fought, traditions challenged, and entrenched values confronted. In my own field of research, Hillman and Samuels have made enormously significant contributions to Jungian psychology precisely because they have been courageous enough to back their own judgement and to be true to their own sources of inspiration. They have resisted Claudius-style or corrupted Jungianism, while remaining faithful to the 'spirit' of Jung, and redeeming his psychology by carrying it into a new era. Post-Jungians can only redeem Jung by going beyond him: to stick to the letter of received wisdom is to debase the work of the founding father. This is a delicate balancing act, and sometimes even the most creative minds can have too much radicalism or too much conventionality. But the supreme paradox is that in holding fast to our own authority, we redeem and further the spirit of the father.

3

CONTEMPORARY DILEMMAS OF FEMININE MEN

Masculine power is exercised either in an inappropriately over-controlling or weakly impotent way: it is failing to be supportive and effective where it is most needed.

Alix Pirani[1]

In these chapters we move from one group of pressing dilemmas to another. We must free ourselves from the stifling influence of the father, yet respect this same figure's life and essence: for his essence is what becomes our own 'spiritual life'. We must embrace and affirm the father, yet to wallow in that embrace or to indulge that affirmation is to regress to the blind unconsciousness and destructiveness of patriarchy. Now we consider a cluster of problems relating to our emotional and psychological connection with the archetypal mother. These problems are similar in the sense that they pose questions about discovering, yet again through trial and error, a 'right relationship' with an awesome psychospiritual figure. The important difference is that, culturally and historically, the archetypal father is waning in power, whereas the mother is waxing. His era of high patriarchy is in decline, but the mother is in the process of experiencing a belated return of power and authority. The once-great and potent matriarchal figures of the ancient pagan world are about to rise again, and if we want to participate in history, rather than become its unconscious victims, then we had better learn quickly to respect these feminine figures.

THE SYMBOLIC REALM OF THE MOTHER-IMAGE

According to Jung, the human mother has been unnecessarily burdened with guilt and blame due to the literal-mindedness of Freudian psychoanalysis.[2] The Freudians correctly noted that the

68

'mother' seemed to be at the bottom of many modern neuroses and mental disturbances, but they did not look deeply enough into the problem. The literal experience of 'mother' was not seen through to its archetypal and mythological foundations: behind the human mother was to be found the archetypal image of the ambivalent mother goddess. The discovery of the role of an unconscious mythology in the lives of modern people, a mythology that power-fully 'distorts' reality by imposing its own images, helps to liberate the human mother from the psychodynamic drama, so that 'she' is no longer seen as the root cause of all our problems. In my view, feminist theory has still to realise the great liberating service that Jung has performed for the experience of womankind. It is not the personal mother or her female representatives whom the male has to 'fight' to win his manhood; rather he must attempt to extricate himself from the primordial strength of this archetypal figure *within himself*.

Thus, before we can get anywhere at all in our relationship with the mother, we must first learn to differentiate between the personal and archetypal mother. The archetypal mother is a powerful content of the psyche, a content that is at first projected upon the personal mother and experienced as synonymous with her. Jung was forced to postulate the existence of an archetype of the mother when he realised that the *fantasies* projected upon the mother did not correspond to the realities of the personal mother. In Jung's view, the highly-charged, fantasy-laden image of the mother is an archaic vestige of the collective psyche, a vestige that gives the personal figure 'a mythological background', and which 'invests her with authority and numinosity'.[3] Psychologically speaking, the 'mother' symbolises the unconscious womb or matrix, that deep psychological substratum that precedes the ego, gives birth to the ego's life, and can readily 'devour' the ego again in psychosis, death, or possession. Goethe called this archaic world the 'realm of the Mothers', to emphasise its complexity, plurality, and autonomy.

If the son is strongly attracted or 'wedded' to the mother in a state of symbolic incest, we can assume that the ego is still too weak to separate itself from the psychic background. According to psychoanalytic theory, every son develops an incestuous Oedipal attachment to the mother, and under normal conditions this attach-ment is overcome by further life experience and by alternative erotic attachments. Freud argued that the human mother can exacerbate the incestuous knot or tie by lavishing affection upon the son or by making him otherwise emotionally dependent on her.[4] By contrast, Jung 'attributed to the personal mother only a limited aetiological significance', emphasising that 'all those influences which the [Freudian] literature describes as being exerted on the children do not come from the mother herself, but rather from the archetype projected upon her'.[5] Hence, if the mother-image appears terrifying and malign, this is not necessarily a reflection of the human mother's behaviour, but an indication that the image of the 'terrible mother' has been constellated in the unconscious. If the mother-image is frightening, this generally indicates that the ego is dangerously close to the unconscious, and it must attempt to develop its own life independent of the maternal matrix. The appearance of the 'dragon' mother is a clear message or warning from the psyche: the time has come to strengthen the ego's ground and to oppose what threatens to overwhelm it.

A future spiritually and psychologically alert culture will take these crucial archetypal insights seriously, developing rituals and rites of passage that allow youths to struggle with an *objectified* and symbolised mother-image, without falling prey to dangerous sexism and misogyny. The more 'objective' the inner opponent to masculine consciousness can be made, the more clearly will men realise their psychodynamic predicament, and the more free women and mothers will be of negative and paralysing male projections.

LIBERATION IN A NEW KEY

In patriarchal society, men have dealt with the dragon of the unconscious simply by slaying it with macho-heroics, rationality, or various other supremacist antics and strategies of the masculine spirit. The hero kills the dragon which symbolises unconscious instinct, the mother-bond, and the 'regressive' attachment to the matrix. He is then 'free' to get on with his patriarchal life and to overcome inner and outer impediments to his heroic career. However, changed historical and spiritual conditions complicate this once very simple fight between the ego and the primordial mother-image. Just as it is no longer socially acceptable for the developing son to gain his personal freedom by putting mother down, by vilifying girls or denigrating women, so too, at the inner level, it is no longer acceptable to simply run the sword into the mother-dragon and leave it bleeding and dying. Here we face a similar problem to that explored in the previous chapter. If we kill, slay, or murder an archetypal figure, we do a lot of damage to the internal ecology of the soul. Not only is the archetypal realm severely brutalised, but the ego itself is diminished by this murder, since it can no longer draw on the incredible richness and libido that the archetypal figure can supply. The ego that continually slays archetypes has become the neurotic or even psychotic ego of our time: it goes on a violent rampage, and then it wonders why it feels so lonely and bereft. Unless we stop killing the monsters of the deep, and the beasts of the forest, we will not have any world left to inhabit, either internally in the soul or externally in nature.

Men still have to free themselves from the imprisoning bondage of primal archetypes, but killing or brutalising is no longer an appropriate style. We have to learn a different language, a new iconography, and different metaphors for liberation. Heroic and violent styles of 'liberation' are most suspect today, and we must all get down to the business of co-existence with our fellow archetypal beings. This is especially important when we come to the mother archetype, because the mother is not only the personification of the deep unconscious, but she also symbolises the entire world of nature, the body, and the organic foundations of life. The mother's realm has to be protected, nurtured, and respected, and psychology cannot add to the patriarchal crimes of the past by insisting that the developing young man or growing boy must kill the dragon-mother and destroy the so-called mother-complex.

On this crucial change in psychological awareness, I am more inclined to turn to the post-Jungians such as James Hillman and Andrew Samuels than to Jung himself. In his major work, *Symbols of Transformation*, Jung explored at great length the need for the ego to engage in a 'Battle for Deliverance from the Mother'.[6] In writing that volume, Jung was very much under the influence of the heroic mythologem, and he did not sufficiently take into account the changes that have taken place in the archetypal structure of the human psyche. In these and other ways, Jung's work has dated, for many dramatic changes have taken place, or have simply become more clearly evident, since Jung's time. Men today must steal themselves out of the mother's primal embrace without wounding her, and remove themselves from the archaic power of the dragon without killing the dragon. As Hillman has said, 'Killing the dragon in the hero myth means nothing less than killing the imagination, the very spirit that is the way and the goal'.[7]

How to liberate without also destroying, how to make free

without also creating horror and devastation? This is the big internal and external problem of our culture, and until we have come up with answers we cannot claim to be a post-patriarchal world. Instead of Herakles who cuts, clubs, and slays, why can't we emulate the style of, say, Hermes, who outwits, outruns, and slips out of sight? If men are caught up in the invisible knot of the mother-complex, why not deftly slip out of the knot like the trickster Houdini, rather than blast away at the knot like the slasher Rambo? Men today are called upon to look for new, more subtle and progressive styles of psychic liberation. A consciousness of the future must be less confrontational and macho, and more hermetic or trickster-like. The 'development of consciousness is not *away* from or *against* matter (mother) but always a mercurial business involved with her'.[8]

MODERN MEN, THE DRAGON FIGHT, AND DOMESTIC VIOLENCE

The 'mother-complex' is such a widespread neurosis, spirit is so immersed in the body of matter [mother], delighting there or squirming to shake free.

James Hillman[9]

However, a growing number of boys and men appear unable to extricate themselves from the retarding influences of the mother-complex. These are the 'passive' boys and the 'sensitive' new men, who are sometimes said to be 'in touch with their animas' (as I have so often heard in general conversation), but who are more realistically awash in the feminine and unable to access their active or phallic masculinity. It is as if, in not being able to conduct the conventional patriarchal escapes from the mother, or the heroic slayings of the dragon, these men remain caught in the primal entanglement with the mother. When the old macho way is no longer promoted or encouraged, masculinity itself appears to suffer from a disastrous lack of imagination. If we cannot cut, hack, or destroy the primal feminine, what then? If we cannot obliterate the feminine from the masculine ego, then what else can we do?

The urgent cultural and psychological task for men's culture is to discover the alternative styles of liberation that I have already alluded to. There is an entire range of styles and possibilities across the masculine spectrum, but somehow the extremes of aggressive masculine heroics, or passive-regressive antiheroics, appear to dominate the psychological styles of a great many men. This means, I think, that the masculine imagination urgently needs to be revitalised, and the way to achieve this is to oppose the ogre father and release the multiple forms he has devoured.

Some contemporary men appear to delight in their incestuous identification with the mother, finding luxury and ease in the embrace of the primal feminine. Lack of phallic strength and direction means lack of stress and tension, and an absence of concern about personal masculine identity. If the ego is not in a collision course with the deep unconscious, so much the better, and these sensitive men are usually pleasant enough, until the milk from the breast of the mother stops feeding them, and then they scream and whimper, blaming others or the government of the day for depriving them of their personal worth and individual identity.

More conventional men find the mother-complex to be burdensome and tormenting. They strive eagerly to fuse themselves with a masculinist culture that can give them a firm sense of identity and worth. The primal connection with the archetypal mother is fought against, but given the increased strength of this archetype in the modern world, masculine detachment and independence is more difficult and by no means guaranteed. As Hillman has said, 'the "mother-complex" is a widespread neurosis . . . affecting everyone with metaphysical affliction. Working out this affliction is individual, which makes therapy a metaphysical engagement in which ideas and not only feelings and complexes undergo process and change'.[10] One could almost say that Western masculinity itself now 'has', or is loaded with, a mother-complex, so that what men present in therapy is not just their personal and tragic fusions with the mother, but Western masculinity's entanglement with an archetype it once thought it had 'conquered'. But the dragon mother is 'back' with renewed energy and force, and therapists can only fully understand this dilemma if they also understand society and the historical process. In the clinical situation, we are not just dealing with personal problems, but with problems of history and the development of culture. Jung was absolutely correct when he insisted that the therapists of neurosis must also be doctors of philosophy.[11] Therapists are perforce engaged in the remaking of collective masculinity, not merely in remaking their clients.

Some men fight against the mother-complex for a lifetime, never managing to free themselves from its apparently retarding influence. According to many stories of heroic adventure, there is just one

73

quick, efficient fight with the dragon-monster, and then the hero is free to 'marry' the supportive and masculinity-affirming anima figure. Of course, the fight for psychological independence has never been this simple, and it is dangerously easy for men today to idealise the past and to imagine that story-book conquests were mirror-images of life. But a *struggle* for masculine independence must always take place, and this is true today even if masculine assertiveness has become relatively unfashionable. Let me explore briefly the problem of domestic violence against this archetypal background.

A modern man who is caught by the primal feminine must struggle toward independence, whether by strengthening the ego, slipping out of the primal knot, or breaking free from the inertia of the unconscious. He engages in external forms of liberation, such as competitive team sport and career development, but inwardly he is still caught by the primal feminine. He will experience this entanglement as increasingly oppressive and tormenting, a torment that is frequently blamed upon wives and female partners. These women 'appear' to be getting him down, undermining his achievements, nagging at him to perform in better ways. In reality, it is the man's own incomplete separation from the elementary feminine that compels him to feel oppressed and imprisoned. At first, the abuse against the female partner is verbal, then it becomes physical. The man 'knows' there is a negative force at hand, a wicked witch, a snake in the grass, and he feels morally justified in taking it out on his wife. Such a man often 'knows' that domestic violence is unacceptable, but he nevertheless is driven to continue it through powerful internal dynamics. I have observed this at first hand, and I know how tragic and dangerous this situation can be for all concerned.

A new-age therapist with a hatred of all forms of violence will tell this man he must stop his wicked ways. He will be told he is simply responding to negative male conditioning, which must be overcome by further development. A profeminist men's group will simply declare that he is perpetuating the violence and hatred of hegemonic patriarchy, and that to become a real man of the present he must adopt sensitive and caring behaviours. An antifeminist men's rights group might simply tell this otherwise 'good bloke' to cool it, and to take his anger out on the feminist influences in the legal system and in other contemporary institutions. Many different kinds of standard advice are delivered today by male and female social workers, therapists, peers, police, and domestic violence interventionists. But the crucial truth can only be made available to him by those with an understanding of psychodynamic process: he must be educated to the reality of the internal plane, and be made to see how he is indeed being attacked and undermined by a feminine opponent. The point is not to get rid of his aggression, but to reframe it, not to repress his violence but to intensify and transform it by becoming alert to the real site of conflict and sources of antagonism. While the surface 'therapies' seek to squash the undesirable contents, the depth therapies work to deepen and transform the unpleasant, macho behaviours. Surface approaches may be vitally important in the short term, especially to protect the safety of women and children, but this man will fight, abuse, and destroy again if he is not alerted to the deeper psychological conflicts at work within him.

I therefore arrive at the homeopathic view that only 'like' can cure 'like', only a deeper understanding of violence and abuse can cure violence and abuse. Only if the therapist has the maturity of vision to work with the ugly images, to insight the problems, to psychologise the (usually mythological) terms of abuse that are directed against women (witch, serpent, dragon, monster, etc.), can a real and lasting cure be effected. Men must be shown that they do not merely live on one plane of reality, but that they live also on psychospiritual and emotional planes, and that the work of liberation must be carried out on these deeper planes. When a man abuses his wife because she is an overpowering dragon, what is happening in this suburban setting must be seen as a failure of secular rationalism and Western society. Of course domestic violence is about the abuse of patriarchal power, but it is also about the absence of spiritual power. The woman is experienced as a dragon because the man has no broader cosmology or symbolic mythology in which to situate his interior life. His psychic life has no depth, no dimension, and it erupts violently into the human plane, destroying our human relationships.

For these and many other reasons, I am a critic of all forms of therapy that do not take the unconscious into account, and do not recognise that our pathetic wife-bashing client is in fact a would-be hero on a journey. Therapy can only work, however, if it grants a secular man a spiritual life; if it opens up a symbolic world in which he can be seen as a hero who must locate the true dragon and liberate himself from its terrible influence. Therapies and therapists that immediately shy away from violence will never work, because change can be effected only if the strong emotions have been located, identified, and released. The education and imagination of the therapist is very important here, because the therapist can show that the desired release from the dragon's grip can be achieved by various alternative methods: tricking, outwitting, confounding, startling, and by other means outlined in trickster cycles and ancient stories. The work of liberation does not have to be violent, but the *urge toward violence* may be the raw energy that gets the liberation started.

FUSION WITH THE MOTHER, SEPARATION AND RETURN

I have taken seriously the modern saying, 'if you scratch a wimp, you will find a wife basher'. In my experience, it is often the more 'feminine' men who are the most dangerous, who are prone to sudden and shocking outbursts of terrifying rage and violence. It is tragically ironic if, in response to the demise of patriarchal masculinity and the increased fashionableness of 'sensitivity', men are forced to remain faithful to the mother-complex, producing an internal suffering that is far more dangerous than most displays of conventional masculinity. In this case, the refusal to oppose the primordial feminine at the internal psychological level means that men are increasingly fighting women in their external lives. Why is domestic violence rising sharply, just at the time when the traditional masculine mystique is waning? The answer is not to bring back the old patriarchal mystique, but to discover, urgently, new ways to deal with age-old masculine problems, including how to separate from the mother without doing damage to the mother or to our own feminine selves.

Paradoxically perhaps, the male personality must achieve a certain level of masculine independence before it can become the mature partner of the feminine. The pattern may be outlined as: original fusion with the mother, masculine separation and relative liberation, and the return to the feminine on a more equal psychological basis. The mother has to be 'betrayed', before a true partnership can begin with the archetypal feminine, which is experienced in a new way as soon as the male ego reaches a certain level of maturity. Genuine relationship requires the coming together of two equal, but independent entities, and as Jung has said: 'Relationship can only take place where this distinction exists'.[12] Here I take issue with the profeminist men's groups, who seem to adopt the view that all masculine struggle and 'squirming to shake free' is merely a form of masculine heroics and social conditioning, which we must collectively outgrow. Unity and harmony between masculine and feminine cannot be had on command, but must be sought through a process of sensitive awareness to the 'alchemical' relationship between these forces.

In my experience, some marriages go through this same pattern of original passive fusion, conflict and separation, and the achievement of a more dynamic unity in conscious relationship. The original unity of man and woman is inspired by unconscious projection-making factors. Things appear to be blissful until either party feels cramped and needs to develop an individual identity. The original unity, based on anima–animus fusion, is smashed, but after 'going separate ways' the marriage can revitalise itself if the partners turn to each other as conscious and complex individuals, rather than as 'halves' of a single whole. This old style of unconscious marriage seems to me to be dated and out of touch with the progressive forces of the time, which are urging for differentiation and conscious relationship. This same process occurs intrapsychically as well. A man is not a real or vibrant partner to his anima or muse until he has learned to differentiate himself from that which he so adores. It has therefore been argued by Neumann and Jung that it is often the anima herself who inspires, or forces, a man to develop his own masculinity. She is fairly demanding of her man, and she wants him to be 'good enough' to be her creative partner.

The archetypal feminine sometimes appears to separate into an elementary and a transformative aspect, or into an inert and a dynamic character. Erich Neumann and Gareth Hill make a good deal of this internal distinction with respect to the archetypal feminine.[13] Neumann argues that the elementary or primal aspect of the mother clutches the son to herself and prevents him from growing up. This aspect of the archetype seems to encourage fusion, dependence, and infantilism, and all of this operates under the symbolism of incest and mother-love. Neumann speaks of a 'transformative' and Hill of a 'dynamic' archetypal polarity that actively seeks change and wills the ego toward adventure, quest, and journeying. This is a very important piece of information which is often overlooked by the Jung-influenced spiritual men's movement. In much popular discourse, it is believed that only the father or his surrogates are capable of 'initiating' the son into activity and self-discovery. The feminine is viewed as clutching, regressive, static – which is only to say that it is viewed through the distorting lens of the mother-complex. There is much more to the feminine than the mother, and there is more to the 'mother', too, as soon as the son is mature enough to be able to see and experience it. But it is certainly no accident that the great works of Western culture reveal that it is the feminine inspi-ratrice (as Laura, Beatrice, Sophia, Euridice, or Cordelia), who initiates masculine consciousness into its higher selfhood.

THE MOTHER-BOND, SPIRITUALITY, AND CHANGE: A PERSONAL ACCOUNT

I am the classic mother's son in many ways. Adored by a loving mother of Irish descent, I was often taken aside during childhood and given moral lessons about how to be a good boy for my mother. My mother asked me to promise that I would never swear when I grew older. I was always to be a 'nice' boy, and to remain faithful to her wishes. I was also to be a religious man, keeping the fundamen-talist Christian faith as she understood it. Despite frequent protestations from my father, who hated this furtive mother–son bond and who tried his best to cut across it, the family romance continued uninterrupted for many years.

The impact of this romance on me was two-fold. First, an inten-sification of my feminine side to the detriment of my conventional masculinity. So, instead of football, I loved poetry; instead of sex, I embraced religion. I was a man of the literary arts at a young age, and my connection with the feminine gave me an attachment to history, painting, and literature.[14] At Alice Springs High School, I was hopeless at what were called 'the boys' subjects': maths, physics, chemistry, and the general sciences. Instead, I did all the 'girls' subjects': literature, history, typing, commerce, art. Needless to say, I was frequently derided by my more conventional masculine class-mates. I was called 'pretty boy', 'cissy', and 'a girl'. Surprisingly, these names did not sting in the way that they were meant to. I was in many ways contented with my feminine lot. I have always had an enormously high regard for my mother, my sisters, and women generally, and was in that sense a feminist long before it became fashionable. In clinical terms, my mother-complex was positive and not negative. My mother adored me and I took strength and secu-rity from her adoration.

However, it was not just the feminine side that got a boost. In Jungian terms, I had also identified with my mother's animus, with her own unlived masculine and spiritual side. Through the agency of her animus, I soared above the ordinary world, full of an amazing religious zeal which has always been hard to describe. I had a kind of redemptive and messianic energy, and my mother's fond hope was that I would one day join the Salvation Army and play the trumpet to herald the coming of the Lord. Flying dreams were very common for me during adolescence; I longed to soar above and beyond the mundane and the everyday.

Just here is a major drawback. It was not until I read Hillman's essay on 'The Great Mother' in the 1970s that I could begin to see the shadow side of this incredible joy. The mother's animus tends to 'exaggerate' the spiritual side in the boy, so that his spirit is no longer convincing or authentic. The 'vertical flights of spirit' become 'a contemptuous soaring over a corrupt and shoddy world'.[15] The spirituality tends to become spiritistic, otherworldly, a mystic flight into the ether. One entirely loses interest in the ordinary, and what for me started out as a Christian flight of spirit becomes an antiChristian, or anti-incarnational, mysticism. It is little wonder that I lost interest in the Church as a young teenager, and started pursuing dreams, occultism, astrology, alchemy, and hermeticism – all matriarchal arts and sciences. 'Without [the Father God], we turn to dreams and oracles, rather than to prayer, code, tradition, and ritual. When mother replaces father, magic substitutes for logos, and son-priests contaminate the puer spirit.'[16]

Playing the trumpet in the Salvation Army band was certainly not what I had in mind. I was reading Madame Blavatsky and Sri Aurobindo at 14, and Nietzsche at 15. At 20, I was studying with women occultists, astrologists, and fortune-tellers, and lecturing on Kundalini Yoga at the Theosophical Society. For me, God the Father, above and beyond creation, did not matter and was a bore. Significantly, it was meetings with intuitive women that led me to the psychology of Jung. Jung was not on the syllabus at my university, but away from the patriarchal academy I feasted heartily on a strong diet of matriarchal wisdom. I also flirted briefly with wicca and neopaganism, with drugs and altered states of consciousness.

Much of this popular spirituality, however, is wrongly titled the 'consciousness movement'. In some ways it is an '*un*consciousness movement', since the object and goal of much of this activity is to seek ecstasy, satiety, and rest. Although operating under the insignia of *spirit*, a fair bit of this spirituality is 'uroboric' as Erich Neumann would say. The goal is to return to the womb-state of unconsciousness, symbolised by the mythological uroboros. The spirit's movement, although 'up and away', actually longs for ecstatic self-dissolution in the matrix. But son-priests never think of themselves as advocates of unconsciousness. As Hillman ironically puts it: 'One can hardly be "regressing" while quoting Hesse, Gurdjieff, Tagore, Eckehart, and Socrates!' And so 'regression is refused as a misnomer'.[17] Freudian or developmental therapists who suspect regression and incestuous passions are rejected or scorned. The son-priest combs the city until he finds a 'spiritual' therapist who 'understands'.

But the son-priest often does end up in therapy. Things never go as well as expected. The boy of high promise comes down to earth with a bang. Relationships are a continual problem: the mother's son gets quickly bored by his sexual partners. As von Franz correctly suggests, the *puer aeternus* is either a homosexual, a promiscuous Don Juan, or both at once. He quickly gets fed up with the mundane, irritated by routine, and always anxious to move on to the next exciting episode. He is often a narcissistic borderline personality. A recurring problem is lethargy, exhaustion, tiredness. There is too much emphasis on the unconscious and on finding ways (meditation, drugs, mysticism, sex) back into it. The ego is not stable or fixed in reality, but relies on bursts of enthusiasm to get anything done. Following Jung, von Franz speculates on the cure for the puer problem:

> What cure is there? you might ask. If a man discovers he has a mother-complex, which is something that happened to him – something that he did not cause himself – what can he do about it? In *Symbols of Transformation*, Dr Jung spoke of one cure – work, and having said that, he hesitated for a minute and thought, 'Is it really as simple as all that? Is that the only cure? Can I put it that way?' But work is the one disagreeable word which no puer aeternus likes to hear, and Dr Jung came to the conclusion that it was the right answer.[18]

Although Hillman has scoffed at Jung and von Franz's suggestion that 'work' cures the complex, I am inclined to agree with the classical Jungian position here. What the puer dislikes about work is its routine quality; its repetition and consistency. But this is precisely what can draw the puer into the world, changing his pattern from transcendental escapism to *bringing transcendence into the world*. This is the great talent and gift of the puer: he can, if prompted and educated in the appropriate way, make the grandeur of heaven become a revelation of spirit and beauty in the here and now. But his innate otherworldliness must be resisted, fought against, and if necessary dragged kicking and screaming into this world. Work is capable of achieving this.

However, there is always the possibility that the son-priest cannot see how he can play a redemptive role in the real world. Sometimes, in making his touch-down upon the earth, something in him dies, or is killed by the real. This is a major crisis and must not be underestimated. Nevertheless, the son-priest must be steered toward the earth, lest he is lost to society and humanity, and the world thereby loses an opportunity to recover an element or spark of its own lost transcendence.

As my own romance with the Mother drew to an end, the negative aspects of this psychological condition became more pronounced. As we outgrow an archetypal condition, we are made to see the negative side of our state in a more intense way, and this becomes an incentive to change. My sexual relationships all seemed to come to the same unglamorous and bitter endings. I was continually bored, frustrated, and impatient. My partners rightly accused me of not being present enough with them; I did not seem to care, my mind was combing the ether; I wasn't interested in the human details, which are so vital in any relationship.

I could not bring myself to work consistently or routinely. As a doctoral candidate at university, I could laze around for weeks at a time, doing nothing in particular, but simply trying to find better and less dangerous ways of dissolving the mind and producing ecstasy. I was too intellectual to become a hippy dropout, but I flirted with the idea. At this time, I began to have dreams in which my father would arrive at my house, unannounced and without warning, and ask to be invited for dinner. I also dreamed that my mother sent me several pairs of underpants for my birthday, but I sent them back with a card telling her that I could buy my own underclothes now. At this same time, my real mother telephoned me to say that she was having disturbing dreams about me. In the dreams, she said, I was rejecting her, and she was waking up with a deep sense of loss and remorse.

It was at this point that I had a simple but very direct dream. At the time of this dream, I was unhappy with my university career, and I was considering moving to another country to commence training to become a Jungian psychologist. I wrote to Marie-Louise von Franz in Zurich, who said in reply that I should seriously consider an analytical career, only she felt I was still too young (I was 26 at this point). But yes, she wrote, the puer problem is a major problem of the post-war generation, and she sent me a copy of her paper, 'Über religiöse Hintergrunde des Puer-Aeternus-Problems'.[19] One evening I dreamed that I received a letter with a message written on the back of the envelope. The message read: 'We think you would make a good analyst, but you must work on your masculine side first'.

At the time I had no idea what my 'masculine side' was, let alone that it needed developing, or that I owed it some moral responsibility. Throughout the 1970s, I was antimasculinist and committed to the nurturing of my feminine side, which I assumed was also the psyche's top priority. So what was this about the masculine side? Ought I to get a second letter saying: look, forget about that earlier message, it was a mistake, masculinity is out of date and ideologically unsound? No, quite the opposite, I had many more dreams suggesting that my masculine growth was stunted, that my relation to the father was dangerously negative, and that I ought to extricate my ego from the power of the feminine and acquire some masculine grounding. During this period I had large numbers of unfashionable dreams, including dozens about competitive team football, a sport I had enjoyed and played as a youth, but which I had decided as an enlightened adult was no longer appropriate for my personal or political agenda. I had heaps of dreams about men's games, men's clubs and sports, cricket, soccer, rugby, and each time the idea of winning was vital. The disgrace in many of these dreams was that I was unable to get the ball and play it toward the goals; sometimes I could not get my legs moving, did not know how to follow the rules of the game, was stuck to the ground, or did not relate to what was going on. I would wake up in a sweat of anxiety, before I set to work grooming my social persona for the day, and this preferred persona was completely opposed to most of the values and attitudes expressed in the compensatory dreams.

My phase as a passive son-priest came to an abrupt and brutal end on 20 February 1980, when a raging bushfire swept through the Adelaide Hills district in which I was living. This fire destroyed my rented shack in the woods, and I lost everything in the blaze, including three years' worth of research on my doctoral thesis. Fate can be so unsubtle! First a blunt, almost curt dream-message, with no elaborate mythic symbolism to decipher. It wasn't a dream as much as a command. Then a very real destruction of the old and a baptism by fire. I had to remake myself after this episode. What I experienced above all was an enormous surge of personal energy. The languishing in the uroboros and the psychic inertia seemed to disappear, and a new spirit seemed to animate my life. Strangely, after the devastation, things went extremely well. I was given so much charity and support that I was the richest I had ever been. I rewrote my PhD from scratch, changing the topic from the mysticism of mandalas to the study of the mother-complex in a major literary figure.[20] After the PhD was submitted, I was awarded a Harkness Fellowship from New York City, and I chose to work with James Hillman in Dallas.

I had travelled to Hillman to conduct what I thought was going to be a postdoctoral academic fellowship. Hillman, true to his puer nature, got quickly bored with our intellectual discussions. He was hungry for soul, not intellect, and he complained that our discussions – any discussion – were too abstract and lacked soul. I found Hillman candid, cheeky, inquisitive, fiery, and capricious. He suggested that we change our academic tutorials into analytical sessions. At first I found this embarrassing: he wanted to turn me from an academic into a patient. He just laughed at my protest, kicked off his smelly tennis shoes, and put his long, ugly feet on the table before us. 'Well, what's it going to be?' I said that I needed two weeks to think about it. There was some resistance on my part, but once this was confronted we were embroiled in two years of twice-weekly analytical sessions. Most of the dreams during this analysis were concerned with my 'masculine side': father, phallus, energy, football, cricket, competition, social identity, place in the world, and rugged shadow figures. This is documented in Chapter 5. The passive son-priest was having to wake up to a new self, to the return of repressed masculinity.

THE POPULAR DISCOURSES ABOUT SOFT MEN

My rude awakening to masculinity in the 1980s coincided with the beginnings of an avalanche of literature discussing the uprising of masculine spirit in the lives of feminine men. The spirit of this writing is probably best captured in a key statement by Russell Lockhart:

All the emphasis on what has been abandoned, neglected, and devalued seems focused too narrowly on the feminine and too rooted in images from the past. There is need of a similar redemption of the masculine spirit and without this the feminine will wander alone.[21]

The tone of this literature appears to be conservative and reactionary, but some of it is not. Only rigidly ideological people imagine that all attention must be focused on the feminine, and that the masculine spirit can go to hell. Although the overthrow of patriarchy demands the liberation of women and the feminine, no social revolution can be properly carried out unless both genders are brought into clear focus and are constructed in new ways. In a sense, what we find in the phenomenon of the new, so-called soft or sensitive man, is an early, very interesting, but largely unsuccessful attempt to reorientate masculinity around the archetypal feminine.

In 1985, Andrew Samuels wrote:

Analysts are beginning to meet a new kind of man. He is a loving and attentive father to his children, a sensitive and committed marital partner, concerned with world peace and the state of the environment; he may be vegetarian. Often he will announce himself as a feminist. He is, in fact, a wholly laudable person. But he is not happy. . . . This man [is a] casualty of a basically positive and fruitful shift in consciousness [and] will stay a mother's boy. He is a mother's boy because he is doing what he does to please Woman.[22]

The 'basically positive and fruitful shift in consciousness' is the powerful resurgence of the feminine in our time, a resurgence which is a necessary compensatory response to patriarchy. This is Hillman's 'archetypal neurosis of the son and the mother', in which the feminine and the mother refuse to be booted around in the manner to which patriarchy has become accustomed. The soft or sensitive male is aware of his difference from other, more conventional kinds of men, recognises he is participating in an historic departure from patriarchy, and yet 'he is not happy'.

The first to deal with these controversial issues was the American poet and essayist Robert Bly. The release of *Iron John* in 1990 represented the culmination of over ten years' work in this field.[23] Although *Iron John* was a huge commercial success, constructing Bly as leader of an international spiritual men's movement, it was in his 1982 essay-interview 'What Men Really Want' that he laid out the essential argument that would later inform the chapters of *Iron John*.[24] I have written elsewhere, and at greater length, on the Robert Bly material, and it will suffice here merely to sketch in Bly's version of contemporary men's experience.[25]

Bly's major point is that men have become distrustful of their own masculinity. From the 1960s on, a great many American men have questioned what maleness and masculinity is, and this has been a necessary part of the general questioning and eventual dismantling of patriarchy. However, according to Bly, the masculine baby has been thrown out with the patriarchal bathwater, so that far too many men today have no sense of masculine identity at all. Canadian analyst Eugene Monick had similarly warned that 'unless masculinity is differentiated from patriarchy, both will go down the drain together'.[26] In 'What Men Really Want', the astute interviewer, Keith Thompson, summarises Bly's position:

> It seems that many of these soft young men have come to equate their own natural male energy with being macho. Even when masculine energy would clearly be life-giving, productive of service to the community, many young males step back from it.[27]

Bly criticises what he calls the '50s male' (a wonderfully apt term), a man who was 'hard-working, responsible, fairly well disciplined; he didn't see women's souls very well, though he looked at their bodies a lot'. The '50s male' was 'vulnerable to collective opinion'; that is, he was a product of the patriarchal collective, and his security and identity were given to him by society at large. Bly contrasts this with his memorable description of the soft male:

> Sometimes when I look out at my audiences, perhaps half the young males are what I'd call soft. They're lovely, valuable people – I like them – and they're not interested in harming the earth, or starting war or working for corporations. There is something favourable toward life in their whole general mood and style of living. But something's wrong. Many of these men are unhappy. There's not much energy in them. They are life-preserving but not exactly life-giving. And why is it you often see these men with strong women who positively radiate energy? Here we have a finely tuned young man, ecologically superior to his father, sympathetic to the whole

harmony of the universe, yet he himself has no energy to offer.[28]

Here we notice many similarities between Andrew Samuels' description of the 'new kind of man' and Robert Bly's intuitive analysis of the 'soft male'. Bly interestingly points out that although the soft male is apparently responding to feminism, a large number of women are actually turned off by the new soft male or sensitive new-age guy. He argues that women have been forced to bear the brunt of both soft and hard masculine positions. In the 1960s, women wanted their patriarchal husbands and companions to recognise the equality of women, to become more expressive, more sensitive and human. In the 1980s and 1990s, however, women recognise that many men have become vague, indecisive, and troubled. Some married women feel they have been saddled with 'wimps', ineffectual men who treat them like mothers and who run to them for guidance and support. Says Thompson, 'We've tried to get strength second-hand through women who got *their* strength from the Women's Movement'.[29] Marriages become disturbed because there is no effective balance of power. Bly argues that 'men have learned to be receptive' but it 'isn't enough to carry their marriages'.[30] Some women obviously agree with Bly's observations, which is why they send his books and essays to ex-husbands, or urge their men to go off to masculinity workshops and consciousness-raising groups.

PROTESTING TOO MUCH: FROM WIMPS TO WARRIORS

A major problem with Bly's position is that he does not make clear enough the distinctions between the compulsive masculinity of the past that is rightly under attack, and the new masculinity that young males must find if they are to recover energy and vitality. Bly recounts the fairytale 'Iron John'[31] and interprets it in terms of 'a different development for men, a further stage than we've seen so far in the United States'.[32] By focusing on the figure of the hairy wildman at the bottom of the pond, Bly argues that modern men need to discover, or recover, the 'wildman' at the bottom of the psyche, an image of primitive masculine energy with which men must find some relationship if they are to develop. Bly idealises this wild, untamed energy, not recognising enough that the *primitivity* of the masculine archetype is what led to patriarchal excess and compulsiveness in the first place. The interviewer is understandably anxious about what Bly is advocating, and asks for further clarification, for some differentiation between old and new masculinities: 'How would you distinguish [this new wildman figure] from the strong but destructive male chauvinistic personality that we've been trying to get away from?' Bly's answer is not very convincing:

> The male in touch with the wildman has true strength. He's able to shout and say what he wants in a way that the 60s–70s male is not able to. . . . However, the ability of a male to shout and to be fierce is not the same as treating people like objects, demanding land or empire, expressing aggression – the whole model of the 50s male. Getting in touch with the wildman means religious life for a man in the broadest sense of the phrase, the 50s male was almost wholly secular so we are not talking in any way of a movement back.[33]

Bly's argument is dangerously naive, and it reminds me of some of the politically naive remarks made by D. H. Lawrence in the 1920s. The '50s male' may have been basically 'secular', but the 1930s European male certainly was not, since fascism as it arose in Germany, Italy, and elsewhere was very much a quasi-religious, ritualistic celebration of the archetypal masculine spirit in all its rawness and pristine glory. Hitler's youth and Mussolini's followers were 'religious', even mystical, about their sworn allegiance to the 'wildman' (or blond beast) in the Aryan psyche. Jung thought that a catastrophic breakthrough of a 'wildman' of Nordic mythology, Wotan, was responsible for the Nazi uprising, and if Bly is the Jungian he professes to be, he ought to be aware of that.[34] Despite Bly's good intentions it is quite possible, as Keith Thompson seems to fear, that this new wildman may end up as a new age cliché which merely provides justification for a return of destructive masculinity.

Bly's 'wild' and woolly-minded generalisations are also a cause for great concern. Although half the young males at his poetry readings are soft, this is by no means an indication that the majority of contemporary men are soft, or in need of his exhortation to seek out the wildman. Millions of North American men would never be seen dead at a poetry reading, millions are ostensibly unaffected by feminism, and far more fill up on a diet of Rambo movies than sit quietly reading Bly's *Sleepers Joining Hands*. Let us not take chronology too literally: not every male in the 1990s is a '90s male'; there are probably as many '50s males' in the world today (this is especially true of my own Australia) as in the 1950s. Men everywhere are at very different stages of development, and generalisations can be harmful if applied indiscriminately. For those many men who still live psychologically in the 1950s, Bly's urgings to toughen up, scream and shout, develop some hard edges, could only exacerbate and worsen their patriarchal condition.

Because Bly's work is clearly aimed at a mass market, the lack of subtlety in the argument and the loss of historical and cultural perspective is not only naive, it is potentially socially dangerous. It seems that Bly is almost intoxicated by a numinous archetypal masculine figure, and the attractive power of this archetype tends to obliterate any concern for the political or social perspective. For instance, caught up in his rhapsody to Iron John, he becomes sentimental about patriarchy, laments the decline of 'Zeus energy' in society, and pays no heed to the historical and archetypal circumstances that have made a relative decline in patriarchy inevitable and necessary.

Bardic praise offered to Iron Hans is socially irresponsible, especially when we notice what is going on today under Iron John's name:

In some Wild Man-type workshops being offered to men across the country, what is being marketed as 'wildness' is often nothing more than thinly disguised anger at women, a militaristic attitude, and familiar patriarchal roles.[35]

Influential feminist Barbara Ehrenreich has said that

Whatever the mythopoetics intend, archetypes like the Wild Man and Warrior embrace long-standing models of the heroic male. I think these men ought to know what strings they are pulling and what these drum beats are evoking for some men.[36]

These criticisms are entirely justified, and the advertisements I have seen for Bly-inspired weekend retreats ('Stalk the Wild Man Within!', 'It is Time for the New Warrior!', etc.) cause me great concern. God help us if Jungian psychology is being used to conjure up a new wave of militarism and fanaticism.

Robert Bly is an ecstatic poet, and he wonders what the political fuss and reaction to his work (including my own) is all about. In a letter to me, Bly strongly refuted my criticisms of his movement, and he argued that I paid no attention to the 'crucial distinctions' he makes 'several times' between 'savage' and 'wild'.[37] Frankly, these distinctions are lost on me, as they certainly are to all the men who seem to view Iron John initiation retreats as new-age versions of boot camp. In another letter, Bly insisted that I could not view his work sympathetically, since I was 'controlled by anti-masculine fantasies' and simply 'repeating feminist clichés in an academic atmosphere'.[38] Bly was especially upset when I compared wildman workshops to the antics and rituals performed in the quasi-mystical youth camps of the Third Reich.[39] Bly is a poet, not a fascist, but what he is stirring up is similar to the 'blood and soil' mythologies that animate fascistic uprisings. To precipitate an extreme right-wing movement, all we need (as Adorno has suggested) is crude religious zeal, intellectual banality, nostalgia for a lost 'organic' selfhood or nationhood, sentimental idealisation of the father or fatherland, toughness, scapegoats, and a few blood-stirring platitudes.[40] All these ingredients are found in large or small measure in *Iron John*. Bly admitted to me, after a fierce exchange of letters, that 'all attempts to teach North European mythology are in danger of being caught up in unconscious militarism', and that 'every movement that becomes public has a danger of enormous shadow activation'.[41] These are important 'after thoughts' and reflections, but it is a pity they were not expressed in the book itself.

Despite his cult of masculinity, my own view is that Bly is not close enough to the masculine archetypes to be able to see them in clear perspective. Bly's true poetic calling, as can be observed from even a cursory glance at his literary output, is to the Great Mother and the Feminine. I believe that Bly is still caught up in the archetypal position of the feminine, and that from this position he engages in a *long-distance fascination for the masculine*. He views the masculine from afar, with incredible homoerotic longing, and this accounts for the excesses and other problems that offend political commentators. The strenuous reaching for the masculine, the feeling-saturated yearning for the father, the idealisation of the hairy wild man or 'deep male', the longing for patrilineal bondings of bygone eras, all of this can be explained in terms of a distant fascination for the masculine in the psyche of a Great Mother's son. And the primitivity of the archetype as Bly sees it, the chthonic quality, the hairiness, nakedness, and ancientness, would indicate that the masculine side is coming up from deep levels of the unconscious. As we find with D. H. Lawrence toward the end of his career, we see in Robert Bly the breakthrough of a frighteningly primitive form of the masculine archetype.

OPPOSITIONAL MYTHOPOETICS: BLY AND HILLMAN

> Assertive masculinity is suspicious. Somewhere we know that it must be reactive to feminine attachment.
>
> Hillman[42]

Bly's work is a crude, muddled, and almost mock-parodic response to the need for 'masculine' development in feminine men. This kind of primitivist, boy-scout, 'wild' masculinity is a far cry from what is required in today's world. When my dream invited me to 'develop' my 'masculine side', it probably did not imagine that I would take this quite as literally, or as stereotypically, as Bly seems to have taken his own masculine development. Masculinity does not always beat its hairy chest, representing itself in macho images and impulses. If the psyche calls for increased masculinity, and we respond by conjuring up John Wayne, Iron John, or Hercules, this merely reflects our own failure of imagination and cultural impoverishment. This is actually an ideal instance in which to learn about differences between archetypes and stereotypes: the psyche's call for masculinity is archetypal, but our response to the call is ridiculously stereotypal. It is not the psyche that is 'reactionary' or 'macho', but it is we who fail the complexity and subtlety of psyche's call.

A demand to 'develop' the masculine could mean, for instance, that we don't act at all, but merely reflect on our situation with greater clarity and precision. The inward need could be for discrimination, judgement, self-criticism – aspects that are often associated with the archetypal masculine. The psyche may not be calling for heroic action but for mercurial insight, so that we might perhaps call upon Apollo, Horus, or Mercury to guide our way through. Only a very narrow and literal response would have us 'fixing' the new male softness by introducing a primal masculinity that is as hard and heavy as iron.

Iron John assumes, along with traditional patriarchy, that masculinity must always be reactive to femininity and the mother. If masculinity is to develop, it must be 'away from the feminine': so Bly exhorts modern men to get out of the influence of women, to bond with lost or shunned fathers, to join with other men in intimacy groups, to participate in sweaty, physical, male-only forest retreats. Women, he states categorically, cannot initiate men into manhood. How, we must ask, does this cultural project further social change? How does it meet the overriding imperative of our time, which is to admit the feminine into all dimensions of psychic and social reality?

Like numerous other people, I have been puzzled and disturbed over recent years at the new alliance between Bly and Hillman. There are considerable amounts of public materials, including books, interviews, essays, audio and video tapes, that make it perfectly clear that Bly and Hillman see themselves as co-workers and leaders of the spiritual men's movement. This unholy alliance was already underway in the early 1980s, when I was working with Hillman in Texas. I warned Hillman against it, but he seemed to have a kind of fatal attraction for Bly's bardic style and charismatic appeal. I pointed out to Hillman that Bly's thinking was confused, and Bly's idealisation of what he then called the 'New Father' seemed decidedly unhealthy. Hillman had his own (often naive and unpoliticised) passions, including a longing for community, belonging, and public mythopoetics, and Robert Bly seemed strangely beyond criticism.

But apart from personal and perhaps commercial gains, there is nothing to be had from the intellectual meeting of Hillman and Bly. Hillman's long-standing insistence on a post-patriarchal and non-heroic style of masculinity contrasts markedly with Bly's advocacy of a primal 'organic' masculinity. Hillman's non-literal understanding of masculinity and femininity, and their appearance in both sexes, contrasts with Bly's simplistic and redneck sexism, which assigns 'masculinity' to men and 'femininity' to women. Hillman's postmodern style and his refusal to think inside rigid categories or blocks of thought is directly contrary to Bly's slow, lumbering reason, with its fixed attachments to binary oppositions. And above all, Hillman's passionate belief that a new, subtle, hermetic style of masculinity must not be '*away* from or *against* matter (mother) but always a mercurial business involved with her',[43] is definitely not to be found in the cult of Iron John. Who is fooling whom here? Has Hillman perhaps decided that his progressive project is too isolating and lonely, and more fame and fun can be had by joining a mass movement? If Bly has short-changed the new masculine spirit by (mis)representing it as an old stereotype, Hillman has short-changed his own reputation by hitching his wagon to a vulgar international star.

ROBERT BLY, TRIBAL ELDER

Bly has a habit of being half right and three-quarters wrong. He correctly identifies a real and pressing problem of the time, and then he puts forward a 'solution' that is wildly reactionary and not of the time. As he gets older, his politics become more transparently reactionary, as we can see from his latest work, *The Sibling Society*.[44] Here he takes on culture at large, and his argument is that none of us can grow up. We contemporary men and women are like squabbling children in a sibling society. Adults in social power today are the post-war baby boomers who believed they would never grow old. In the 1960s and 1970s, we celebrated the gods of sex and vitality, we lifted the repressions of the fuddy-duddy 1950s, and now, in the 1990s, we reluctantly face our ageing and the social responsibility that goes with it.

Bly argues that people are growing old but not up; in fact we have lost the entire 'vertical' axis of our culture, and now everything is horizontal, equal, democratic, reasonable and dreadfully flat. We should restore what he calls 'vertical thought', and have some 'exultation in the midst of flatness'.[45] As in *Iron John*, the possibility of Bly's cure leading to right-wing solutions is left dangerously open. He writes, 'Most of us feel grief and fear at the newest developments, but we also know that what is happening is simply a part of the levelling process that has been going on since the time of the French Revolution'.[46] So what does he want? Is he saying we need a new era of authoritarianism or a militant dictator to help us restore the vertical axis? Bly's prose is full of nostalgia and longing for an idealised former time. We are always made to feel ashamed about modernity, and guilty about the advances of democracy.

The notion that my own generation cannot properly grow up, or complains bitterly as it does so, is not new. We have seen much journalism and a lot of books on this subject, including Christopher Lasch's *The Culture of Narcissism* and Robert Hughes' *Culture of Complaint*.[47] But Bly is explaining these arguments to a popular audience who apparently missed this debate because they do not read difficult books and are not part of high culture. After the intellectuals come the popularisers, and they are the ones to make the real financial killing out of explaining the big picture to ordinary people.

In some ways, Bly is right about our time; it is flat, lacking a sense of grandeur and spiritual magnificence. But if *Iron John* urges us to return to a time when men were solidly and securely identified with their maleness, *The Sibling Society* implores us to go back to an era when adults knew they were adults and were not just kidding. Fifty years ago, good American citizens accepted their maturity and they even spoke and dressed like real adults. Today, Woodstock and the 1960s has messed us up. As sociology, this is excruciatingly bad.

But what does ring true for me is Bly's notion that my generation refuses to grow old, not simply because of its fear of mortality and death, but because it resists the spiritual or religious attitude toward life that inevitably comes with growing up. Bly argues that we only enter full maturity when we 'understand that the world belongs primarily to the dead, and we only rent it from them for a little while'. What brings wisdom, and what turns an ordinary adult into an 'elder', according to Bly, is a heightened spiritual awareness that lifts us out of narcissistic and ego-related concerns. The baby boomers resist this awareness because they are into power, not responsibility, and are victims of a modern secularism that will not allow them to mature emotionally.

But moments of lucidity are rare in Bly's garbled gospel. His work exemplifies the left-wing fear that 'spiritual' awareness leads inevitably and always into a right-wing clamp-down and rigid conservatism. Why does the call of 'spirit' frequently appear to result in such depressing social scenarios and political agendas? Does spirit destroy our imagination and creativity, so that whenever it arises all we can imagine are predictable and entirely conventional responses to its call? In his late career, Bly has become indistinguishable from an old, kill-joy puritan father who chastises naughty children for not respecting their elders. Not because they are wise, but because they are old. But if we cannot look up to them, the book seems to be saying, we can always take a short cut and revere Robert Bly, tribal elder. He constructs himself as the epitome of everything in his preferred human type: very old, wise, hairy, and certainly not vertically challenged.

RETURN TO THE MOTHER AS A PATH OF DEVELOPMENT

In contrast to Bly's insistence that only old men, fathers, the Deep Male, and the Hairy Wildman can initiate men into manhood, I want to reflect in closing this chapter on a contrary point of view:

returning to the mother and the feminine can be a legitimate path of initiation for men. In his essay on 'The Great Mother and the Puer', Hillman refers to an alchemical motif in which masculine spirit and maternal matter are conjoined, and that this 'close union' reflects 'an incest that is a virtue'.[48] Similarly, in his early essay on 'The Feeling Function', Hillman speaks of the *necessary* incestuous return to the mother.[49] If energy is tied up in the mother-image, then the exhausted and depleted male ego must, at certain critical moments, return to that image to be renewed. Sometimes making love to the archetypal mother – rather than running away from her upon the shoulders of a Hairy Wildman,[50] or heroically attacking her with a masculine weapon – is the way to psychological liberation. The following is my 'house of incest' dream, a dream of 1979 that opened a window to the dynamics of my own soul:

> I enter a large, dark, haunted house. It is eerie, and I wander through its dimly lit halls. I come to a bedroom and see my mother lying on a bed in a highly seductive and erotic manner. I move toward the bed and am soon engaging in sexual intercourse. There is a deep sense of guilt and wrong-doing, but I go on with it anyway, feeling waves of ecstasy flow through me. After sexual climax, my mother invites me to make love again, but I feel reluctant. She looks at me longingly and says, 'Let's do it again'. Looking down at her thighs, I suddenly notice that large pointed teeth have grown inside her vagina. I look at her face and there is no sign at all that she is aware of this change; she still seems seductive and erotic.
>
> But the teeth convince me that I am not to engage in further intercourse. I walk out of the bedroom and notice how wretched the whole place is – how full of malignant spirits, ghosts, presences, spiders, old skulls chattering on antique tables. An unknown woman comes up to me and asks: 'Is this house haunted?' 'No,' I answer, lying, and at once I regret the lie, feeling that I have betrayed something. After a moment I correct myself: 'Yes,' I say, stuttering at first, 'Yes, this place is quite haunted.' With these words the entire house begins to change. All the ghosts and bizarre forms rush out of corners, cupboards, and hiding places and come together in one miraculous whirling ball of energy in the centre of the room. The house feels lighter now, as if released of a great spell or burden. Then a form gradually emerges from the whirling ball;

it is the form of a young woman, but she is not exactly human. This woman rushes out of the house and dives into a nearby river. The water begins to stir and 'she' charges along just below the surface, following the river to the sea. Some way out to sea, five jet planes shoot up out of the water, in perfect formation, and move swiftly across the sky.

The pattern of development imaged here involves a return to the maternal source, penetration of the maternal womb, and the possibility of a permanent fusion with the mother in repeated psychological incest. This initiatory pattern is perhaps only for those son-lovers who have not experienced a 'normal' separation from the mother through conventional masculine development. Speaking of the incestuous return, Hillman says:

> It is a Tantric way, if we see it through Hindu eyes. One immerses oneself in the *kleshas*, the attachments to the Mother Goddess. It means going where the heart really is, where we actually feel, even if in the fists, guts and genitals.[51]

The appearance of the mythological image of the *vagina dentata*, the toothed maw, indicates how potentially dangerous this incestuous condition is. The dream indicates that the forbidden incest can by ritually enacted once only. After that, the son's phallic life would be 'devoured' by the toothed vagina. But it is doubtful whether we can, in patriarchal fashion, blame the mother for being devouring, or whether the male ego, being weak and prone to states of regression, is merely projecting its own self-destructive impulse upon the mother. Jung, always ready to protect the mother-figure from psychoanalytic bashings, wrote:

> Always he imagines his worst enemy in front of him, yet he carries the enemy within himself – a deadly longing for the abyss, a longing to drown in his own source, to be sucked down to the realm of the Mothers.[52]

In this sense, the mother's destructiveness is given by the *self*-destructiveness of the son. The male ego has remained too long in its state of incestuous regression, and the teeth are the much-needed 'sign' from the unconscious that it is time to put an end to this ecstatic embrace.

The initiative now lies with consciousness. The dream ego must recognise the teeth, see the danger, and make a decision about its present reality and future course. The responsibility that rests with the ego is made clear by the question put to it by the unknown woman: 'Is this house haunted?' The psyche, through the agency of a creative anima-figure, is calling for greater awareness about the state of things in the house of personality. The ego must admit that incestuous regression has led it into a weird, haunted, deathly place. At first, the ego refuses to admit that its house is haunted. To say 'yes' is a blow to the pride of the male ego, and it resists the humiliating acceptance of its own powerlessness. Such an admission is a defeat for the ego, yet a gain for the psyche as a whole. The need to say 'yes' to hauntedness is perhaps comparable to the demand placed upon characters in fairytales to 'kiss' something or someone who is loathsome and ugly. A negative figure or situation needs to be transformed, and the only way to achieve this is to force the ego to know it intimately and befriend it. In the same way that a fairytale 'kiss' can bring immediate transformation to a beast, monster, or frog, so here the uttering of 'yes' is a liberating act that transforms a psychic house full of inert energies into a dynamic force that achieves focus, form, and power.

In a conventional hero myth, the male ego is compelled to defeat, combat, or kill the toothed mother-dragon that stands before it. As Hillman has said, '[The conventional] way out of this embrace of mother and son' has been 'in terms of a heroic mother–son battle for which St George and the Dragon has become the major Western paradigm'. In patriarchy, 'to be conscious has meant and continues to mean: to kill'.[53] In the present dream, the ego's only action is to give voice or expression to its own situation. This is very Buddhistic and nonviolent: *self-awareness is the liberating act*. Through awareness, development can take place, release can be achieved, and the archetypal mother is still alive and part of the story. The primal mother simply moves into the background and is no more the centre of the son's psychic universe.

Conscious awareness gives birth to the dynamic anima. The dream presents a powerful portrait of the bipolar or dual nature of the archetypal feminine. The reclining, ecstatic mother, who entices the son to continuous incestuous fusion, is Erich Neumann's elemental feminine. This figure, the source of pleasure but the bringer of terror, appears to want to dissolve the son in incestuous sexuality. The unknown woman who asks the world-changing question, and the dynamic ball of feminine energy, are clearly Neumann's transformative feminine, which seems to be opposed to the static/reclining/restful character of the mother. The archetype has split along its dynamic–static fault-line, and this split is apparently necessary to create movement in the overwhelmingly feminine psychic landscape of this mother's son.

First a whirling ball of energy, then a not-quite-human young woman, then an ominous 'stirring' in the waters of the river, and finally a group of jet planes soaring across the sky: the dynamic anima reveals its staggering versatility and its miraculous capacity for shape-shifting and self-transformation. What all these stages of representation have in common is energy or libido. In mythology, the wondrous Aphrodite was born from a turbulence in the sea, a turbulence generated from the fallen genitals of Ouranos after he had been deposed by Chronos. Here a 'stirring' in the depths similarly results from a transformation of a regressive psychic situation. Only there is no violence; simply a refusal to indulge in further incestuous sexuality.

There is nothing particularly feminine about five jet planes flying in formation: indeed this image has a distinctly masculine character. In feminine men, the anima sometimes has a masculine quality, simply because the unlived masculine potential falls into the unconscious, where it conditions the anima, who then carries bisexual attributes. Perhaps the flying anima and jet planes in this dream can be compared with the winged horse Pegasus. Pegasus (in Greek, *pegai* = spring) sprang from the neck of the terrible mother Medusa, after Perseus had heroically cut off her head. Pegasus moves swiftly across the sky, a 'symbol of liberated spiritual imagination'.[54] However, the Perseus myth involves killing and cutting; this modern 'myth' does not:

> The son does not have to force a break with the mother. It has happened. It is given with his condition. He is no longer only her child. The only-natural has been broken because the spiritual has intervened, and so a separation of puer consciousness from mother occurs without the necessity of cutting or killing. Evidently another archetype is activated to which the son also belongs, and this other archetype is as signal to his fate as is the mother from whom he is separated.[55]

Within a few months of having this dream, my shack in the woods was burned to the ground, and everything took place that I have previously described. A dramatic shift was experienced, and virtually everything in the dream 'came true'. However, a real danger in this dream is that the fierce ball of energy and the soaring, skyward jets foreshadow a future development in which all energy moves upward toward spirit, sky, and the heavens. The anima seems rather too keen to leave the body of the mother, and to move toward the archetypal territory of the Heavenly Father. The problem is that if the earth, the body, and sexuality, are linked with 'mother', then to leave mother is to be alienated from these basic realities and desires. Of course, it is only because the attachment to the mother has been so intense, and so long-standing, that the psyche is forced to compensate with an exaggerated 'spiritual' emphasis. In my mother-based mythology, and in my compensatory vertical flights of spirit, I sensed a common heritage with the pathways of Indian Yoga: 'Does not Vedanta and its transcendence of matter reflect a spirit so entangled in the great world mother that it must resort to disciplined exercises to find liberation?'[56]

But another archetype has been activated, and this is the archetype of the spiritual anima, who traditionally stands close to the Great Father. In Chapters 5 and 6, my symbolic experience of the Father, foreshadowed here, is discussed in great detail, and in Chapter 7 the skyward anima is shown to be interested in coming down to earth again.

4

RITES AND WRONGS OF PASSAGE

Men are beginning to divine that only the spirit can give life its
highest meaning.

Jung[1]

TIME-HONOURED SEXISM AND INITIATORY PROCESS

I would now like to focus on the problem of initiation into
manhood, a problem implicit in much of the foregoing, but yet to
be considered in its own right. It is not only our time which is
anxious about manhood, but it seems that all peoples have shared a
basic anxiety about the achievement of masculine maturity.[2] Most
traditional cultures adopt the view that manhood is an achievement, not a given.[3] Although biological development may 'force'
change upon us, we have to respond in the appropriate way, and the
achievement of maturity (however it may be defined) is by no
means automatic. Traditionally, manhood must be earned, won, or
fought for through various trials and ritualised sufferings. It seems
to me that male rites of passage were devised to facilitate a major
transition from a 'given' psychological identification with the
mother and maternal society to an 'acquired' identification with the
father and paternal society. This accords with basic psychoanalytic
understanding, which has the son first fused with the mother in a
symbiotic relationship, and only later emerging from this maternal
field to enter into an 'ambivalent' identification with the father.[4]

The transition from one state to the other is fraught with
emotional difficulties and psychological dangers. Among these difficulties, we could include: a characteristic 'separation anxiety' as the
son leaves the mother, resulting in incomplete separation, strong

feminisation of the son, and a hatred for the father; and, on the other hand, an over-hasty, over-reactive flight to the father, which damages the essential relationship with the mother and the feminine. In contemporary men's experience, the 'left wing' of the men's movement reflects some of the first set of problems: a continued identification with the mother, a championing of her cause under the banner of radical political protest against a depraved and degenerate father. The 'right wing' of the men's movement, however, takes the over-hasty flight to the father, representing the matriarchal position as pathology and folly (the 'soft male' with his 'maternal domination'), and idealises the new identification with the patriarch. Between these two extremes, individual modern men must chart their own course of individuation. But whatever the outcome, and whatever one's political tastes or affiliations, a *break* in the early identification with the mother must take place, lest the son never embark on his own individuation or discover his own selfhood.

According to Ray Raphael, initiatory rituals were meant to complement and intensify the 'natural' developmental process, and to boost the differentiation of the male ego from the maternal matrix or background. 'Through the use of structured initiation rites, [tribal] societies have been able to help and guide the youths through their period of developmental crisis'.[5] In this way, culture 'improves' on nature by providing a kind of public psychodrama in which the symbolic processes within the developing youth were carefully crafted and manipulated to produce socially desirable results. In tribal rites, boys were often seized from their mothers during the night by the male elders of the tribe. Sometimes the elders were dressed and decorated in the likeness of the Gods, to indicate that what was about to take place was ordained and sanctioned by the divine masculine figures.[6] In some rituals, the mother was supposed to weep and wail at the initiation wall or at some other demarcated barricade, to demonstrate the painful separation which had taken place. The mother was expected to ritually mourn the 'death' of her son, who was often given a new name and a completely new identity. Once the ceremonies were finished, the mother was sometimes prevented from 'recognising' her son for a prescribed period of time, to give further support to the new masculine self and the developmental process.[7]

With all these safeguards, rituals, regulations, and taboos, we can appreciate how difficult this emotional transition or rebirth was felt to be. The contents and activities of the rites of passage were closely guarded because the integrity of the male society was believed to rest upon strong and effective rites. Patriarchal control is in this sense a compensatory reaction to the natural power and authority of the given matriarchal situation.[8] In depth psychological terms, patriarchy got behind the developing ego, while the mother was associated with the unconscious source that had to be opposed and, in a sense, betrayed by the ego that would tear itself free from its own psychological background.

One of the arguments of this book is that the son must free himself from the mother, but that the old ways of achieving this are no longer desirable. Most of the ancient rites of passage I have studied, or have observed close at hand in various ethnic contexts, are not desirable in today's world, and as such we must view with utmost caution the desire of the right wing of the men's movement to 'revive' these old male customs and ancient rituals. Most of these social rituals are unduly sexist, and commit the basic error of identifying the mother-complex and the regressive 'tie' to the source, with the actual human mother, and, by extension, to all members of the female sex. The responses of patriarchal cults of initiation to mothers, girls, and women, are clearly phobic and extremist, due to the contamination of archetypal contents with the human and social sphere. If we believe that boys must still be 'initiated' into manhood, we must not be tempted to revert to these archaic practices, and must work toward a postmodern, not a premodern, understanding of ritual masculine process. As I will go on to suggest, I believe that a revival of an appropriate religious or spiritual attitude could produce the necessary 'authority' to facilitate transformational change from childhood to adulthood.

'GOING PRIMITIVE' AND THE POPULAR IDEALISATION OF MANHOOD

There is in many men today a nostalgic longing for the simplicity, efficiency, and finality of the tribal initiations. As one interviewee responded to Ray Raphael's summary of an indigenous American initiatory rite:

> I wish I had it that easy. Run through the fire, step on the coals – then it's over and done with. You're a man, everyone knows you're a man, and that's the end of it. For me it keeps on going on and on. I've got to keep on fighting for money

and respect. The fire never stops; I keep running through it every day.[9]

If only, some men cry, the state of manhood could be locked in by this or that psychodrama or pattern of initiation! That way, they argue, modern men would be exempt from much personal anguish, psychological pain, and social alienation.[10]

Almost inevitably, the popular appropriation of ancient rites degenerates into a kind of mock-parody of the distant past, where bored office workers and alienated moderns pretend for the duration of a weekend retreat that they are tribal warriors, and that their gathering in the forest has the power to initiate men and hopeful boys into the state of manhood. This kind of weekend primitivism, which has reportedly 'worked' for some individuals, can rarely hope to get beyond the level of ineffectual parody, and may in some cases be injurious or harmful. The main problem is that there is a grossly insufficient grasp of the psychological and inward dimension of the process of initiation. The forest retreats get caught up in literalism, in copying old forms and ancient rituals, and do not sufficiently engage the raw psychological energies of the present. No 'initiation' occurs at all, unless the psychological process and situation of the participant has been understood from the inside and has been engaged with empathy and understanding.

As someone who grew up living alongside the tribal indigenous cultures of central Australia, I have too much respect for tribal rituals to reenact them in a workshop setting or to appropriate them wholesale in a consumerist bid to fill the void of our contemporary Western culture. I have never believed that we either can or should steal another culture's sacred rituals and pretend that they belong to us.[11] Our spiritual longings make us very curious about tribal rituals, and urge us to move close to them. Our political awareness, however, correctly distances us from those same rituals, pointing out that history and culture separate us from them, and that to imitate or borrow them is tantamount to cultural imperialism and gross impropriety.

The rites associated with an initiation into manhood cannot be copied or imitated because those forms and rites are specific to a particular time and a particular place. The condition referred to as 'manhood' is not static, but varies greatly from one society to another. By definition, 'manhood' means acceptance into the adult male compact of a specific group. One group's notion of a dignified

102

manhood may be another group's idea of oppression or hell on earth. It is very wrong for starry-eyed participants in the popular men's movement to reify or freeze this concept of manhood. The whole business about 'manhood' contains a large dose of social engineering, and we are dealing as much with artificially constructed stereotypes as we are with metaphysical or *a priori* archetypes. The world of initiation and rites of passage is at once complex and paradoxical. The impulse to be initiated into manhood may well be archetypal, but *how* that longing is fulfilled, and *how* manhood is defined, is socially constructed. As Jung made clear, at the level of archetypal content, nothing is fixed or stable, and everything is supplied by temporal conditions. Cultural history fills the 'empty' archetypal pattern with its own contents and definitions.

Traditional male initiations are works of socialisation and indoctrination. Ancient societies, especially the small nomadic tribes of the Australian Aboriginals, could not afford to have their male members incapacitated by psychological distress or paralysed by existential uncertainty. As Margaret Mead observed in a different context, there is little room in the tribal compact for 'the unplaced person who has yet come to no terms with his society. . . . The [unplaced youth] could not be endured; the social sanction of ridicule would be too great'.[12] As soon as healthy and able-bodied youths could be put to productive service for the community, initiations were arranged to turn boys into men. The neophytes upheld their new status with considerable pride, and shirking or refusing to perform the role allotted to them by the tribe was met with general disapproval.

Alienated moderns tend to idealise the tribal initiations from afar, as we wince at our own isolation. However, anthropologists who work in these fields rarely romanticise these rituals, because they are alert to the fact that although the puberty rites offer a firm identity and a strong context, they also severely limit individual choice and drastically curtail the freedom of the individual will. Initiations induct the novice into what the society of the time regards as correct behaviour, right attitudes, and desirable manners. It is ironic that those modern men who tend to idealise the tribal initiations of the past are also the first men to attack any modern authority or tradition if it deigns to condition their own responses or limit their choices. This is a classic case of idealisation accompanied by splitting, demonisation, and projection of the shadow side of the desired impulse. The tribal initiations only worked well if the

103

novices did not complain about the social and political forces that were attempting to shape them into adult men. One cannot have it both ways: one cannot idealise an ancient form of social engineering, and then rail against all modern collective forces that would attempt to mould our being and compromise our individuality. Belonging and conformity go together, so that stable initiations are synonymous with stable institutions. Ancient initiations and the modern ideal of freedom of will and action do not sit happily together.

What we find in the popular men's movement is an almost systematic confusion of archetypal calling and stereotypal response. Men feel a 'calling' to initiation, but fail to understand that a *new* calling demands a *new* response. Too often, the calling to initiation is simply collapsed into old or outmoded cultural forms. What this tells us is that the psychic impulses are way ahead of the cultural forms, so that the psyche is forced to wait on the culture to change its structures and practices. The psyche can provide us with the impulse or desire, but how that desire is put into practice is up to us. However, we continually short-change the new spirit by forcing it into old bottles. A comparison might be made with the problem of religious fundamentalism. If, say, the psyche calls us to spiritual rebirth, and we then decide to enlist in the local 'Born Again' religious cult, we may well have betrayed our finest and deepest spiritual impulse. Joining the cult is simply to literalise or falsely concretise a legitimate spiritual calling.

THE FATHERING CAPACITY AND NEGATIVE CAPABILITY

Frequently, the archetypal calling to initiation meets with the response: but where are the fathers, uncles, elders, wisemen, patriarchs, to conduct this men's business? Everywhere in the international men's movement we meet this deep, sonorous, emotive crying out to personal and social fathers, who are expected to rescue contemporary men and youths from their uncertainty and insecurity. But we have already seen in Chapter 2 how problematical this longing is. The new idealisation of the old patriarch simply reflects the moral conservatism and spiritual rigidity of the men's movement. The social-political father, or patriarchy, is in decline: why should we initiate our sons into a morally bankrupt and declining institution? The figure who symbolises the dying and decaying past cannot be expected to lead the young men of today into a new vision of manhood and maturity. What we are concerned with here is really a crisis of modelling. Who can model for us the new images of a post-patriarchal masculinity? The honest answer is that no-one can model for us what has still to be born.

When stereotypes come crashing down, when social figures can no longer perform in the expected way, we can only return to the archetypes themselves and 'dream the myths onward'[13] to new and future manifestations. When the father is ineffectual or absent, the archetypal reality of the father may have to present itself directly in the psyche of the son. We may have to 'turn inward' to find the new father who will show the way to the future. The son may have to 'father' himself, or initiate himself, largely through trial and error, into a more mature psychic state. Or we have to look into all kinds of new directions for the fathering capacity or initiatory potential, such as the dynamic aspect of the feminine. Important new visions and values, such as environmentalism, feminism, post-colonialism, the new sciences, new spirituality, gender studies – all these major new cultural preoccupations have the capacity to 'father' us and to initiate us into our own creativity and into the larger social world. Where we get caught, where we fail the inner calling, is when we imagine that the initiatory impulse simply wants us to fuse our identity with an unquestioned or unbroken cultural tradition.

Too much of the Jungian literature fails us in this important regard. In numerous books and essays we find a profoundly nostalgic longing to revive or boost the lost, diminished, or weakened masculine rites of passage. Often we find that the diminished importance of the Jewish *bar mitzvah* is lamented, and that the passing of Christian rites of spiritual maturity is bemoaned. But it is not sufficiently realised that there is a larger historical importance behind the disappearance of these old-style patriarchal rituals. Jungians too often want to see the ego 'mature' and 'develop' at all costs. But mature into what? And develop into what? Initiation is too often valued for its own sake, and questions are not asked about what the novice is being inducted into. There is an enormous privileging of the individual developmental process and a general lack of concern about the developmental process of society itself. Can't society be allowed to break down? If its spiritual buffers and reinforcements are weakening, can't this also be a cause for celebration for what the future might bring?

It stands to reason that the much-hallowed 'initiations' of the past cannot take place when the foundations of social structure are moving. What faces us today is a huge opportunity to recreate the social world, and to move beyond the stultifying and narrow confines of psychological patriarchy. But we have to learn to cope with large amounts of uncertainty while this rebuilding takes place. What is required of the present is an attitude that the poet John Keats called 'negative capability': the ability to be in doubts, mysteries, uncertainties, without any irritable search after fact or reason. We must recognise that boys need to 'change into' men, but our definitions of manhood must be flexible, open, receptive to the new and unanxious about enforcing the past. We must, writes Samuels, 'allow ourselves to exist in a temporary but creative vacuum', which 'might allow a new, antitotalitarian position to emerge'. Samuels cleverly turns the rhetoric of masculinity back upon itself: 'Perhaps the manly thing to do nowadays is to try to live without the guidance and structures that defined manliness in the past'.[14] In this somewhat precarious position, we can learn from the past, but we must not simply succumb to it.

THE AUTHORITY OF SPIRIT AND POLITICAL AUTHORITY

Initiation implies a subordination of the personal will to a trans-personal authority. When I said before that some of us today have to discover the fathering capacity within ourselves, what I meant by this was that we must locate, and submit to, an internal authority which is greater than the ego. The contemporary concern with psychotherapy is really an attempt to explore one's own self-initiatory potentials. The whole point of therapy, at least as I have experienced it, is to discover an objective dimension of subjectivity (a strange contradiction?) that we can learn to trust and obey. With so many of us today unable to trust external authorities, it becomes even more important to provide an introverted alternative to the object-relations and power-relationships that are usually conducted at the social and political level. But not all of us have the money to go into long-term psychotherapy! Nor do we all possess the introverted-intuitive consciousness that could make sense of an 'inner journey' to discover the 'fathering capacity' or 'initiatory potential' within. For many natural extraverts, these phrases make very little genuine sense. All the more reason, then, for us to revive and renew the sociopolitical sphere, to develop new values and visions that can lead and guide young people into a larger moral and spiritual universe.

Social authorities have always been responsible for turning boys into men. In tribal societies, spiritual authority derived from the Gods and Goddesses, Deities, and Creator Beings, and this authority was, in turn, appropriated by the tribe and used as a justification for its own traditions and practices. 'Enlightened' anthropologists may quietly smile at this claim, viewing it as a transparent work of social engineering and political manipulation, but I have no reason to believe that this claim means other than what it says: a direct link with an archetypal source is fostered and nurtured through the social and political compact. For the modern West, patriarchy itself has stood in for the 'higher authority' of spiritual or religious revelation. The links between the Western capitalist system and Christian theology have been much explored and discussed. To ensure its effectiveness and longevity, it was necessary for patriarchy to mythologise itself, to invest itself with absolute and larger-than-life significance. Until recently, patriarchy was not challenged or questioned; it was simply assumed to possess awesome power and to be a kind of earthly extension of God the Father's dominion. Boys became men by following the career paths of their fathers, by becoming absorbed into conventional trades and practices that enabled patriarchy to rule and to run smoothly. Youths were transformed into 'real men' by fusing their identity with the moral and political authority of patriarchy.

It is clear to me that my personal father, John Edward Tacey, achieved his own sense of manhood by these means, and that both my grandfathers had done likewise before him. For good or ill, I broke this patriarchal line because I could no longer *believe* in the authority of patriarchy. It had little authority over me, I had grown wild and feral, and I paid it hardly any respect. Maybe it lacked authority for me because I could not sense the glow of transpersonal values within it. It seemed to me to be an institutionalised system of unfairness, which benefited some people, but which disadvantaged many. Patriarchy unwittingly began its own undoing when it distanced itself from its original source of religious authority. As the West became more secular, the divine 'inspiration' behind the patriarchal system became obscure and difficult to discern. The post-Enlightenment West eventually stopped dispensing religious truth, and instead began to espouse a purely moral or social gospel under the umbrella of secular humanism. The archetypal father had 'down-sized' to the social-political patriarch, whose only authority was derived from tradition, habit, and ideology. Without any religious mystique, the old patriarch had rendered himself vulnerable to all sorts of reasoned, intellectual, and ideological attacks. Patriarchy had rendered itself easy to 'see through'. Where there is no vision, the political system perishes.

All true authority derives from the spirit. Unless spirit animates a social or political institution, it cannot initiate anyone into a higher state, because it lacks the spiritual authority to do so. Patriarchy can no longer recover this spiritual capacity because the spirit has deserted it. It cannot align itself with the creative spirit of the time, because this spirit is feminine, radical, and transformative. When I was a student in the 1970s, Marxism, an alternative political philosophy, appeared to possess spiritual authority. I was never sure what this authority was, until I read in Mircea Eliade that

> Marxian communism . . . takes up and carries on one of the great eschatological myths of the Middle Eastern and Mediterranean world, namely: the redemptive part to be played by the Just (in our own days the proletariat), whose sufferings are invoked to change the ontological status of the world.[15]

Broadly speaking, in my student days, most conventional men unquestioningly identified with mainstream patriarchal ideology, while many 'thinking' men took on Marxism and began to see their own lives as profoundly related to the revolutionary cause. If you will, Marxism was the big idea or the 'scale of the Gods' that gave many students a link to a larger and potent life, a link that cancelled their own insignificance and 'initiated' them into a greater philosophical world. Importantly, with this initiation went profound social awareness, a very active public conscience, a high regard (often amounting to romantic idealisation) of the working classes – all important features of initiatory process insofar as they lead the novice away from private pleasures into social action and political responsibility. Marxism, for some of my own peers, was itself a *rite de passage* into maturity, and although I have never been passionately involved in Marxism I have always respected the transformative role it has played for many people.

With the world-wide collapse of Marxism-Leninism, this alternative political programme now has the same kind of dubious initiatory status as mainstream capitalistic patriarchy, namely, it is something of a museum-piece, an institution that once possessed enormous transformative potential but is now being emptied of meaning. It may be that the modern era's love affair with politics is in decline. In today's world, it is increasingly difficult to pretend that this or that political system can lay claim to absolute truth or can act as a dignified container of our spiritual energy. Our political systems of the left, right, and centre, seem all too human, prone to corruption, and incapable of being idealised in the way that is essential to initiatory process. With both rival political systems now divested of their mystique and exposed as institutionalised systems of bias and prejudice, there is an urgent need to replace these fallen idols with something else.

Beyond the artifice and the antics of human endeavour, a living transpersonal force must be felt to reside at the centre of social structure. That force, if actively constellated, is what actually transforms and initiates the novice. In his illuminating essay, 'Initiation and the Modern World', Mircea Eliade draws particular attention to the spiritual dimension of adolescent initiation in ancient tribal contexts:

> The tribal initiation introduces the novice into the world of spiritual and cultural values and makes him a responsible member of the society. The young man learns not only the behaviour patterns, the techniques, and the institutions of adults, but also the myths and the sacred traditions of the tribe, the names of the gods and the history of their works; above all, he learns the mystical relations between the tribe and supernatural beings as those relations were established at the beginning of time. In a great many cases puberty rites imply the revelation of sexuality. In short, through initiation, the candidate passes beyond the 'natural' mode of being – that of the child – and gains access to the cultural mode; that is, he is introduced to spiritual values.[16]

Eliade makes clear in this essay that the tribal youth becomes a man not merely by glimpsing the tribe's mysteries or by having them narrated to him, but by becoming the *living embodiment* of an extra-mundane source of truth. The youth believes that he has actually contacted a new mythic source, which has dramatically altered his identity and shifted his sense of self. Our youth seem instinctively to realise that they must forge a connection with a higher authority, even if we adults have forgotten that the passage into adulthood is for the novice a profoundly spiritual experience. Youths realise that they must awaken to a force greater than themselves, a force that is ultimately transpersonal, before their identity can be transferred from that of the egotistical child to an engaged, socially committed adult. The experience of spirit is the powerful force which carries the promise of their own transformation. Teenagers, I think, instinctively look to adulthood as an initiation into big values, great stories, and spiritual realities.

TOWARD A SPIRITUAL RENAISSANCE

The signs are that we may well be experiencing a revival of spirituality, which I for one see as a positive development. It is not that politics will disappear or become unimportant, but simply that politics may no longer carry (or be capable of carrying) our spiritual idealisations. As a university student, I used to think that I was the exception to this rule, but now the tides of change are moving toward my own personal orientation, and, somewhat strangely, my own views are now increasingly 'in vogue'. Large numbers of youths and adults are now involved in new (or new–old) religious philosophies and spiritual practices, and the attraction of increasing numbers of men to what is broadly termed 'mythopoetics' and spirituality has become widespread. More teenagers are talking about spirituality, in the same enthusiastic way in which students two or three decades ago spoke about political systems. Adolescents realise that they must be able to connect with something that is large, grand, and archetypal.

When my students tell me they are interested in spirituality I am excited for them, but also I feel professionally frustrated, since so little that they encounter at university will help them articulate and develop their spiritual lives. On the contrary, the secular education paradigm, which, like the materialist health paradigm, is severely dated and out of touch with the needs of the young, will encourage them to repress their spirituality and to study a whole range of highly abstract and intellectual subjects which are often unrelated to their immediate longings. Students will be applauded for studying all kinds of sexual practices and politics, the more radical the better, but they won't be given the space or the opportunity to attend to the spiritual dimension. Our secular mainstream culture is still suspicious about spirituality, and it does not seek to encourage what it hopes is merely a passing fad in the lives of our young people. I think the public education agenda will change if enough students put pressure on it, but for the time being God is still too much of an embarrassment for the education system to cope with. I guess that is why my wife and I have chosen to give our daughter a Catholic education, not because we are supporters of dogmatic Catholicism, but because the Catholic system will at least provide her with myths, dreams, and images large enough to create space for a transformative spiritual life.

My students who say they are interested in spirituality are often quick to deny an interest in 'religion' as such. It is as if 'religion', like politics, is too man-made, too limited and perhaps incapable of containing idealisations. Religion no longer holds a monopoly on the spiritual lives of adolescents, and it is time our established faiths took full note of this. Today, spirituality has become separated from church, synagogue, temple, and mosque, suggesting that there is a surprisingly large amount of free-floating spiritual energy in the human psyche. This could be the energy that builds a new (or a reconstructed?) world religion, one that fulfils the spiritual and cultural needs of the time. If I suggest to my students that they should attend their local church, they often look at me as if I am an agent of the establishment, not on 'their' side. Clearly, what is on their side is a notion of the living spirit which they feel is not catered for or encouraged by the traditional faiths.

It could be that environmentalism and eco-feminism, for instance, are potentially great containers of adolescent spirituality. The only problem with these two ideologies is that they need to deepen themselves in the direction of the spiritual before they can act as symbols of a larger universe. Environmentalism must reach into the mythic sources that could add depth and vision to its activist program, such as Buddhism, Zen, Christian and Jewish mysticism, and especially Taoism. Similarly, feminism must deepen its political platform into religion and spirituality, and in the United States it has already accomplished this in the burgeoning field of feminist theology. These are important examples of how we can fuse political concern with religious depth, outer-world interest with inner-world experience. Youths appear to me to want two things: they want their religious lives to be 'relevant' to the contemporary world, and they want their involvement in the political world to be passionate, or 'spiritual'. Only contemporary social movements that search for deep religious roots, or ancient religions styled to meet the contemporary situation, will satisfy the needs of youth today.

If our materialist society is too small and mean to develop any cosmic scenarios, then our adolescents will create large visions of their own. Although cosmic visions may be given short shrift at school, and do not appear on the public education agenda, students develop enormous appetites for astrology, occultism, wicca, Tarot, I Ching, yoga, reincarnation, channelling, and many other esoteric sciences and hermetic arts – all of which appear to offer them doorways into the cosmic dimensions of the world. I am frequently astonished by the huge interest in the esoteric arts and sciences in today's youth. I am sure that more of my students understand the language of astrology than they do the cultural history and mythology of the Christian Bible. Many adults think this interest is dangerous, wrong, or ill-conceived, but personally I try to tolerate this interest, since it is simply a symptomatic expression of the lack of religious vision in our mainstream culture. If we presented youth with a living and dynamic religious life, the appetite for the 'seeing arts' and the esoteric sciences would undoubtedly diminish. As it is, let them have these esoteric paths, so long as they do not become demonic or dangerous.

Many youths today do not search for an esoteric path, but actually turn consumerism itself into a religion. Society is encouraging them to do this all the time. Advertisements and television commercials deliberately employ religious themes and mythological elements in their images and narratives, anxious to make commercial value out of our unfulfilled religious longings. Copywriters and film producers look up motifs and themes in Joseph Campbell and Jung, making a literal travesty of the notion that myth and symbol are the rich treasures of civilisation. Many youths today are saturated with quasi-religious compulsions and worshipful obsessions, and some actually 'believe in' media celebrities, cinema personalities, and rock stars. These are, as it were, the degraded and cultic substitutes for genuine spiritual relationships with sacred or mythological figures. If our culture has no pantheon of living Gods, it will quickly develop clusters of human idols and commercial gurus. This is a very dangerous situation, because the human need for worship and surrender before cosmic forces is instinctive, and youths will throw themselves before commercialised interests that can only exploit them.

Commercialism dominates not only the entertainment industry, but also the new-age philosophy industry. Hundreds of new-age sects, cults, and groups are happy to accommodate the initiatory fervour of today's youth. One simply has to pay the required fee, and keep paying for boosters and 'advanced' programmes, and a carefully designed doorway to cosmic truth will open before you. What we notice about the new sects and cults is how *certain* they are of themselves. They are convinced that their spiritual product is genuine, that it works, and that it gets the Gods on line. This is an important popular element, because the certainty of the cults appeals to the initiatory urge in adolescents. In our postmodern world, governed as it is by relativism and plurality, *certainty* is most attractive to adolescents who want to leave childhood behind and enter a larger world.

We can, therefore, observe a series of compensatory mechanisms at work in our current social situation. As public education becomes more dryly intellectual, detached, critical, the adolescent's world outside the classroom becomes more obsessional, frantic, and full of emotional longing. As our official humanist culture loses its heat and becomes tepid and cool, unofficial subcultures develop enormous energy, each one with its own fire in the belly. As postmodernism decides that all knowledge is relative, socially constructed, and arbitrary, cults and sects trade on absolutism and fanaticism. We have to understand that it is our own spiritual emptiness that wills the new cults into existence. We could put it this way: as official culture loses sight of, and confidence in, the moral and spiritual *fundamentals*, a tide of *fundamentalism* is being set into motion at the fringes of society, threatening to overwhelm the lifeless thing that official culture has become. Education and fundamentalism are caught up in a kind of binary opposition: as the one relinquishes truth, and even doubts that truth exists, the other will start peddling confidence tricks and grotesque parodies of truth. Youth will get its fix of truth, either officially from education and culture, or unofficially from cults, media, and the new-age supermarket.

Mainstream culture must attempt to rekindle the fires of truth, but this recovery can only take place within a revisionist programme. 'We cannot go backwards by propping up senex religion.'[17] As Jung has said, 'Eternal truth needs a human language that alters with the spirit of the times'.[18] It is no use protesting that we have not yet enough scientific data to construct an image of cosmic truth, or, as one of my own professors said, that 'we do not yet know enough about reality to start talking about spirituality'. While we fiddle with these stupid rationalistic reservations, our adolescents burn with unrequited spiritual fires and unchannelled emotional longings.

113

SEXUALITY AND ADOLESCENCE

In the important passage from Mircea Eliade quoted above, we read: 'In a great many cases puberty rites imply the revelation of sexuality'. It may be worth reflecting on the meaning and implications of this statement. Sexuality and adolescence go together, and it is proper that the mystery of sexuality is revealed to the novice during the initiation process. In ancient religious practices, sexuality is dignified by linking it with the procreative forces of nature and with the spiritual goals and truths of the social group. Only our own 'modern' Western culture has had a hard time facing up to this existential problem. Those in the West who are interested in spirituality generally do not include sexuality in their understanding of the life of the spirit. And the secular majority do not see any reason at all why sexuality and spirituality should be brought together. Here, tribal and ancient cultures are far in advance of our contemporary society. Long before Freud had to enlighten the modern world, early humanity recognised that the sexual instinct was the basic and primal source of human energy. If we ignore sexuality, we leave out the libidinal source of life itself. And so tribal initiations were designed to reveal sexuality as a sacred force that linked the novice, in his bodily and biological urges, to the vitalistic life of the ancestors and the creator-spirits. By so linking sexuality with the life of the spirit, the sexual impulse was humanised and civilised.

It was felt by many tribal groups that sexuality which had not been initiated in this way was potentially disruptive to the social compact. If sexuality was not allowed an official outlet into society, if it were not granted a higher status by linking it with spirit, then the sexual impulse could not be utilised as a vital energy source at the service of society. Sexuality would remain trapped at a personal level, locked into private fantasies and trapped in infantile expressions. This, I think, is the experience of many adolescents today. There is a blockage in the energy gradient: a depressed, empty, or exhausted outward persona, while inside, below the surface, there is a veritable torrent of energy caught up in genital sexuality. Because society appears to offer little or no spiritual outlet for the generous surplus of emotion which is found in adolescence, our youthful fervours turn sexual and genital, so that many modern youths invest a much larger than normal amount of energy into sexual matters. The sexuality of our adolescents has not been 'initiated', not released into higher cultural channels, and so instead of expressing itself in both higher and lower forms, that is, in cultural creativity and in genital procreativity, it all flows down and out through genitality. And we sit back and wonder why teenage culture seems to be drenched in ever-larger measures of sexual desire: because that is precisely where the life-energy is held. Until our spiritual disciplines can learn how to reach into that ocean of libido, our age will remain saturated with untransformed sexuality and our teenagers burdened by quantities of desire which are not so much antisocial as they are presocial in their nature and direction. Christianity in particular has much work to do before it can respond to these fundamental problems of human desire and expression.

CYNICISM, BRILLIANCE, AND DEPRESSION

If many young people today appear confused, unsure about which way to turn, who to believe and who to disbelieve, it is because they have internalised the chaos that is around them. The cynicism with which some youth treat social and educational authorities is, I think, a fairly natural, if unfortunate, response to the fragmented nature of the times. I sometimes encounter angry or jaded students who say to me, after I have lectured on some topic, 'But that's only your view!' They are absolutely right, and I do sympathise with their rejection of my authority – which is, until I have earned their trust, just one more authority in the confusing supermarket of contradictory authorities. My job is to receive their cynicism without too much personal hurt on my part. If I accept their distancing of my authority in a mature way, they are, paradoxically, all the more likely to take my counsel seriously later on.

In a culture giving out mutually exclusive messages, the brightest and best minds are forced, sometimes at remarkably early ages, to hold counsel with their own souls. It is not uncommon for me to meet teenagers who have tried to construct moral maps and metaphysical systems of their own. When the official culture cannot be trusted, when the world is torn and unstable, many of our teenagers valiantly attempt to become their own authorities. Some children appear to be born old (*puer senilis*), to be robbed of their childhood, because the state of childhood cannot be properly lived in a climate of fear and uncertainty. When trust is absent, innocence vanishes – hence many kids struggle to be cool, all-knowing, tuned-in, fully aware, even if this is merely a pose to hide the fact that, underneath, they are merely frightened and in need of love.

The mixed messages of society create confusion and uncertainty about which way to move forward. While some enjoy this challenge and become highly motivated in their attempts to steer their own course, for others the efforts required to meet the challenges of the day are daunting and overwhelming. There are, for some teenagers, too many big decisions to be made, too many life-choices, and too many existential questions to be answered. Depression and chronic fatigue appear to be inflicting people at younger and younger ages. 'Major depressive illness, once regarded as a malady of the middle-aged and elderly, is becoming increasingly common among teenagers and young adults'.[19] The spiritual and moral effort of living creates a mental heaviness that soon manifests as a physical inertia. Some young people feel under too much pressure – peer groups are moving in one direction, while parents urge them along a different road. Decisions about how to face the world, or what face to wear in the world, can lead to chronic depression, if not to bouts of mania followed by depression. All kinds of external factors are blamed for the malaise: difficult friendships, parents, the stress of school exams, the inability to find a job, but how many of these areas are simply excuses for deeper spiritual problems which are far more difficult to name and identify?

Research has shown that choice creates stress, and a lot of choice creates a lot of stress. Ancient tribal societies were severely regulated and controlled. One's social role was chosen by the elders of the tribe, and one's daily rituals and activities were all regulated by a conservative social agenda. In the tribal context, the big existential questions were the job of the shaman, or the men and women of high degree. The normal person simply did not have to bother himself with problems of being, morality, and spirit. Many of our youth today feel that they have to carry all the big questions on their own backs. They have to deal with a series of large spiritual questions, and every time an answer is found to a question they have to reinvent their lives in accordance with the new revelations. No wonder more youths are suffering from chronic fatigue and depression. We are asking our teenagers to carry impossible burdens, as mainstream society manages to shirk the big moral and existential issues that culture is supposed to be shouldering.

SUBSTANCE-ABUSE, DRUGS, ALCOHOL

If youths cannot build a new and brighter self with the assistance of cultural values, they may decide that it is easier to hack away at the personal self than it is to transform it. Here we enter very dangerous psychological territory. If our personal energies are not permitted an upward outlet, they may move down and backwards into violence, crime, anger, and a kind of cult of self-destructiveness.

The symbolic destruction of the old, childhood self was actually a crucial part of ancient initiatory process. According to Arnold van Gennep, the classic authority on rites of passage, the so-called 'death phase' was an integral part of all traditional initiations.[20] This part of the ritual process was usually surrounded by the strictest taboos, because the tribal cultures understood that a kind of psychic surgery was being performed, and this was connected with all manner of moral, spiritual, and physical dangers. The old self and identity had to 'die', and a new self be allowed to be born. In most ceremonies, the rites and symbols of loss, deprivation, or pain were in some way enacted. In some contexts, lacerations to the chest, back, and other parts of the body were enforced. Other common components of the death-phase included hunger and deprivation (sometimes to the point of near-delirium), minor bodily injuries, the knocking out of a tooth, running on hot coals, circumcision, or subincision.[21]

These rituals often appear brutal, harsh, or downright crazy to contemporary taste. We call these acts 'uncivilised' and 'inhumane'. However, the tribal view was that the transition to the adult state involved unavoidable pain and suffering. Paradoxically, the aim of tribal initiation was to *reduce* and *ritualise* the mental suffering of youths, to construct limits and boundaries to the psychological tortures involved in moving from infantile self-absorption to a responsible life in the adult community. Contemporary youths who succumb to the archetypal suggestiveness of the death-phase of self-initiation can spend months or even years in this self-destructive cycle, precisely because there is no cultural containment or ritual form to their period of mental disorientation. If some of us today spend months or years in this extremely dangerous state, while tribal novices spend three days or a week in states of near-delirium, then who are the civilised ones, and who are the primitives?

In many ancient rituals, hallucinogenic and other drugs were often ceremoniously deployed to further the dissolution of the old self and the transition to a new identity.[22] For instance, intoxicants have long been used in African and New Guinea initiations, and the mescaline-rich peyote is used in Mexican and Amerindian rituals. I believe that the contemporary adolescent abuse of intoxicants, hallucinogens, and other drugs can be viewed against this archetypal background. Adolescents take drugs for the same reason that tribal initiates were given drugs by their elders: to help dissolve the boundaries of the self, to expand to a fuller or different identity, and to gain an ecstatic experience that links them to a wider cosmos.

It is as if contemporary youth knows instinctively that it must overcome the habitual and stable self in order to move to a new state. However, as with everything that can be compared with tribal experience, the modern experience of the liminal stage is protracted and extended. Youths do not simply dissolve former boundaries and then move on. Rather, they can become addicted to liminality and danger, and engage in a chronic and repeated attempt to dissolve the self in drugs. In this event, drugs do not lead forward to a new birth, but actually lead backward into disintegration. In tragic cases, there is an ego-death of sorts but no rebirth, no embrace of a wider reality that would enable the youth to develop a new moral centre. What we have in our drug cultures is a negative and symptomatic enactment of the need for initiatory transformation. The fact that drug cultures are full of special code languages, secrecy, closure, a society that conducts behaviours that are not understood in normal society, shows that this culture is a kind of unconscious parody of initiatory experience, with its own esotericism, secrecy and its separate realities.

Drugs hold out the prospect of a new world, a prospect that an increasing number of teenagers are finding irresistible. It is fine for us moralistic adults to be appalled at the increasing drug problem, but our moral stand is faulty if we cannot provide youths with an alternative to drugs. It is no good just to demand that they stop taking them, when the hunger for a life beyond the childhood self is at the root of the drug problem and must be fulfilled in some way. And again, when official society cannot offer any experiences of ecstasy, dark subcultures will move into the void and exploit commercially the neglected side of contemporary experience. These are the drug cultures, the pushers, the marketing networks, who profit from the disorientation of youth, peddling parodies of ecstatic experience. In fact, one of the designer drugs on the market today is called 'ecstasy', indicating the archetypal basis of the drug industry.

I am not ruling out the possibility that drugs can sometimes provide the desired transition to a new state of being.[23] However, more often than not drugs are abused rather than used, because their use is not regulated, and youths do not know what they are actually doing. The hippy philosopher Alan Watts once said that drugs are like a telephone call from the cosmos: when you get the message about the new and expanded self, you hang up the phone and get on with your new life. Unfortunately, youths themselves get 'hung up' on the message itself, becoming addicted to, and imprisoned by, what in other circumstances might have set them free.

RISK-TAKING AND SUICIDE

In some indigenous Australian rites of passage, the novice is painted white (to symbolise bones and death), and buried in a shallow grave covered with leaves and twigs. In Joseph Henderson's version of this ritual (supported by extraordinary photographic materials), Aranda Aboriginal youths are decorated and placed under blankets to 'die', before the sacrificial operation of circumcision is performed.[24] The point is that an old self must be put to death. In secular society, where we have no respect for the symbolic language of the spirit, some teenagers feel compelled to live out this destructive impulse in tragically literal terms. In this category, I would place drug overdoses, binge drinking, dangerous risk-taking behaviours, and attempted or actual suicides. More recently, the disturbing new 'sports', such as running between speeding cars, or 'surfing' the rooftops of trains, or reckless bicycle riding or car driving, apparently provide the heightened emotional atmosphere in which life is tested and death almost tasted.

Reckless or 'delinquent' youths feel impelled to change. We could say they are responding to a 'call' from the psyche to exterminate the old self, but because this call is not understood symbolically, the youth does not ask: 'what or which self needs to die?', but simply assumes that his whole life must be sacrificed in direct fulfilment of this inward call. Thus, the youth feels justified in carrying out life-threatening practices, since he is acting from the authority of the soul. The soul's longing for dramatic change can make the youth addicted to danger and actually drive him to death. Such cases show that the raw impulses of the psyche should never be allowed

119

to replace the wisdom of society and cultural practice. True, the contemporary youth gets his signals directly from the soul, but the soul gives its directions in a primitive form. The soul never says to the teenager, 'by the way, this must be treated symbolically': the soul provides the urge and desire, but it cannot provide the spiritual understanding. This can only be provided by culture.

RITES OF WAR: A TRADITIONAL INITIATION BACKFIRES IN VIETNAM

Men and boys long to be embraced and contained by a big idea, and through that idea they are reborn to their higher masculinity. After the 'first birth' from the mother, there is the rebirth or 'second birth' through the symbolic father. In a culture devoid of transformative values, spiritual rebirth is difficult to achieve, leaving many men caught in the 'liminal' or threshold state of disorientation. I want to use the Vietnam War as an example of where many men are trapped at the moment.

In Arnold van Gennep's text, *The Rites of Passage*, all initiatory processes are analysed in terms of three basic phases: separation from the childhood scene; transition to a new state (involving the 'death' of the old self), and reintegration into the community as a newly inducted adult member.[25] The archetypal notion of spiritual rebirth through the father corresponds to van Gennep's 'third phase' of reintegration into the community. This three-fold initiatory pattern is clearly apparent in traditional war experience.

In both world wars this century, many men greeted war with a high degree of enthusiasm, and, most famously in my country, underaged youths pretended they were older than their years so they could be included in the war effort.[26] What were they after? Today's anti-war sentiment says they were after blood-lust, legalised violence, and gory heroism. I doubt this very much. What they were after was an authenticating experience that would lift them out of boyhood into manhood. They wanted to be linked to something beyond themselves, a great cause, which would bestow maturity upon them. In a secular culture devoid of ceremonialism, war experience is one of the last vestiges of initiatory process.[27] First, there is enforced separation from the childhood domestic scene. Second, there is a dissolution of the old self and an acquisition of a new identity. Boys were made to wear uniforms, had their hairstyles changed, behaved in regimented ways, and adopted new names:

Corporal, Private, Sergeant, and so on. Youths were initiated by men into a society of men, with its own language, its distinctive ritual behaviours, its esoteric codes and rituals. In military service, male bonds were formed that lasted a life-time and sometimes even transcended life itself. The risks and dangers of war also served a function: the old self was to be threatened with death. Initiation has always been a risky business and a symbolic encounter with death has always been part of it. If the young man survives the ordeal, there is finally the hero's triumphant return to the community. The young man has helped to save the nation from the common foe, he wins the admiration of society, and the nation feels politically and spiritually regenerated by his efforts.

It is not my task to glorify war or to suggest that it be revived as a theatre of male initiation, but it is beyond doubt that war has long acted as a cultural site for the making of men. I grew up in a family that was steeped in the war ethic, and in a moral atmosphere that almost grimly assumed the centrality of war. My father fought in the Pacific theatre of the Second World War, and my grandfather fought in Turkey and Egypt in the First World War. Growing up in the 1950s and 1960s, I was surrounded by books and literature which enshrined the traditional masculine values of courage, endurance, valour, and heroism. These values were taken for granted and were certainly not open to debate. The men in my family often referred to the facts of war, but they rarely discussed 'war' as a topic. This reticence is not only a defence against a painful past, but a respectful stance toward a system of values which played a crucial part in their psychological development. The well-known laconicism of returned soldiers is a code of conduct that protects their initiatory experience from the onslaught of intellectual suspicion and outside enquiry. No initiate emerges from sacred rituals and exposes his archetypal experience to the profane eye.

Although the elders of my family were initiated into manhood under the sign of Mars, I questioned this martial system and doubted the validity of war as a site for identity formation. I was very much a product of my time, as my father and grandfather were of theirs. Many of my generation were opposed to war in any form, and, with the advent of the Vietnam War, the case in favour of war seemed especially vulnerable. I protested against the war, and did not submit my papers to the compulsory national draft. I felt morally righteous at the time, but I imagine that if a full-scale world war had been declared I would have felt inclined to become involved. I studied the anti-war literature, and quoted Gandhi and John Lennon. My father was bitterly disappointed in my attitude, since he not only felt I was denying my male duty but I was also indirectly criticising his own rite of passage. During heated arguments, my father would remind me of the initiatory functions of war, and of my failure to perform in the expected way. 'You ought to wake up to yourself, boy,' he would say. 'A few years in the army is what you need to smarten you up! It would make a man of you'.

Although at the time I could only see my own side of the argument, I can now appreciate his side. I think he was probably right, given the values and background he was bringing to the debate. I did require some kind of initiatory process; I needed to be jolted out of my romantic dream, and to have my masculinity consolidated. However, the tragic irony of the Vietnam War was that even those sons who willingly enlisted did not achieve the initiation into manhood that their fathers had achieved in previous wars. Those who protested the war remained uninitiated, and those who engaged in the war effort experienced a very ineffectual initiation. Many of the Vietnam soldiers were left in a torturous psychological state.[28] They were not reintegrated into society but were, and still are, arrested at the stage of liminality and transition.

War only serves as an initiatory vehicle if society believes in it. The Vietnam War was considered by many, not only by rebellious youth, to be unsound. Many felt that the Americans and Australians had no business there, and were interfering with another nation's internal politics. The idea of fighting to win freedom for one's own country was lost, and instead this idea was reversed: our soldiers in Vietnam were dirtying the name of their home country. They were not heroes abroad, but anonymous men engaged in atrocities and terrible accidents. This was not a dignified enterprise but merely a dirty war.[29] It was also a war that the Western nations lost. The extensive media coverage worked to support the 'dirty war' image, and the ennobling values of the warrior tradition were dramatically eclipsed. When war is questioned as an initiatory vehicle for young men, and as a self-legitimising enterprise for the nation, we are already in a post-patriarchal time, even if we lack any replacement rituals.

When the Vietnam veterans returned to Australia, they did not feel welcomed back, much less celebrated as heroes. Many felt rejected as they entered a social scene which continued to debate whether or not Vietnam had been a just war. Some managed to pick up the pieces of their lives, but a large number lived in a condition of nightmare and mental turmoil. This turmoil is often commented on but rarely understood. Popular sentiment has it that these men are deeply disoriented by the atrocities of war. I am not doubting that atrocities can scar men for life, but the crucial disabling factor is the breakdown of the initiatory model. Men experience atrocities in every war, but the larger ideals enable men to place them in a context where the bad is counterbalanced by the good. In a dirty war, the redeeming values are absent and transformation does not take place.

There is separation from the social compact, but no real return. Australia recognised this when it staged a very belated official welcome for the Vietnam boys. Engraved on the Vietnam War Memorial in Canberra are these words: 'On 27 October 1987, 25,000 Vietnam veterans marched in a welcome home parade through Sydney to the cheers of hundreds of thousands. It was the greatest emotional outpouring witnessed in decades.' Indeed it was an outpouring, where the nation's guilt and despair over the failure of our time-honoured collective ritual was released.[30] But it was a case of too little, too late. The damage had already been done: Vietnam veterans both here and in the United States had long suffered from low esteem, disorientation, liminality, depression, free-floating anxiety, panic attacks. Some have killed themselves and others have attempted suicide. Some have taken refuge in drugs, alcohol, and psychedelics. Some appear obsessively attached to the music, folklore, and iconography of the 1960s. Some have joined biker gangs, communes, or cults. All of this is characteristic of youth experience, but the intensity and protracted nature of this behaviour indicates that this generation of men has remained pathologically trapped in the second phase of male initiation.

The term 'Generation X' has been invented by Douglas Copeland to describe the contemporary youth experience in which values have been eroded, idealism annulled, and personal identity cancelled out. In this nihilistic world, the ego feels defeated, and the object of life then becomes the astute avoidance of work and the pursuit of a pleasurable narcissism. If development won't take place, then the psychic energy flows toward an imagined utopia or an infantile paradise of pleasures. In this sense, the Vietnam boys, with their desperate search for context, their drug and music addictions, and their longing to transcend the self, are the original X generation, and the true casualties of the new post-patriarchal dispensation.

MEN (OBSESSIVELY) AT WORK: THE SEARCH FOR VALIDATION

At the other end of the scale from those who are lost and disoriented, are the young business executives and over-achieving professionals. While seemingly so different from Vietnam veterans, they share with these men a profound anxiety and a feeling that they are not really 'part' of society. The upwardly mobile professionals are engaged in compensatory behaviours, anxious to 'prove' themselves and to demonstrate their essential worth to peers, employers, and society. They too are victims of a social context which does not bestow meaning, spiritual value, or moral worth upon the young who are entering the adult world.

Today the chosen profession or career path becomes dangerously contaminated with initiatory fervour and intensity. While tribal men 'proved' their worth by enduring several days of masculine testing, many modern men have to keep proving themselves in the workplace, on the sports field, or in any context where they can feel themselves moving toward the competitive edge. There is nowadays an almost terrifying burden of proof and self-validation attached to the experience of work. Work is not just a service to the community which has accepted the man as one of its own. Rather, work becomes the site of self-validation itself. There is an obsessive-compulsive aspect to work, as can be found, for instance, in this newspaper report on young medical practitioners: 'Many trainee doctors have a "tribal" mentality that encourages them to work continuous shifts of up to 36 hours to prove themselves to their peers'.[31]

Employers and senior staff sometimes capitalise on this deep-seated anxiety in younger men. Instead of acting as 'elders' who put men at peace and provide a sense of affirmation, managers and supervisors will sometimes whip men into a frenzy of over-achievement. They encourage anxiety and give fuel to the neurosis of low self-worth. They want the newcomers to prove their substance, to test their mettle. Obsessive traits in young men are met with approval and compulsive elements are encouraged. Bosses and employers assume the role of the negative senex or devouring father, leading men into a spiralic condition of performance anxiety, where the emotional rewards are very few. Maybe these older men are themselves 'uninitiated', and are plagued by the same condition. But for whatever reason, they are familiar tyrants who lead men into states of burn-out, unless the employees wake up to the game that is being enacted.

A related problem is the competitive frenzy of the professional world. Today we are encouraged by commercialism and late capitalism to feel discontented with our lot. There is always the elusive incremental increase, the movement up the scale, or the sideways-and-up approach which encourages us to take on new and more difficult tasks. If initiatory validation is fused with the concept of upward mobility, then by definition self-validation can never be achieved. The next milestone has to be gained, not as part of an organic career development, but as another illusory mark of one's authenticity. This is a professional syndrome which sends some men rocketing into increasing levels of stress, with little sense of real achievement.

Traditionally, initiation has meant being accepted into the social compact, so that one's identity is united with the group. But if initiation as the 'granting of self-worth' is often not achieved in the modern world, then initiation as 'admission to the group' has almost been lost altogether. The modern concept of upward advancement within a hierarchy of power leads not to integration within a group but to further separation and aloneness. In order to prove oneself, one demonstrates that one is better at the task than the next guy. Today's corporate warrior and ambitious executive does not overcome his own egocentricity in order to fit into the group; rather he defeats and incorporates others so that he can make himself bigger. The large vision or transpersonal container needed for initiation is missing, and perversely the 'largeness' is parodied by the ego itself, which bloats to inflated proportions. Enlarging the ego cannot bring largeness of character, because the development of personality can only be granted by an experience of an Other which stands beyond the ego. Paradoxically, the ego must be made to serve something else, and that is how it is validated.

CLUBS, GANGS, BUDDIES

Initiatory fervour seems to be behind the establishment of fanatical sports clubs, amateur associations, 'little leagues', street gangs, and all manner of contemporary male bondings where emotions run high and enormous claims are made on human feeling. As spiritual and moral authority disappears at the centre of our culture, these various 'local' groups and associations appear to want to reinstate authority and absolute value at the local level.

Recently, I entered the locker-rooms of a local sports field during the half-time break of a little league grand final. It was clear to me then how much initiatory process and feeling survives in our sporting culture. These boys had shed their personal identity, and had taken on an abstract number, and a set of uniform colours, that were part of a common team identity. They were playing hard and training regularly for a local, and intensely masculinist, conception of the 'common good'. The screaming coach was imploring the boys to become conscious of their 'transpersonal' identity: 'You have worked hard all year for this last game, and now you must give it your best, not for personal fame, but for the glory of the club'. 'Do it for the club's colours; win the game for the brown and gold!' The appeal to such abstract entities as the team's colours, the animal totem of the club, and the amateur tradition, seemed to fire the boys up as never before. Yes, they did care about these abstractions, and yes, they would run out onto the ground and play all the harder because they had been activated by the animated coach. They would risk all and give everything for the sense of belonging to a greater reality.

On a lower level, macho clubs, street gangs, or teams of buddies can also be understood as spontaneous, if also vulgar, expressions of initiatory feeling. The all-male group acts as a *de facto* patriarchal society, which substitutes for the lack of masculine brotherhood and phallic support in a society in which the Father is absent. In this sense, gangs represent a form of secular retribalisation. Groups or gangs frequently get caught up in chronic or symptomatic enactments of initiatory processes. Because the authority of the gang is invented, it may not actually transform the participants. The street gang, like the sports club, automatically acquires an animal totem or mythic figure as its ruling logo, obviously to mythologise its power and increase its authority. But if the brotherhood lacks direction, mature guidance, and higher meaning, it will almost inevitably get stuck in empty and meaningless acting-out of masculinist ritual. Assertiveness, autonomy, independence – all these important aspects of masculine maturity will be parodied and exaggerated, in forms such as bullying, violence, stealing, defying authorities, taking the law into one's own hands, and so on. The ingredients for a mature transformation are present, but no real transformation takes place. Like so many of the modern secular rituals, such as drug-taking, binge-drinking, risk-taking, and living in the streets, what began as a transformative process ends up being mostly destructive to society and to the individual participants. When developmental processes are not guided or encouraged by culture, the possibility of harm or sheer destructiveness is always present.

INITIATION INTO WHAT? GROWING UP IN A MORAL AND CULTURAL VACUUM

An Aboriginal worker in Alice Springs once told me that I belonged to an infantile culture that could not grow up. He gestured toward the commercial centre of the town, and said:

> You mob are like silly children who only believe in the things you can see and touch. You delight in material objects, as if these had some magic of their own, but you haven't got any Dreaming. That's why you are always restless and very busy. Always trying to find some magic, but you can't find it, because you have not been initiated.

Ironically, my own white culture saw Aboriginals as basically infantile because they chose not to pursue lives of material comfort and security, but to live in what the West would call 'primitive' conditions. Aboriginals, in turn, saw the white society as infantile because it was spiritually immature and had no sense of the living reality of the spirit.

The Aboriginal view accords profoundly with the universal spiritual perspective. According to this view, only spirit can induct us into a larger and greater world, and only spirit carries the authority that can lift us out of the landscape of childhood and move us toward maturity and self-validation. When spirit is absent, there is no heart or soul in anything we do, because nothing connects our small human tasks and tribulations with a larger, redemptive vision. It seems to me that we are learning the hard way the ancient truth that, 'Where there is no vision, the people perish' (Proverbs 29: 18). Or in the present context, where there is no vision, boys cannot be transformed into men.

It is senseless for commentators to complain that youths today are not growing up as quickly as they should, or are not maturing in the expected way. If we adults cannot supply a moral and spiritual universe of values that can bring about the desired transformation, then we had better stop complaining about the younger generation,

127

since they are simply mirroring our own spiritual hollowness and immaturity. Adolescence appears to become more and more protracted, and can extend from about age 12 (or earlier) to 30 or even 35. According to psychologist Andrew Fuller, 'because of better nutrition, adolescence is getting earlier by about one third of a year per decade, so that the average age of onset for a girl is now 11.7 years'. 'Adolescence starts earlier and lasts longer'.[32] Our society is being overtaken by 'adolescence', a condition that hardly existed before the modern period. In early tribal societies, 'adolescence' lasted as long as the initiatory trials and rites of passage. The novice entered the trials as a boy, and came out as a man. As mentioned, tribal societies could not afford to carry people with incapacitating identity crises. Each member had to be effective, efficient, and contribute to the common good of the community. Only today do we find that young adulthood is about rebellion, protest, and individuality. Adolescence is only terminated when the individual is gathered into a greater reality, in other words, when selfish 'individuality' itself is transcended by identification with a larger whole.

With adolescence lasting longer, society is forced to sustain more abuse and negative treatment. As the 'transitional' or 'hazing' phase is protracted, adolescents are likely to inflict more damage upon themselves and upon society, in risk-taking behaviours and in acts of rebelliousness. So long as they are made to feel alienated and separate from the social compact, they are liable to want to hit out at what they feel excludes them. There is a dramatic correlation between the protractedness of adolescence and the increase in youth suicide, youth crime, and juvenile delinquency. As the rites of passage which enclose and contain the 'death' of the infantile self decrease, social damage and personal harm experience a corresponding increase. In a recent study, up to 93 per cent of males in New Zealand acknowledged some delinquent behaviour prior to the age of 18.[33] Achenbach and Howell argue that the behavioural problems of American adolescents have increased over the past ten years.[34] In Australia, the youth suicide rate has more than trebled since the 1950s, and Australia now competes with Norway for the dubious distinction of having the highest youth suicide rate in the world. The most dramatic rise in the Australian suicide figures is found in young males aged between 15 and 24.[35] The destructiveness of the adolescent 'hazing' period can only be reduced if we reconstruct a sense of cosmos and meaning in which individuals can find relief from egotism and liberation from the infantile self.

I do not believe that tinkering with the fabric of society, and artificially reinventing or reviving ancient rites of passage, is going to make much difference in the long run. This puts me at odds with new-age spirituality, which seems to value ancient rites of passage in and for themselves. The problem of initiation leads us to the 'big questions' about the moral and spiritual structure of mainstream society. Adding some new age frills, or covering over our moral void with indigenous decorations, is diversionary and misses the mark. It is not the rituals themselves that heal us, but the larger realities toward which the rituals point. If the greater realities are not present, are not lived or creatively reimagined for our time, then we are wasting our energies on paraphernalia and ritualistic trimmings. I agree entirely with Sol Kimball when he writes that 'ceremonialism alone cannot establish the new equilibrium, and perfunctory ritual may be pleasant but also meaningless'.[36]

If we are concerned about our youth, then we should not purchase them places in shamanistic retreats or sign them up for rites of passage workshops, but develop with them and for them a morally coherent world into which they can be inducted. The bourgeois response always falls short of the goal, and it always parodies in a vulgar way the essential nature of the problem. We must construct dreams and visions powerful enough to lift youth out of the ego and to connect them vitally to the wider community. Marie-Louise von Franz has said:

> It is increasingly clear that our cultural values have been undermined, so that even among the masses, and especially among today's youth, there are individuals who are seeking, not so much the destruction of the old, as something new on which to build.[37]

We must see the rebuilding of our spiritual culture as a matter of utmost urgency, and avoid the dead-end of perfunctory ceremonialism. We do not engage in this resacralising project for personal enjoyment but for the survival of society itself.

Meanwhile, every man to his own pattern of initiation. Kimball writes: 'An increasing number of individuals are forced to accomplish their transition alone and with private symbols'.[38] When society shirks its role of spiritual educator of its youth, the individual psyche has to pick up the burden of development and show the way through the maze. Although these problems are collective,

129

general, and widespread, I suspect that the solutions will have to remain personal and individual until we enter a new phase of collective spiritual wisdom. In the painful interregnum, it is crucial that we learn to differentiate between the inherent or archetypal *impulse* to initiation, and the historical *forms* that have arisen in the past to answer the initiatory need. We must search for new forms, and pay close attention to individual requirements and differences, so that we do not get caught up in the terrible nostalgia for historically outmoded and culturally inappropriate rites of passage.

5

HOMOEROTIC DESIRE AND THE FATHERING SPIRIT

the homosexual advances made to him by the psyche are precisely the
healing that could open him up to taking in another spirit; being
penetrated, opened.

James Hillman[1]

Homosexual individuation processes are not confined to homosexuals but can be found as well in the psychic development of heterosexuals. This psychological fact arose in my own personal analysis, and it challenged my preconceptions about my identity as a heterosexual, and about the usually hard-and-fast categories 'homosexuality' and 'heterosexuality'. Taking these social categories too literally, in a narrowly conventional way, can be injurious to the psyche and can block the inner processes of both homosexual and heterosexual individuals. This sometimes comes as a shock to heterosexual men in therapy, who often assume that they *ought* to have only heterosexual dreams and individuation processes, and may become edgy when homosexual elements arise in the analysis, especially if the analyst is of the same sex.

PSYCHICAL BISEXUALITY AND THE UNCONSCIOUS

By speaking of 'homosexual elements' in heterosexual men, I refer not only to the repressed desire for genital contact with other men, but also, and especially, to the constellation of *images of same-sex union* in dreams, fantasies, and psychic material. 'Homosexuality' and 'homoeroticism' in this chapter refer in part to a metaphorical state of soul, and in particular to the libidinal situation that arises when a young man's individuation brings him to the stage of reconciliation with the father, and to images of *puer–senex* intrapsychic union. At first glance I may appear to be taking too much licence,

131

but both Freud and Jung understood sexuality in a much wider sense than is popularly conceived.

In her impressive study of Freud's approach to homosexuality, Christine Downing points out that 'Freud's understanding of sexuality was always transliteral, always encompassed much more than genitality. ... Freud saw us as having defined sexuality too narrowly'. 'When Freud speaks of sexuality he means to include all sensual and affectional currents, all the ways we experience bodily pleasure, all our intense emotional attachments.'[2] And in *Jung, Jungians, and Homosexuality* Robert Hopcke writes, 'Homosexuality, as Jung uses the term ... is as much a psychic state of same-sex attraction as the behavioural expression of this sexual attraction with another man or woman'.[3] Similarly, James Hillman has said that 'Homosexuality is far more than [genitality]; it is homoerotics, the eros between men, between women, or between "likes" – similars, familiars, sames'.[4] Metaphorical or psychical homosexuality cannot be entirely reduced to frustrated desire for same-sex genital contact, but must be regarded as a legitimate condition in its own right, a state of soul which both 'homosexuals' and 'heterosexuals' can and do experience.

Freudians disagree among themselves about the status and nature of homosexuality. Some argue the legitimacy of homosexuality as an authentic mode of male sexuality; others, such as Reuben Fine in his *The Forgotten Man: Understanding the Male Psyche*, dismiss adult homosexuality as 'mere pathology', at best a 'sexual orientation disturbance'.[5] Fine rails against his Freudian colleagues who have (as he claims) 'surrendered' their professional integrity to a militant gay rights movement, reflecting their 'susceptibility to political pressure' and their alienation from 'a considered scientific opinion'. Fine argues that,

> Exclusive homosexuality, in which normal sexual relations are completely absent, is in the common sense of most people a sign of pathology. All this hullabaloo [about gay rights] should not blind anyone to the simple fact that continued homosexuality into adult life is merely an adolescent hangover. Boys remain boys; girls remain girls. No one becomes exclusively homosexual if they have had warmth and love from their parents and are given a chance to enjoy themselves heterosexually. Gay immaturity should not be confused with a real resolution to life's problems.[6]

Despite these dogmatic assertions, Freud believed that homosexuality and heterosexuality were, at least in part, socially constructed. Although Freud considered heterosexuality to be the norm, he entertained the view that we are all psychically bisexual, and that for convenience and stability we repress a part of our sexuality. Reuben Fine dismisses Freud's 'alleged statement' about human bisexuality, claiming that this statement is 'a common misquotation and misunderstanding'.[7] But in *An Autobiographical Study* Freud did in fact speak of 'the constitutional bisexuality of all human beings',[8] and in his clinical practice he was constantly alert to the ambivalent nature of human sexuality. It looks to me as if the conservative Freudians have reinvented Freud in their own image.

Let me quote at greater length from the father of psychoanalysis:

Psycho-analytic research is most decidedly opposed to any attempt at separating off homosexuals from the rest of mankind as a group of a special character. By studying sexual excitations other than those that are manifestly displayed, it has found that all human beings are capable of making a homosexual object-choice and have in fact made one in their unconscious.[9]

Through social conditioning and the efforts of an often over-zealous ego, one set of sexual priorities and impulses are privileged and another set are forcibly repressed.[10] What is very often discovered in the unconscious, as was true in my own case, is a sexual orientation opposite to that which is professed and practised in conscious reality. This is not to say that any given heterosexual man is 'really' a homosexual underneath, but simply that one side of our psychical bisexuality has been repressed and almost invariably comes to the surface in the course of a successful analysis.

Indeed, Freud felt that the fear of encountering one's denied homosexual longings constituted 'one of the most powerful elements in resistance to analysis'.[11] It is significant that, as Downing has shown, homosexuality either manifest or latent, literal or metaphorical, figures prominently in every one of Freud's case studies.[12] Reductionists will say that Freud's patients were all latent homosexuals; cynics will proclaim that Freud projected his own homosexual conflicts upon the lives of his patients. But a more productive reading is to suggest that the human depths that Freud explored are always and everywhere characterised by an essential psychical bisexuality. We are psychosexually androgynous, and every journey into psychic depths will yield insight into our unexpressed or latent 'other' mode. This means that, for heterosexuals, psychoanalysis is virtually synonymous with an experience of psychical homosexuality. The more ardently or fanatically heterosexual one is, the more actively constellated homosexuality will be in the unconscious, and – most likely – the more emotive and fierce is the resistance to psychoanalysis. This is especially helpful in understanding the long-standing and entrenched resistance to psychoanalysis in Australia,[13] a country where, as I shall soon explain, homophobia is endemic in the prevailing national character.

POLITICAL REALITY AND PSYCHIC REALITY

Freud was aware that in drawing parallels between homosexual and heterosexual development he was challenging the claims of then contemporary gay men to represent a 'distinct sexual species', a 'third sex'.[14] Just here we face a particularly difficult and sensitive problem, where psychoanalysis and contemporary gay politics appear to collide. The emphasis in the gay movement on difference and distinction must be considered in its social context. In our political and social discourse it *is* important to make real distinctions between gay and non-gay men, since in a society which privileges heterosexuality above other sexual modes the excluded and marginalised sexualities must emphasise their *differentness* in order to achieve recognition and social standing. At the social level, any bland, all-encompassing, totalising project is likely to make homosexuality invisible again, and to turn the clock back with regard to collective understanding and appreciation of gay lifestyles. But in the realm of the psyche, our sexual categories may be less important and may be revealed merely as social constructions. Here I agree with Freud, who felt that phobias abound whenever our thinking becomes too rigid and whenever we make a dogma of sexual preference. When we enter psyche we enter a relativistic universe, where the values, attitudes, and assumptions of our socially constructed selves are challenged and sometimes even reversed.

HOMOPHOBIC MATESHIP

I spent my teenagehood in Alice Springs, central Australia, which is possibly the homophobic capital of the world. The psychosocial situation of present-day outback Australia is similar to that which existed in the 'Wild West' of premodern America. We are speaking of a frontier society, with little or no evidence of civilisation, where men gather together to provide mutual support and security, where women are held at a distance, where uneasy or explicitly hostile relations exist between the colonising settlers and the indigenous peoples, and where a general sense of siege pervades the psychic atmosphere. In this situation the famous Australian 'mateship' is born, that particular kind of behavioural code in which a man will do anything to protect or support a 'mate'. Mateship, felt the writer Henry Lawson, is not only a code of conduct but a religious creed, something to believe in.[15] In Australia, mateship reigned supreme and unchallenged for some time, but in recent history its shadow aspects have been exposed by historians,[16] feminists,[17] and sociologists.[18] It is misogynist, racist, sexist, bigoted, and repressive. It supports a narrow definition of manly behaviour and acceptable masculinity. Homophobia is the most recently discovered shadow aspect of this great Australian institution.

For Freud, homophobia is an expression of repressed homosexuality. He sees homophobia as an attempt to prevent admission of unconscious homosexual desires by activating 'vigorous counter-attitudes'.[19] In mateship, the homophobic response stands in direct relation to the intensity with which male-bonding is pursued. Precisely because there is so much feeling in the male-to-male bond, the social ego constructs an all-powerful taboo against physical intimacy, sexual attractiveness, and the expression of feeling, whether verbal, emotional, or physical. Men adore their mates, but there will be no obvious caring, no touching, no outward display. Friendship is expressed as it were negatively, by shadow-boxing each other, by punching your mate coyly on the arm, by offering terms of abuse and by swearing at each other when we meet ('You bloody great bastard, how are you?').

Alice Springs is a long way from the San Francisco Bay Area. Here, if two men walked down the street arm-in-arm, well, they would most likely not get to the end of the first city block. If aggressively homophobic 'ordinary citizens' do not intervene, the homophobic police force would, since in the Northern Territory (as in the state of Queensland), homosexuality is still a criminal offence. Under sections 208 and 211 of the Criminal Code, any male found guilty of sexual acts 'against the order of nature' can face a maximum prison sentence of seven years' hard labour. It is entirely irrelevant whether the homosexual events took place in private between consenting adults; if the police can prove they occurred, then a criminal sentence is handed down.[20] Homophobia is thus enshrined in our mental attitudes as well as our legislation, every bit as much of a national institution as the mateship which it unconsciously shadows. Gay men in the Northern Territory and in Queensland go into hiding, develop flawless masculine personae, or move to the inner suburbs of Sydney and Melbourne.

Although I moved south to Adelaide, spending ten years in a university environment, the legacy of my upbringing remained. Homophobia had been a strong element in my psychology for over thirty years, and it took a vigorous analysis to confront this bogey and to work through it. Strange and perverse as it may seem to any one of my central Australian 'mates', homophobia became a psychological block to my heterosexual masculine development. I am referring in particular to an internalised homophobic response, to a refusal to engage in a full and erotic manner with same-sex psychic figures, to a resistance to psychical homosexuality. My university education had effectively banished homophobia from my consciousness (it was considered backward), but it had fallen into the personal unconscious, serving as a censor of internal processes, causing me to 'forget' certain dreams, and blocking me off from my own experience of that dark symbolic force *phallos*.[21]

It may sound ironic, or contradictory, but acceptance of homosexual imagery, and a change of attitude in relation to homosexuality itself, brought with it a complete transformation of my character, and a more profound experience of my heterosexual masculinity.

HOMOEROTIC DESIRE IN ADOLESCENT RITES OF PASSAGE

Before I continue with my personal story, I would like briefly to revisit the topic of male rites of passage. I have already said that in psychological wisdom the so-called 'primitive' cultures are more advanced than our modern culture. This is especially so in the recognition of the importance of the homoerotic element in heterosexual men. Not that homosexuality *per se* was condoned in ordinary social life; in most ancient cultures I have studied this has proved not to be the case. A taboo against homosexuality seems to be present in many patriarchal societies. But in ritual activity and religious symbolism the taboo is deliberately violated so as to access and release the archetypal power of *phallos* and the masculine spirit. In *Ritualized Homosexuality in Melanesia*,[22] Gilbert Herdt explores the role of homosexual practices and symbolisms in the components of male initiation and in secret men's business. What Herdt finds in Melanesia is discovered in numerous other tribal contexts: namely, that a ritualised homosexuality is central to the symbolic experience of becoming-a-man.

When psychoanalysts and sociologists comment that homosexual activity is a common feature of contemporary adolescence,[23] they are simply rediscovering and recontextualising the findings of anthropology and ethnology when these sciences assert that a 'phase' of homosexual exploration is typically part of traditional adolescent development. In tribal initiations, the taboo against homosexuality is dropped so as to strengthen the symbolic meaning and spiritual significance of the induction into masculinity as a 'mystery'. Central to the mysteries of masculinity is the erect and potent phallus, which is the major symbol and archetypal bodily experience of mature masculinity. In some ancient ceremonies, tribal men and youths engage in mutual, joint, and public masturbation, because they are being made to experience their own specifically male potency and life-force.[24] The initiate's developing sexuality links him not only with his own primal, bodily powers, but with the procreative forces of the tribe and the cosmos itself, as these are represented in tribal symbols and in the procreative, fructifying Father God. Ritualised homosexuality is a concrete display of masculine power, and a celebration of the cosmic-procreative forces to which the youth has suddenly been introduced by virtue of his own biological and sexual development.

It is difficult for us today to grasp the symbolic significance of homosexual elements in rites of passage. We are very literal-minded about sexuality, and we no longer appreciate the cosmic forces and dimensions at work in our own sexual experience. Some anthropologists see these rites purely in terms of political and social power: the erect phallus is the symbol of patriarchal authority, and in the 'sacred space' created by ceremony, youths are inducted into patriarchy in its most bodily and physical aspect. Freudian anthropologists, such as Bruno Bettelheim, read these sacred homosexual rituals as patriarchy's vain and futile challenge to the procreative powers of the mother and of women.[25] Most frequently, these rituals are explained away in terms of social structure, or as a masculine protest against women's power. Our secular consciousness seems constitutionally incapable of receiving or understanding the larger archetypal significance. Traditionally, sexuality was authenticated by its connection to a divine cosmic source, and the full awareness of this extra dimension endowed the tribal man's sexuality with a dignity unknown in the guilt-ridden West, where sexuality is profaned by reducing it to the personal. Eliade writes that 'puberty rites imply the revelation of sexuality – but, for the entire premodern world, sexuality too participated in the sacred'.[26]

In modern times, we have our own versions of the all-male or same-sex sacred ritual, which we call 'adolescent homosexuality', and this is undoubtedly on the rise in Western society. In adolescent homosexuality, the motivating force is to experience a specifically male potency and erotic-creative power in a sort of ritual worship of the erect male penis. In her brilliant essay 'Homosexuality at the Fin De Siècle', Camille Paglia intuitively grasps the religious and sacramental dimension of teenage homosexuality:

> Teenage boys, goaded by their surging hormones, run in packs like the primal horde. They have only a brief season of exhilarating liberty between control by their mothers and control by their wives. . . . Teenage gays are guardians of the masculine impulse. To have anonymous sex in a dark alleyway is to pay homage to the dream of male freedom. The unknown stranger is a wandering pagan god. The altar, as in prehistory, is anywhere you kneel.[27]

Unlike tribal cultures, we have no way to ritualise the primal and universal male impulse to join with like in a celebration of masculine power. These impulses are relegated to the profane and sordid margins of social experience, although they still retain their essentially religious character, as Paglia's language so clearly demonstrates. In toilets and dark places of the street, contemporary adolescents gather together to celebrate what was once ritually contained in ceremonial process. How many 'pervert' priests and paedophiles are engaged in an unconscious form of male initiatory process? The high incidence of abusive homosexual practice among the Christian clergy worldwide indicates that, in some peculiar way, religion and homosexuality are very much interconnected. The social and cultural forms for these activities have disappeared, but the archetypal impulses are still real and alive. However, only a very few, including Paglia, poets, and psychotherapists, can still recognise the imprint of the divine hand in and through the veil of pathology.

To speak about homosexuality as a 'phase' of adolescence is problematical these days, in view of the ongoing discourse about homosexuality as an authentic alternative to heterosexuality. In this discussion about phases and transitory experiences, which draws on facts from anthropology and ethnology, I hope I am not being disrespectful toward constitutional homosexuality. I believe there are many different kinds of homosexuality, and here I am particularly interested in the form which is associated with a *rite de passage*, and as such, is actually a part of the broad experience of heterosexual development.

I also believe, along with Paglia, that this kind of homosexuality is increasing in modern society. Some argue that the rate of homosexuality in society is constant, and that through the gay movement and public discourse it is made more visible than before. However, I think teenage homosexuality is increasing in direct proportion to the decreasing effectiveness of male rites of passage. When the desire to connect with the mystery of *phallos* is not realised in ritual or religion, we will naturally find an increased enactment of this impulse in social behaviour. This impulse will be fulfilled in *ad hoc* expressions, or, as in my own case, it will fall into the unconscious and generate there a series of dreams, fantasies, and unconscious symbolisms.

DREAMS OF SAME-SEX LOVE AND FATHER–SON REUNION

During my Jungian analysis with Hillman in the 1980s, I was made aware that I carried an extremely negative image of my personal father, and that this fixation was blocking my experience of masculinity and my personal development. Hillman tried to get me to see positive elements in my father, and my idealising transference to Hillman was itself a major catalyst to my new feeling for the father and a new yearning for the fathering spirit. In the analysis I experienced a great longing for the father, a desire to reconnect with my personal dad, and I had several dreams in which I was forced to recognise my father's talents and virtues. In one dream I entered a room in which my mother and father were sleeping in separate beds. As someone with a history of dreams of mother–son incestuous unions, it was with some surprise that I told my analyst that the dream ego approached, and kneeled beside, my father's bed. The father was in a poor physical condition, and I would have to care

139

for him and nurture him to health. All this was fostered by my positive transference toward my same-sex analyst. Although I did not
see it at the time, the analysis began from the start as a healing of
the relationship to the father and as an intense exploration of the
puer–senex bond.

Homoerotic dreams began to arise. In one early dream a sailor
directed me to a house where, he said, I could get my fill of sex. I
went in search of the house, found an attractive woman, and began
to undress her. When I took off her underclothes I noticed she had
balls between her legs and then I saw a cock. 'You are really a boy!'
I said. 'Yes', he or she smiled. 'But I don't make love to boys', I
said. He looked disappointed as I backed away and prepared to
leave.

Here the ego makes a firm decision that terminates the erotic
interplay between itself and the 'boy'. The transvestite figure is of
great interest since either the anima has become masculinised due to
the repression of masculine contents into the unconscious, or the
masculine is hiding itself beneath a feminine persona in order to
arouse the sexual desire of the ego. Another reading could be: the
ego has been led to a deep realm of psychical bisexuality, where the
desired love-object is neither strictly male nor strictly female, but
both, being 'polymorphous perverse' (Freud). But however we inter-
pret the dream, the fact remains that the ego cannot cope with what
is going on, and has decided not to make love to a figure with same-
sex characteristics.

What we see here is the effect of an internalised homophobic
attitude. The fear of homosexuality is so strong that it is introjected
into the psyche, where it acts as a prohibition against the commin-
gling of same-sex figures. The ego cannot fully 'know' other
masculine members of the psyche while it is identified with the
homophobic attitude. 'Knowing' other psychic figures means, as it
meant in the language of the Old Testament, knowing intimately, or
'carnal knowledge'. Sexual interaction is the psyche's favourite
metaphor for deep psychic connection, for a bonding which is at
once passional, emotional, and instinctual. It is clear that connection with my masculine side involves an erotic embrace and a
libidinal investment which the ego is not yet prepared to make.

Other dreams emerged at this time that took me back to childhood, during which I had some prepubertal genital play with a male
cousin. This aspect of my early experience had been lost to my
adult consciousness, or should I say the homophobic censor had

'edited out' this childhood homosexual experience from my present image of myself. A number of dreams in which my cousin and I were developed sexually and paraded full erections before each other indicated that the psyche was now calling for a reactivation of my earlier same-sex erotic model into the sexualised atmosphere of adult reality.

I had several other dreams in which the ego was drawn toward an erect phallus of another male, and occasionally the ego fondled the aroused penis. In one dream I watched an erection begin to swell and grow inside the trousers of an anonymous man, and I pulled down the trousers to release the throbbing erection. In the major dream of this series, the ego was imaged in a state of excited craving for an erect penis. It was not clear who the other male was, since I was unaware of anything above or below the genital region. This was an impersonal, or archetypal, encounter with *phallos*. The dream involved considerable foreplay, and then the ego took the penis into its mouth, and, after much oral stimulation, eventually swallowed the hot sperm that was shot out at the moment of climax.

The ego was inseminated with masculine seed and, like the New Guinea youths who must digest semen during their rites of passage into manhood, the sexual fluid contained the seeds of my own developing masculinity. This dream marked the birth of my new, or renewed, masculine self.

HOMOPHOBIA IN SO-CALLED 'CONSCIOUSNESS-RAISING' MEN'S GROUPS

Recently I discussed this dream in a large, all-male therapy group in Melbourne, and it met with a very mixed response. The atmosphere in the room was tense, and all were listening carefully. But later, during the coffee break, there was a fair bit of laughter, some of it perhaps a natural response to a release of tension and seriousness, but some of it decidedly defensive and homophobic. During the informal discussion that followed, a number of 'manly' men were quick to inform the group that they had never had dreams like this, and that if they had had such dreams they would be very worried about the dreams and about themselves. The effect of this response was to construct me as the homosexual other, and to relinquish themselves of their homosexual elements by projecting these elements upon me. I was not prepared for this transference but I ought to have anticipated it, knowing what I already knew about the prevalence of homophobia in Australian men. I was surprised to find that even a gay therapist in the group found my dreams heavy going, possibly because they challenged the stability of his persona, and possibly because he felt these very explicit dreams were too highly charged to be dealt with in public.

The homosexual transference of the group challenged my privileged position as group leader, since not a few began to wonder what they were doing submitting themselves to an intensive course in men's issues in which the leader was indulging his 'poofter' fantasies. My counter-response was to stand back from the dreams and to emphasise their 'symbolic' dimension. I think I even made a few jokes about the dreams, in order to claw back the authority which I sensed I was losing. I attempted to recover power by deliberately withdrawing into my own homophobic attitude and by asserting my superiority over the powerfully homosexual dreams.

In the next session we switched to another topic (male violence and aggression), and homosexuality was not mentioned again. All the men came back for future sessions – all except the homosexual participant, who was undoubtedly driven away by the constellated homophobia of the group. I was aware of my failure to transform the homophobia of the group, and I realised later how far away I was from the 'therapeutic' reality of the dreams and from the attitude my analyst had adopted toward them.

The main thing I learned, apart from my inability to deal with any activation of group homophobia, was that defensive heterosexuals are almost incapable of experiencing the healing power that can arise from same-sex psychic imagery. In fact, many cannot even begin to respond therapeutically to internal homosexual imagery, since the homophobic attitude is triggered whenever such imagery arises, thus preventing these same-sex symbolic processes from being realised as significant processes of the psyche. No wonder so many men remain boyish or puerile, no wonder they continually seek to prove their manhood, if a precondition to maturity, and to puer–senex union, is the ability to respond to the psyche's unconventional sexual patterns and especially to male–male psychosexual conjunctions. A few years after my analytical involvement with Hillman, I discovered his characteristically succinct and insightful summary of the homophobic problem:

Men patients who are quite closed in on themselves are very

resistant to the homosexual advances and attractions that appear in their dreams. Usually these images are interpreted as proof of latent homosexuality and therefore the patient's closedness is seen as a result of his latent homosexuality. But this has it backwards because the homosexual advances made to him by the psyche are precisely the healing that could open him up to taking in another spirit; being penetrated, opened.[28]

THE ANALYST'S RESPONSE TO HOMOEROTIC MATERIAL

My homoerotic dreams placed a considerable demand on the analyst, as well as upon myself. Any homophobic residues in him could have proved injurious to my development, and to the erotically charged puer–senex bonding that was taking place in the soul. It was important that the analyst, as bearer of the senex image, became an enabling father figure by adopting a positive, sexualised attitude toward the erotic images. Even a hint of puritanical reaction could have set the process back. Fortunately, he was fully involved in the psychic imagery and able to further the process by his careful attention to the psyche's demands.

After presenting the dream in which I sucked on the penis and ingested the seminal fluid, the analyst simply said, 'Go for the cock; grab it; grasp it'. Obviously he said more than this during the hour, but these words are the only ones I remembered later. At this stage I dreamed I was discussing sexuality with my paternal uncle, and he spoke warmly to me about male sexuality. As he spoke, my own body seemed more alive, more sensuous, more manly. In reality, my family and relatives were all narrowly puritanical, and they had instilled a fear of the body and an antagonism toward sexuality into me as a child. Now the internalisation of this body-denying puritanism, as well as the internalised homophobia, were being dissolved by the dreams, the inner process, and the analysis.

The analyst's response enabled me to experience the erotic imagery fully and immediately. There was no attempt on his part to hide behind Jungian theory, to emphasise that the homoerotic images were 'only symbolic'. In the inner world, I was being ravished and inseminated by archetypal *phallos*, and for this to have any effect in reality it was important that I allow myself to feel this as a ravishment, as a deeply erotic experience. Adolf Guggenbuhl-Craig writes that some Jungian analysts who have not confronted

their homophobic attitudes are inclined to withdraw from homosexual images presented by a same-sex client:

> Jungian psychologists may, however, try to evade this involve-
> ment in eros by not following up veiled or even relatively overt
> sexual statements by the patient, or immediately trying to
> interpret such statements on a 'higher level'. They make refer-
> ence to the patient's relation to the spiritual-masculine, to his
> own creative masculinity, etc. A homosexual dream is
> instantly interpreted as 'a search for, and an attempt to under-
> stand, one's own masculinity'.[29]

Guggenbuhl-Craig says that analysts often 'clothe [themselves] in an
endless variety of theories and run for cover'. If the analyst finds
the material 'painful and repugnant', his use of clever interpretations is 'of no use whatsoever to the patient'.[30]

What is of use to the analysand is a felt, full-blooded, libidinal
response to the homosexual images. Chances are that the kind of
client who seeks out Jungian therapy already 'knows about' the textbook explanations that a defensive analyst would provide. Men in
Jungian therapy have already read in Erich Neumann or Robert
Johnson or elsewhere that sexual imagery in a fantasy or dream is an
expression of a symbolic process of union within the soul. The
analysand in Jungian therapy often 'knows' far too much, and that
can be a real obstacle to change. The point of therapy is not to collect
bits of theoretical information but to experience the psyche directly.
The only kind of knowledge that is important is that old-fashioned
'knowing' which meant to know intimately, sexually. What
analysands want from therapy is carnal knowledge of the psyche.

Patricia Berry has said in a lecture that the two golden rules of
psychotherapy are: don't repress, and don't act out. Some people
think that these laws are mutually exclusive, that they cancel each
other out. If I cannot repress, and I cannot act out, what can I do?
The answer is: *experience the psyche*. Given what Guggenbuhl-Craig
has said, it seems that not a few analysts fail to discover this third
way of psychic experience. All too readily, we rush into theory, into
pronouncements about higher meanings and archetypes, which
leaves the libidinal ground in favour of intellectual knowledge. The
other side of the coin is where analyst and patient go to bed
together, the erotic tension so great that only 'acting out' can give
release and fulfilment.

The therapeutic attitude consists in being present with the mythic material, in sticking with the images. What repression and acting out have in common is that they impose a reductively personal attitude upon the material and refuse to acknowledge psyche. The analyst represses the homosexual image because he imposes his own homophobic attitude upon it, because he does not want his client to act out the impulse, or because he attempts to forestall the homosexual advances of his client. Alternatively, the analyst acts out the erotic impulse with his client because he feels the Eros constellated in the analysis involves himself, that the dreams or longings of connection are indeed about him and directed to him. These personalistic reductions amount, in Robert Stein's phrase, to a betrayal of the soul.[31]

THE HETEROSEXUAL ANALYSAND'S RESPONSE

If the heterosexual analysand engages in actual homosexual activity at this point in the analysis, is this 'acting out', or is this a perfectly natural expression of his homosexual longing? A heterosexual onlooker, perhaps, may see it as acting out (in accordance with his own set of preferences), but a homosexual observer may say that he has finally lifted his inhibition and is now exploring the same-sex dynamic in the truest possible way. Interpretation, as every hermeneut and postmodernist knows, is surely a matter of perspective, and largely dependent upon where one stands in relation to the event or thing to be interpreted.

If, for instance, after imploring me to 'go for the cock' in one analytic session, I came to the next with reports that I had indeed engaged in homosexual relations subsequent to that session, would the analyst think this appropriate? Presumably, he would not be shocked, but would he think it psychologically sound? Much would depend upon my former sexual history, and if the analyst felt that my active homosexuality had arisen solely as a response to a phase in the analysis, then he may be critical of it. Would my homosexuality be read, not as enactment of an archetypal impulse, but as an *avoidance* of the more difficult *intrapsychic puer–senex union*?[32] It would appear that Jung and traditional Jungians would view homosexuality as an acting out of same-sex archetypal dynamics, and therefore as symptomatic behaviour which obscures the intrapsychic process.[33] But how come, some of us have begun to ask, they do not apply the same reasoning to heterosexual activity, and see this as obsessive or defensive acting out of the need for the feminine matrix? Why perform a psychological reduction on only one sexual mode? Obviously, when prejudices govern our thinking, we use psychology against whatever it is that offends us or we wish to exclude. The new, relativistic view is that 'any sexuality, or no sexuality at all, can be pathological'.[34]

Every analysand must arrive at his own individual response, not necessarily as a result of answering these tortuous questions, but by intuitively deciding what is right for him. A merely intellectual decision is not enough, and may even be a grave mistake. I must confess that in my own case none of these questions were posed. Such questions only arose years later, when I was situationally outside the analysis and outside the intensity of the puer–senex libidinal reunion. Such questions have been put to me, too, by anxious men in consciousness-raising groups; the same men who said that they would be 'worried' if they had dreams similar to mine. Doubts and questionings came to me before and after my analytically assisted passage into masculine maturity, but at the time I found the images so enthralling, the analysis so stimulating, and the inner process so demanding that thoughts about my social classification as 'gay' or 'non-gay' never arose. They seemed, and indeed were at the time, irrelevant. I was in Victor Turner's 'liminal' or transitional state, betwixt and between two stages of development,[35] and this sacred condition might have been profaned by a too hasty attempt to impose sociopolitical classifications.

Now I view the process outlined in this chapter as a ritualised homosexual phase that was essential for my heterosexual masculine development. My relation to the masculine side was so undeveloped, so deeply unconscious, that nothing short of a powerfully erotic upheaval could have aroused the masculine from its slumber (pun intended) and brought it into contact with consciousness. However, my own analytically-assisted homosexual journey is not available to everyone, and even those who are fortunate enough to enter therapy are not guaranteed a therapist who is able to achieve a state of full symbolic receptivity to the powerful images.

Today, everyone demands to know from the maturing young man his *true* identity and his *real* sexual preference. But if he is on an initiatory journey, in a liminal state which is betwixt and between, he won't know who or what he is! The whole point of the journey is to discover identity in an ongoing process of development. I believe that any rigidification of the categories 'straight' and 'gay' is a menace to all of us and an impoverishment of culture. We must become tolerant toward ambiguity and sexual exploration. On the one side, the sexually adventurous young man receives pressure and anxiety from mainstream homophobic culture, which hopes and prays that he will 'return' to the straight and narrow and resume his place in heterosexual society. On the other side, pressure also arises from the anti-establishment youth culture and activist gay groups. Youths who appear ambivalent or bisexual are encouraged to 'come out of the closet' and admit to themselves and the world that they are gay. But in a climate of transition, such demands for ideological clarity are insensitive. A strident gay community emulates straight society in its lack of negative capability, and its insistence that men in various stages of development make definitive pronouncements about their identity. Ideological rigidity is destructive, not only to the bonds of community but also to the fluid world of the psyche, which ebbs and flows according to its own innate currents. Once we take seriously the fact of our psychical androgyneity, we enter a larger universe where fanaticisms melt away, divisions blur, and where all life is wild and unpredictable.

BODY, PSYCHE, FATHER

During the period of my analysis outlined here, I referred to my fifty-minute hours as 'body-work' sessions because my body seemed to be responding in definite ways to the analysis. I felt a number of body-sensations which are difficult to articulate now. I felt more grounded in my body; this sounds like a new-age cliché, but it will have to do. I developed a positive body-feeling and an awareness of my physical maleness. My body changed shape. I developed muscles where there were before just bony arms and legs. I put on several kilograms of weight and no longer looked like a half-starved student. I experienced as well a new relation to my anger and rage, which had been buried before, but which were now within range of consciousness.

Most intriguing of all was the new relation to my personal father, a new sense of warmth and connection, which I had not experienced since I was about 8 or 9. During my fourteenth year, my father announced to my astonished family that I was no longer his son, because the gap that separated us was too obvious to ignore. My rivalry and dislike were intense, and I made no attempt to make amends. But after this phase of analysis everything changed; intellectual and ideological differences were still evident, of course, but

147

there was now an emotional understanding and acceptance that transcended these differences. My father related to me as man to man, rather than as parent to wayward child. He sensed the change and seemed to relish the new dispensation.

He once told me in Alice Springs that all gay men in Australia should be transported to a desert island and left to starve. So I did not or could not explain to him that a psychically homosexual phase had made a man of me. He could not appreciate that the spunk and male energy which had entered me had done so because I had performed fellatio and sodomy in my dreams. My new-found maleness was thanks to my new willingness to 'make love to boys', and my masculine energy due to swallowing and ingesting the hot sperm-seed of logos.

6

STRUGGLING WITH THE INTERNAL TYRANT

We do not want the turmoil which the senex–puer struggle within ourselves releases.

Hillman[1]

The next stage in my spiritual reunion with the father was not as happy or wonderful as the previous chapter might suggest. At first, the return to the father is indeed a joyous occasion, and to the son this is like a homecoming to his own spiritual self. This is especially the case to the previously mother-bound son, who has been emotionally estranged from his father-self, or paternal self-object, and who is delighted to be able to turn an Oedipal rival and foe into a personal psychological foundation. But every archetypal figure brings with it its own set of dangers and difficulties. There is no simple 'integration' of the father, but an ongoing struggle to maintain one's own individual identity in the face of this potentially overwhelming archetypal figure.

I have already discussed in Chapter 2 the problems of the 'father-devoured' personality. In the spiritual men's movement, new-age 'soft' men overcome their incestuous ties to the mother by 'embracing' the father and becoming *like* the father in a *puer–senex* reunion. This embrace feels wonderful to the estranged son, but it often leads to conventionality, conservative politics, regression to patriarchy, and the restoration of the same hegemonic (sexist, homophobic, and conquistadorial) masculinity that society was plagued with *before* the advent of the new 'soft male' culture. The sensitive new-age guys simply swap an imprisoning mother-complex for a devouring father-complex. To Robert Bly and his followers, this is called being 'initiated' into the patrilineal line. Having sounded off at what the spiritual men's movement gets up to, it is now time to explore and confess my own personal experience of a similar archetypal shift from maternal domination to paternal complex.

DANGER FROM ABOVE: THE SPIRIT FATHER AS DEVOURER

The difficulties of contact with the archetypal dimensions of the father are exacerbated in individuals such as myself, where there is a relative absence of a solid childhood relationship with the personal father. In *Ego and Archetype*, Edward Edinger points out that

> When the personal father is missing . . . there is no layer of personal experience to mediate between the ego and the numinous image of the archetypal father. A kind of hole is left in the psyche through which emerge the powerful archetypal contents of the collective unconscious. Such a condition is a serious danger. If, however, the ego can survive this danger, the 'hole in the psyche' becomes a window providing insights into the depths of being.[2]

If the personal father is absent, the son may be directly exposed to the awesome Spirit Father, a situation reflected, and successfully negotiated, in the life and career of Jesus of Nazareth. The Spirit Father is a formidable archetypal force, or a part of universal mind. He is not concerned with 'my' welfare, and knows nothing of or about 'me'. His task is to take care of himself, to ensure his survival by replicating his own patterns. If his archaic power is to be challenged and humanised, this can only come about by initiating conscious interaction with the archetype. Here Christ is our paradigmatic example: through an intense relationship with the Father, during which the Son maintains and defends his own individual humanity, the archetypal character of the Father is transformed from archaic, wrathful judge to a loving and caring redeemer. This transformation can only eventuate through the struggles and passion of a consciousness committed to its own archetypal pattern. By taking up the burden of Sonship and individuation, the ego actually succeeds in humanising and advancing the Father. This is no easy task, as Christ's sufferings so fulsomely demonstrate. The path of consciousness is and must remain an heroic undertaking, and even if Christ's life makes no theological sense today, it can provide us with a powerful psychological model for tasks that we mere mortals have to fulfil in our own small and individual ways.

Mythology and dreams reveal that the primordial father can emerge in the beginning as a cosmogonic monster or beast who must be 'humanised' by consciousness. The Great Father might first appear in prehuman or theriomorphic symbolism, indicating the archaic quality of the depths that have been activated. He is not yet 'father' in any recognisable human sense, but is the paternal or procreative principle, as represented in animal symbolisms and biological mechanisms. In my own case, the early appearances of the father archetype took the form both of semi-human objects and non-human symbolic forms. The earthly aspect of the father first assumed the form of the erect phallus, and these symbolisms were outlined in the previous chapter. The spiritual or 'pneumatic' aspect of this archetype, however, assumed the symbolic form of a dangerous, man-eating eagle. Significantly for me, as someone who tends to value the spiritual above the earthly, the most dangerous aspect of the father emerges from 'above', from the realm of the heavens, whereas the earthly phallus had a primarily invigorating or stabilising impact on my development.

At the time of my mythic shift from the mother to the father, I experienced a number of dreams about large predatory eagles flying overhead, often sweeping downward from great heights to pick up prey and quarry. In some dreams, I was simply aware of gigantic eagles flying above me, watching my movements in a menacing or ominous way. In one dream I noticed the eagle diving to the ground and carrying off sheep, dogs, and other animals. The huge talons would be extended, poised, ready to strike into the sides of its prey. Sometimes the victims were human: boys and girls were carried off to the eagle's nest high up in the mountains beyond human settlement. As this archetypal motif was developed over many months, the figure of the eagle became more menacing. In one dream, I stalked the eagle with a rifle, anxious to restore order to the land, to rid the place of this danger. I aimed, fired, and missed. In another dream, my gun clipped one wing of the eagle, and it momentarily fell to the ground in a flurry of feathers. The eagle recovered, blood dripping from its side, and flew to the top of a fence-post, where it stood, unimpressed, its eye fixed intently upon me, so that I began to tremble, wondering what revenge it might have in store.

There are many large eagles in central Australia, and some key moments of my adolescent years involved sightings of or encounters with this bird. In the 1960s my favourite camping site was the 'Valley of the Eagles', a wonderful rocky gorge or canyon east of Alice Springs. I was impressed by the sheer size and majesty of the wedge-tailed eagles that flew above the desert landscape. Once, on a dusty outback road, an eagle swooped down upon the car ahead of us, its wings so vast that it seemed to envelope the proportions of the puny vehicle. I can recall hearing the comment: 'That's no bird, it's a bloody flying monster!'. Later, during a week-long camp in the desert, I attempted to climb the wall of a rocky canyon. At one point I slowly dragged myself up to a horizontal ledge, only to come face to face with a wedge-tailed eagle that was basking in the heat. As well as being terrified, I was struck by the power of the bird, the size of its beak and claws, and in particular by the detailed markings upon its face, which I had never seen before. I quickly scurried down the cliff face, much faster than I had climbed up, and in fear I jumped into the freezing cold water-hole below, as the fastest means of escape. The eagle, however, remained motionless and did not seem perturbed. I got out of the water and went to my guitar to scratch out a song about the eagle.

The eagle represents for me something otherworldly and quintessentially nonhuman or Other. It assumes mythological status in its magical quality, its uncanny appearances or revelations, and its terrifying power. In its preference for high altitudes and remote places, the eagle represents archetypal spirit in its lofty aspect, and in mythology the Sky Gods, including Zeus, sometimes assumed the form of an eagle. The dreams suggest, I believe, that as I enter the archetypal field of the Great Father, the pneumatic element of this archetype presents itself in the guise of what Erich Neumann calls 'the frightening Spirit Father'.[3] Any archetype is 'frightening' to the ego, not only because it encapsulates an aspect of eternity but because it can readily disintegrate the ego with its power. This disintegration, however, can be experienced as pleasurable and desirable, because the ego may in fact identify with the aggressive force that threatens to attack and overwhelm it.

Indeed, at the time of having these dreams I was largely oblivious to their ambivalent aspect. I interpreted them, under the influence of studies on shamanism, as the glorious awakening of my spirit guide or totemic power. I don't know how I interpreted the act of firing at the eagle with a rifle, an act which clearly contrasted with my day-world veneration of the great bird. Nor do I recall how I responded to the images of animals and children being carried off to their death in high places: a classic image of psychological death through spiritual inflation. 'Annihilation through the spirit,' writes Neumann, 'is a motif that occurs as early as the Babylonian Etana myth, where the hero is borne up to heaven by an eagle and crashes to earth.'[4] Insofar as I was prone to inflation through identification with spirit, the Sky Father represented a danger to me and the archetypal encounter could prove disastrous. I was unable to see this negative aspect at the time because I was spiritually identified with the eagle, and the dreams were clearly warning me of the potential disaster.

Just here we have to move very carefully. We should not look at dreams through the oppositional lens of pathology *or* spiritual vision, but we must have the courage to see both aspects at once. The coming of an archetypal force is positive and negative, and it transcends any simple-minded moral evaluation of the ego. The truth is paradoxical: I am being assailed by a spiritual force which could empower the personality *and* I am in danger of being disintegrated or – to use the language of the dream – 'carried away' by this same archetype. It is interesting that children are carried off in the dreams, because this provides a hint that it is the naive or childlike part of me which is most vulnerable to spiritual elevation and uplift. But again there is a double side: it is also the childlike part which is receptive to flights of enthusiasm, wonder, and divinity. Our psychological nose must rightly smell danger, but our mythic imagination must also be alert to the spiritual possibilities of the dream. Combining psychoanalytic suspicion and archetypal affirmation is the best way to work with dreams, so that we can see both sides.

A further dream at this time brought greater clarification to these dilemmas. An enormous eagle, with a wing-span of about fifty feet, is menacing a quiet village. It lives on a high mountain and regularly swoops down upon livestock and children, carrying both away to its exalted abode. The situation is grave, as several children have disappeared, and the flocks of sheep are under constant attack. The town calls an urgent public meeting at the church, which is built on a green at the centre of the village. Everyone asks what can be done, and there is a lot of angry discussion and argument that gets nowhere. Then, exploring the contents of a bookcase, I find a small pamphlet called, 'What to do when the eagle comes'. The text says:

When the Great Eagle comes down from the mountain to menace the land, the people must all gather together in the church and worship together. Supplies should be brought to the church, and children kept inside for three days. After prayer and devotion, the Eagle will return to the mountain and the land will be restored.

The text is read out to the community, and stores are gathered for our period of retreat.

This dream is very unambiguous in its emphasis upon danger and menace. The eagle is a flying monster, and if the people do not do something (if consciousness does not intervene), the land and the people will be destroyed. The cure of the situation is most interesting. One is not called upon to obliterate the eagle with force or violence. Nor are we instructed to interfere in any direct way with the bird of prey. Rather, human consciousness must get itself into order, or achieve a new kind of order, and then the bird will no longer be destructive toward the land or the people. The people must gather together in prayer and worship, in a kind of enforced spiritual retreat. There are two basic lessons here, both of them instructive to all men and women who make a direct connection with the Spirit Father.

The first lesson is the rediscovery of our 'common humanity'. The act of gathering together in shared community is a healing process for any individual who is in danger of spiritual inflation. *Communitas* is a healing force because it gets things in the right perspective, and one's own common humanity is recovered in fellowship with ordinary people. Interestingly, it is inside the church filled with villagers that the ego discovers the vital pamphlet which spells out the cure. Then, after several days of enforced community and fellowship, the world will be put right again, and life can proceed without danger of spiritual annihilation.

The second lesson concerns the achievement of 'common humility'. We are instructed to engage in prayer, worship, and devotion: these are propitiatory acts concerned with recovering a right relationship to the archetypal powers. By acknowledging the divine, we recognise in that same act that we are not the divine, but that we must serve the archetypal powers in and through our lives. By subordinating the ego, we at the same time objectify the archetypal source: 'The words that I speak unto you I speak not of myself: but the Father that dwelleth in me, he doeth the works' (John 14: 10). We are also reminded of the central question put to Parsifal in the Grail myth: 'Whom does the Grail serve?'.[5] The Grail, symbol of spiritual power, must serve the Grail King, who is also the image of God. In this dream the ego is encouraged not to fly off in ecstatic identification with the spirit, but to *serve* the spirit within the modest enclosure of the church. Humility and humanity restore the ego to its rightful place. Then, the Spirit Father returns to His rightful abode, no longer acting in invasive or lethal ways upon the human-social world. The dream reminds us of those many folk tales and legends where the cure of a supernatural blight (such as a man-eating monster or an invasion from 'above') is found not in direct combat or violent acting-out, but in recovering a sense of spiritual order in the condition of consciousness itself. As Jung consistently reminded us, when consciousness fails to separate itself properly from spirit through the agency of the 'religious attitude', spirit becomes a demoniacal monster, a force of destruction rather than of good.[6]

I should briefly mention in this context the American journal of the spiritual men's movement, called *Wingspan: Journal of the Male Spirit*. This journal, which began in 1987 under the editorship of Christopher Harding, is the most widely circulated men's movement publication in the world. The journal is full of optimistic and 'uplifting' articles that speak about spiritual matters, with titles such as 'Longing for the Great Father', 'In Quest of Archetypal Masculinity', and 'A Walk with the King'.[7] It frequently contains 'mystical' photographs featuring men dressed as eagles or hawks, covered in feathers, arms outstretched, as if about to take flight. I recognise in this journal the signs of spiritual inflation and archetypal grandeur that I have had to struggle with myself. This journal most often represents the 'ecstatic' side of identification with the eagle archetype and the Great Father, and yet I read very little there about the dangers of this so-called spiritual work.

Loss of self through identification with the archetype, loss of the reality principle by being 'borne up to heaven by an eagle', being devoured by the primal masculine, the disappearance of social and political problems in a seductive mystical haze: these perspectives would undoubtedly be constructed as reductively rational or 'Freudian' by the many readers who are using this publication to 'get high' and take leave of the ordinary. The addictive nature of these images and messages, the fact that the same themes are reiterated in every issue, suggests to me that the great eagle has carried more than a few contemporary men to its lofty abode at the top of the mountain. Although my North American feathered friends think only of shamanism and ritual, they should perhaps be observing their dreams to discover the repressed pathological side of this same archetypal experience. 'The danger from the senex lies just in the fact that we are unaware of it as dangerous.'[8]

MY FATHER, MY RIGID-CONSERVATIVE SELF

We have already had occasion to refer to the rigid conservatism that afflicts men who fall under the father's sway, but I would now like to view this psychodynamic process at close range, and with my own experience in mind. In my youth, with my anti-establishment attitude, I could never imagine that I would fall victim to rigidity of mind and behaviour. I think I always had the notion that such rigidity was 'out there', in other people, in institutions and social forms. If I kept a safe distance from the world and its structures of power and control, I could escape the hegemonic masculinity that binds and constricts. I did not sufficiently realise that this tyrannical structure could arise within my own being, devouring my spontaneity as swiftly as the bird of prey swoops upon lambs in the meadow.

When I entered the university system as a full-time staff member in the mid 1980s, it was with the vain hope of changing the system from the inside. I would preserve and promote my own youthful creative spirit, challenging the rational, dry, and patriarchal structures with my own 'feminine' mythopoetic vision. Perhaps predictably, I was rapidly devoured by the system, and within a few years I had almost forgotten what my original vision was. I walked into my profession with an interest in Jung, spirituality, myth, and poetry, but I soon began to repress or displace these concerns in a bid to become professionally integrated into my work environment. I lost the courage to be independent, and looked for acceptance and recognition from others. Clearly, such recognition would not be forthcoming so long as I emphasised Jung and Hillman in an era infatuated by Derrida, Foucault, and Lacan. I recall presenting a staff seminar in 1986 on Hillman's concept of the soul, and it fell flat. What was I talking about, referring to Gods and Goddesses as if I were addressing a medieval gathering? My professional integrity was offended by these cross-currents. I tried becoming an 'eccentric' who might be tolerated for his 'difference', but this didn't work. I found myself isolated and alienated, and I started to resent my own interests.

Professionalism is the absolute bane of creativity. As I became more professional, technical, efficient, and precise, I found that my imagination emptied out and my soul lost connection with my intellect. I immersed myself in conventional scholarship, in the Freudian tradition, and in postmodern theory. At conferences and public events, I would present as a post-Freudian, and this won me some acceptance. But there was a lot missing. I was merely average at these mainstream materialist discourses. Any bright postgraduate student could surpass me in understanding contemporary intellectual theory. I knew that I was performing well below my level. I was caught between competing desires, but the desire to fit in was stronger than the desire to be myself. I lost touch with my interests, my body, my emotions, as some strange internal force urged me to lofty heights where I did not belong. The archetypal father was pushing my ego development, but it seemed to occur at the cost of my individuation.

In his chapter on 'The Slaying of the Father', Neumann writes that the 'terrible father . . . functions not only as a principle that disintegrates consciousness, but even more as one that fixes it in a wrong direction. It is he who . . . upholds the old system of consciousness'.[9]

This certainly explained my situation: lost in a rigid collective system, with my consciousness 'fixed in a wrong direction'. Neumann says that the Terrible Father 'acts like a spiritual system which, from beyond and above, captures and destroys the son's consciousness'. He refers to this condition as 'patriarchal castration', which he defines as '[being] bound by traditional morality and conscience, and . . . castrated by convention'.[10] This explained my feeling of numbness, my sense of being ineffectual, lacking flair and drive, and bound to conventions that made me appear mediocre. Murray Stein provides a memorable description of what he calls the 'father-devoured' personality:

> The phenomenological reflection of this negative side of the father archetype is consciousness tied, bound, swallowed in convention and habit, in attention to duty as defined by prevailing collective norms. A gastric flood – of values, thought patterns, tastes, dispositions, attitudes, opinions – from the prevailing culture digest away all traces of individual experience and spontaneous reaction.[11]

157

The mythological resonances here are deliberately related to the figure of Chronos-Saturn, who devours everything into himself, and whose 'gastric juices' annihilate all distinctions and individual differences. Stein goes on to describe how this affliction causes loss of identity and self-alienation, but when the father complex rules the psychic situation the personality is forced into submission.

Augusto Vitale argues that there is in the consciousness of the son, or *puer aeternus*, a dark longing to be put to death by the negative father. If the puer stands for creativity and individual expression, this spirit undergoes a crisis where it sacrifices itself to the life of the Father. Vitale writes that 'Puer and senex are the personifications of the two extremes into which the libido in a certain condition splits'.

> In the old man the [psychic] process has stopped in an excess of egocentric differentiation which has exhausted the transformation potential; it has become petrified, and the old man, detaining the power, tends to block and petrify the process around him. By now Cronus is hardened by his thirst for power and by his fear of what is new.[12]

This is a dark and dingy condition. All of one's energy appears to be diverted into ego development. Whereas before one was concerned with creativity, music, dreams, travel, receptivity to the beyond, suddenly one becomes obsessed with real estate, mortgages, fitting in, conformity, getting on. The psychic 'flow' has stopped; puer becomes senex, mercury turns into lead. But this transformation takes place almost imperceptibly. As Hillman has observed: 'Identification with the senex occurs subtly; we learn the role slowly. It is a chronic disease, creeping upon us unnoticed'.[13] One simply begins to live life in a different mode, a new key. I started to take my authority very seriously, I forgot the constructed and arbitrary nature of all authority, and I desired to impose my authority upon others and upon myself. At this time, I became not only a senex figure at work, but a father at home. Responsibility, limitation and order became my primary goals, or in other words, I unwittingly killed my puer spirit.

While still in analysis with Hillman, and just before taking up my position as an academic, I had the following dream which provided a most explicit warning about what was to follow:

> Grey-haired men in grey suits, grey ties and shiny black shoes

had taken over the back-yard of my childhood house. They looked slick and professional, but they were demons of destruction. They had turned the garage into a chamber of torture and execution. Their task was to torture, then murder, rebellious, wild, creative young men. It seems they had been involved in this work for some time. When I arrive on the scene and realise what is going on, I am shocked but unable to do much about it. Their evil doings seem too well established and beyond my control. Upon entering the garage I am appalled to see that Toby [a young man from my student days] is about to be strapped to a conveyor belt and murdered. At the end of the belt is a huge mechanical saw, which will cut him into two halves. I try to stop this from happening, but Toby is resigned to his fate, and he even seems to be joking with his executioners, having a cigarette with them before the horror starts. He just assumes that I cannot help, and places himself on the belt, ready to be killed. As I protest and rage, he is conveyed toward the saw, which I cannot see because it is hidden in the darkness.

Hillman advised me to pin this dream on the wall above my university desk. 'Make sure', he said, 'this isn't the life you find yourself living as a university professor.' Hillman himself had not had much luck with universities; he could not reconcile the blue fire of his own Dionysian imagination with the senex dryness and dullness of university tradition. Hillman was strongly opposed to my embarking on an academic career. He tried to talk me out of it for several weeks, as he thought I should become a writer, and not squeeze myself into the academic mould. He was probably right, but I obviously could not escape the encounter with the negative senex, when it seemed to be willed by fate itself.

As a self-confessed puer type,[14] Hillman has a keen nose for the presence of the negative senex, and a genuine and abiding fear of his crushing and destroying capabilities. 'Is there a way out of the saturnine convention so that we are not eaten by the senex complex, swallowing our individual redemption?'[15] Elsewhere he warned: 'This desire in the father to kill the child we ignore to our peril'.[16] Surely two *pueri* working together in analysis could outwit the dark designs of the old senex! But even as we worked through this dream, looking for signs and clues, I had the feeling that something was foreshadowed that could not be avoided.

In the dream, it is fascinating how the puer willingly submits to the devices of the demonically destructive senex. There is complicity and agreement between them, and here we find the shadow side of what Collins calls the 'shared selfness' of father and son.[17] The grey fathers are determined to slaughter the creative sons, and the sons are prepared and willing to offer themselves as sacrifices. The ego protests, but its protest is ineffectual. There is something archetypally correct in what is taking place: we might say that this kind of puer creativity is destined to be destroyed in this way; part of its archetypal 'life' is to be put to death by slick, professional fathers. On the other hand, this can be read as the fatal flaw of the puer: he cannot stand up for himself in the face of senex authority; he may be adventurous, vigorous, engagingly wild and sexy, but the one thing he cannot deal with is the negative senex. The senex imposes its separate power and authority, causing the puer to surrender its consciousness. The ego's *late arrival* upon what seems to be an established and entrenched scene indicates that consciousness is lagging behind, and even when it finally 'sees' what is happening in its own backyard, it is unable to do anything about it.

REBELLIOUS YOUTH AND CONSERVATIVE AUTHORITY IN SOCIETY

Watching this process unfold within myself helped me to come to a better understanding of the fate of my own generation. My generation was wild, rebellious, creative, full of challenge and bluff. The 1960s and early 1970s were exhilarating while they lasted. We saw horizons expanded, vistas opened, a release of new libido, and a worship of Eros, earth, nature, creativity. The puer-inspired rebels of these years had declared war on the authority of the father and on conventionality, and we wanted to set up the youthful God Dionysus against the old Father-God of Jewish-Christian tradition. We protested, demonstrated, wore flowers, experienced ecstasy, attacked traditions, and by the example of our personal and political behaviour we hoped to inspire a revolution that would replace the old order with our new social vision.

But what happened? After the failed revolution of 1968 the puer-spirit began to wane. The puer is not a long-distance runner; he comes onto the social scene in fits and starts, often lighting up the cultural order with brief episodes of brilliant creativity. Like John

Lennon or Jimi Hendrix, he inspires the world with his Dionysian energy, and then he dies young, or is killed, and mourned. Collectively, Dionysian brilliance quickly burns itself out. My generation gave up on revolution and decided it wanted to make money. Archetypally, the puer spirit was devoured by the senex. The hippies and rebels of the 1960s became the grey-haired stock-brokers and grey-suited merchant bankers of the 1980s and 1990s. Creativity was returned to the collective unconscious, the mytho-poetic lights went off, a Big Chill set in, and we were down to business, often very big business. The free-spirited youth had turned greedy, selfish, and ego-dominated.

The 1980s saw the emergence of unprecedented greed, corporate mergers, inflation, stress, futures markets. The senex was back in town and he was meaner than ever, devouring whatever he could before – what? Before the puer-spirit gathered new momentum to challenge his hegemony? Social-political life over recent decades has seen a rise and fall of senex and puer extremes. Both styles have positives and negatives, but it is clearly apparent that they have a kind of invisible confluence or shared archetypal reality. Creative puer and negative senex constellate each other; there is a powerful secret symmetry between them. The puer-spirit disappears and is strangely transformed into the conservative authoritarianism of the senex.

Journalists and commentators often ask: what became of the radical 1960s generation? My own dream is the best answer to that question that I am aware of. It is not exactly that the flower children 'betrayed' their cause and engaged in a breach of faith. As this dream indicates, the *pueri aeterni* did not deny their mythic pattern but followed it through.

The real psychological and political task, however, is to *become conscious* of the ways in which creativity is repeatedly devoured by tradition, freedom by authority, imagination by intellect, and youth by age. Puer is the progressive spirit, and if he is continually devoured then society will always 'revert' to patriarchy, and creativity be destroyed by convention. Our task is to become aware of this tragic psychocultural pattern, and to develop ways, or strategies, in which senex control can be subverted and his characteristic repressions lifted.

161

HOOKED ON PETER PAN: PUERILE MEN AND THE UNCONSCIOUS POWER DRIVE

These psychodynamics are interestingly explored in the recent movie *Hook*, directed by Steven Spielberg.[18] This film, which features Robin Williams as Peter Pan and Dustin Hoffman as Hook, is a psychological reconstruction of the Peter Pan books by J. M. Barrie, and it provides an interesting perspective on the internal father-tyrant and how his power can be challenged.

In his book *The Peter Pan Syndrome*, Dan Kiley argues that men governed by the image of eternal youth typically experience a dramatic psychological shift as they enter adulthood. 'During their late teens and early twenties, these men indulge in an impetuous lifestyle.' Narcissism holds sway and 'locks them inside themselves'. Then, after years of poor adjustment to reality, they suddenly appear to be ruled by a very strict reality principle. 'Life seems to reverse itself: "I want" is replaced with "I should".' 'Pursuit of other people's acceptance seems their only way to find self-acceptance.'[19] Kiley says that the modern-day Peter Pan imprisons himself in an extremely narrow image of maturity, almost a parody of mature responsibility, and that he quickly becomes stressed, tense, and angry.

In the movie *Hook*, the Peter Pan figure has dumped his 'Pan' nature and has become an aggressive business entrepreneur. He is occupied day and night with big deals, takeovers, and mergers. This is a perfect metaphor for the devouring father: the commercial senex 'devours' whatever it can find. Peter consumes other businesses at the same time as he is himself consumed by this relentless power drive. Peter's wife, Moira, begins to oppose his neurotic condition, witnessing the disintegration of the family and the alarming absence of human care or concern. At one point she seizes his mobile phone – just as he tries to clinch the biggest deal of his career – and throws it out the window. She recognises that his neurosis requires desperate measures.

Peter has no time for his children. His son Jack feels deprived of his love, and we find again the common image of the father who destroys by being emotionally absent. Peter promises his son that he will be present at an important baseball match. However, the father is held up by urgent business, and he arrives at the stadium too late to see the game. 'My word is my bond' promises Peter to his son before the big game; 'Yeah, a junk bond', replies the resentful and already cynical son. Peter is a false father, a man play-acting at maturity, and as such the idea of a 'junk bond' is an appropriate image for false fathering and for the fraudulence and emptiness of modern society.

When Peter reports to the elderly Wendy about the state of his life, she exclaims, 'Peter, you've become a pirate!' He attacks, ravages, and lays waste like Captain Hook himself, whose very name symbolises the impact that the negative senex has upon a man: he becomes 'hooked' by greed, fast money, and savage dealings. But the film cleverly insists that Peter has become a prime candidate for the negative senex because he is still, at the deepest level, 'hooked' on his Peter Pan nature. The movie indicates that he has to journey back to Never Land, regain contact with his buried and repressed inner child, and release energy into his consciousness so that he can live authentically as an adult. His energy is still trapped at a primal level, so that his present life is really a half-life. Living within such narrow limits, the ego goes into negative mode and the senex-devourer takes over and coordinates consciousness. The negative senex rules best when our psychic energy is not available to challenge him.

When the psyche demands change, it sometimes takes away something that we truly value, so that we are forced to go in search of a fuller consciousness. In this film, Peter's two children are magically abducted by Captain James Hook and taken back to Never Land. This forces Peter to journey into the otherworld, luring him into the unconscious where his lost self can be recovered. What he encounters in Never Land is a more dramatic version of what has already taken place in his life: the loss of creative youth to the negative senex. He must free his children from the dreadful Hook, thus liberating both them and himself by defeating the hold that the negative senex has upon him.

At this point, too, the 'other' woman suddenly emerges. The new, exciting, often young woman who represents the man's lost vitality and who points the way to his re-experience of instinctual childhood existence is represented in this movie by the figure of Tinker Bell. She is the anima-woman who classically emerges at the midlife crisis, who lures a man away from his sterile life and leads him by the hand into Never Land. The role of the anima in extricating a man from the clutches of the negative father will be discussed in the following chapter. Suffice it to say that she is, as Jung often stated, the bridge into the deep unconscious and into a man's creative transformation.

In Never Land, Peter encounters the rebellious Lost Boys, who represent psychic vitality caught in a stunted, infantile condition. These boys believe that adulthood is depraved and degenerate. 'All grown ups are pirates!' says the truculent leader, and he adds: 'We kill pirates'. The Lost Boys apparently view adulthood as a state of 'adulteration', synonymous with a fatal loss of youthful creativity. In her book *Puer Aeternus* Marie-Louise von Franz makes the same point.[20] She argues that the *puer aeternus* cannot envisage a creative adulthood; the puer looks at maturity and age and sees only the truncated half-life that is represented by the negative senex and the pirates. Von Franz suggests that not only the fear of adulthood, but also a fear of death and mortality, holds the puer back from his own development. A real fear of death underlies the cult of youth, and this is evident in the discussions that take place between Peter's abducted children and the Lost Boys.

Peter's task is to recover his Pan nature, reconnect with his childhood creativity, and resist the tyranny of Hook. In psychological terms, this means that he must forge a direct link between his adult life and the condition of childhood, allowing for the hitherto impossible state of 'creative maturity', a fusion of the two sides of himself. When this connection is made, 'Hook' is automatically defeated, because the tyrannical child-killing part of himself is overcome. We cannot, in this movie, afford to think too literally about Hook, despite the splendidly convincing, flesh-and-blood characterisation of Dustin Hoffman. The film's visual display encourages literalisation of Hook, but the plot and story move in the opposite direction, toward Hook as a metaphorical figure for an aspect of Peter's nature. It is commendable that the film should be able to move in both directions at once, toward literalising and psychologising the same dramatic figure.

The pirate-king, who is symbolised throughout by ticking clocks and the passage of time (*chronos*), attempts to brainwash the abducted children. He works to erase positive memories of the real parents and strives to force Jack and Maggie to devote themselves to him. The girl resists this brainwashing, but Jack succumbs to Hook's indoctrination and becomes a *de facto* son of the pirate-king. Significantly, the boy who has been ignored by his own father becomes the most likely candidate to perpetuate the role of the negative senex. The pirate condition feeds on anger, resentment, and narcissistic rage. In this way the cycle of emotional abuse is perpetuated, puer becomes demonic senex, and the archetypal pattern is reinforced.

As Jack changes from neglected boy to angry pirate, Peter transforms from negative father to playful child. Peter allows himself to be 'tutored' by the Lost Boys, who facilitate his reconnection with bodily nature, physicality, and primal aggression. The film argues that over-senexed men must recover their puer nature through the agency of the shadow. Peter becomes impish, immoral, crude, feral, and through this reverse 'initiation' is reunited with his vitality and power. Peter must also recover his capacity to fly. This is the ultimate symbol of the puer state: the ability to soar on the wings of youthful spirit. He must 'fly' to Never Land to recover his children, and he must use imagination and spirit to access the world of the unconscious. In order to fly, Tinker Bell informs him that he must think a happy thought. The only memory that succeeds in recovering his boyhood flight is, ironically, the memory of his first moment of fatherhood.

The psyche works by paradox and reversals, not by linear or logical sequences. When he emotionally re-experiences the joy of fatherhood, and his capacity to father, then he is released again to his own boyhood. The joy of fatherhood connects to the joy of youth: the same joy, the same ecstatic source. Joy or ecstasy awakens the spirit of Dionysus, the 'loosener', and as Peter admits this spirit into his life he is freed from the killing embrace of the negative senex. As Pan and Hook shape up for their long-awaited fight, the daughter Maggie screams out from a suspended net in which she has been trapped by Hook. Peter flies up to release her from bondage, and Maggie recalls him to his true mission, which is to rescue his kidnapped children, not to lose himself in macho-heroics with the pirate. This is an important moment of the story, because it is only the negative senex who wants to engage in battle. Combat and warfare are central to his archetypal style, and to become embroiled in the games of war is to continue to be subject to his tyranny. The film indicates that the way to defeat the internal tyrant is to refuse his structures, to call up different spirits and different styles, and to introduce ecstatic energies that dissolve the rigid boundaries of senex control.

Hook is a comedy with a happy ending. Peter Pan is returned to reality to lead a fuller and more creative life after having journeyed into another world to meet the archetypal elements of which he is composed. In my opinion this movie is not too far-fetched or overly sentimental, because if men follow the directions suggested by the soul, we can be released from the fatal grip of the negative senex. The main thing is to *recognise* that we have fallen victim to a tyrannical force, and many men are unable to reach this first stage of liberation, because untying this complex goes against the grain of the masculinity that has overtaken us. The negative senex actually fuses with our male ego and our power drive, and men tragically fail to realise that the very thing that presents us with the illusion of power is the source of our crippling pathology. As Jung would say, if we are lucky, we get a terrible neurosis, which prevents the personality from continuing along its 'normal' course.

THE BALANCING ACT OF CREATIVITY AND AUTHORITY

Another instructive work of popular culture which maps out the terrain of the negative senex, and especially the conflict between youthful creativity and traditional authority, is that justly famous narrative, *Zen and the Art of Motorcycle Maintenance* (1974).[21] Robert Pirsig's autobiographical novel presents a vivid account of the senex–puer conflict enacted simultaneously at internal and external levels. Internally, the narrator of the story is divided between his present senex-based personality, and his split-off puer self, called with appropriate irony Phaedrus. A brilliant youth who dared to question the authority of the ossified and pedantic Chairman at the University of Chicago, the narrator became inflated with his own puer grandiosity, and, like Icarus or Phaethon, rose dangerously high, burned up, and collapsed. After being committed to an asylum, the narrator switches suddenly from creative puer to rigid senex.

Years later, he rides across the high country of Montana with his 11-year-old son, in search of the lost essence of youth (which is called 'Quality'). Ironically, even as he quests for the puer spirit, the narrator fears a return to Phaedrus, who becomes a threatening presence. To the older man in search of lost creativity, the puer is indeed threatening, since the present personality, based on a senex adaptation, will have to be dissolved to make way for the excluded element. This is starkly emphasised in the fact that the puer self bears a separate name, a different identity, and almost a different history. The narrator lectures his own son about the necessity of honouring Quality, but a structural irony in this story is that the father's authoritarian stance and teachings about the necessity of

166

the puer spirit become senex-obstacles for the son. (I know all about the 'inspired teacher' syndrome, and the reverse effects it can have upon the young.) Eventually, the son clashes with the father in a bid to honour his own puer essence.

There is much here for contemporary men to feast on, but when I first read this book in the early 1970s I was fairly oblivious to the psychological depth of this complex moral fable. Nor could I have been aware that my own puer self was reading or 'constructing' the book then in terms of its own myth, whereas now, as I reread the story, I am approaching the same book as practically a dried out senex, a curmudgeon looking for clues about how to recapture teenage spirit. What *Zen and the Art of Motorcycle Maintenance* reveals is that puer and senex can never be reconciled in any bland, glib, or optimistic formula. Each has substance, power, a different *kind* of spirit, and each has to be honoured in its own way. Puer and senex are both liable to become split-off sub-personalities, creating havoc in the individual who identifies wholly with one figure or style at the expense of the other. 'Motorcycle maintenance', which the narrator sees as both rational and intuitive at the same time, is his personal blend of senex and puer. He learns that accepting the otherness of the puer in himself means also honouring the otherness of his son's puer spirit. Psychologically, he learns that senex is the ability to order experience and to teach this order to others, but puer is the capacity to remain open to mystery and revelation. Senex defends wisdom by closure, whereas puer creates spirit by openness. Coming to this lesson slowly and painfully, Pirsig eventually realises that it is torturous to engage in both conditions or styles at the one time. Nevertheless, this self-division, duality, or psychological complexity must be endured if some integration is to be achieved.

THE FATHER WHO INCLUDES THE SON

The kind of men's movement I am interested in is the kind that understands the necessity of working along the puer–senex axis. Robert Bly is fascinated by the challenge of making the 'soft' male become hard, whereas I am interested in the problem of making the 'dry' male become moist. Moisture comes from the soul, dryness from the intellect. Our culture is full of dryness, and as soon as the puer steps into mainstream culture he faces the prospect of taking on a soul-destroying dryness. One of my university colleagues, a man no longer operating within the system, once commented to me that in our professional lives we seem to be 'gargling with talcum powder'. The moisture of the soul evaporates in the excessive dryness of our over-senexed culture. Indeed, Hillman once defined 'senex consciousness' as 'the basic Western condition'.[22] Certainly the senex is not on the endangered species list, but the *puer aeternus* is. We must struggle to keep the puer spirit alive at all costs, since it is so readily devoured by conventionality and hardened authority.

In this respect as well I seem to be on the opposite side to Robert Bly. In his recent book, *The Sibling Society*, Bly argues that modern American (but I think he means 'Western') society is suffering from an overdose of youth, and he bemoans the fact that age, wisdom, the father, and the senex structures of authority are no longer respected as they once were.[23] While it is true that the Great Father of our high culture continues to decline, and along with his demise we find a degeneration of truth, moral values, and spirit, I nevertheless believe that the old father still represents, as Hillman says, 'the basic Western condition'. It is simply the exalted face of the Father, or his spiritual life, which is rapidly deteriorating. Meanwhile, the low life of the Father, his life as ordering social senex, who constricts, limits, opposes, and says no to the forward-striving spirit, is thriving as never before. The Spirit Father may be dead, but the mean-spirited father is dominant today, gripped as it is with the disease of pettiness, orderliness, constriction, rigidity. The liberating father who 'provides not bread but spirit through meaning and order' is definitely absent, but in his place we have 10,000 parodies of the father: a style that provides not order but bureaucracy, not spirit but repression, not meaning but regulations. The 'end of high patriarchy' does not mean that the father goes away; it simply means that we become consumed by low-grade versions of the archetypal father.

Our task today is to attempt to liberate the archetypal father from all this negativity. We certainly do not achieve this goal by treating the father kindly or gently, by indulging his obsessive pettiness and his crippling cruelty. Nor do we redeem the father by idealising a lost past, or by trying to turn the clock back to a time when youth 'respected' their elders. We redeem the father best by going beyond him. In other words, we take up the fight for the youthful spirit, championing the puer spirit in a time ridden by the negative senex. The puer spirit is simply the father's own spiritual life; but it is a life he will not recognise unless we push it into his face. The father in his old age, or late patriarchy, suffers from loss of memory and loss of recognition. He cannot recognise or applaud the puer spirit because he is alienated from his own spiritual life. There is no point in being sentimental about the decline of patriarchy: let it fall, and give it a push or two for good measure. Our job is to revivify the spirit of the father, and we achieve this by supporting the forward-driving puer spirit in ourselves and in society at large.

The men who want an 'expressive' men's movement, who want to discover their feelings and explore their emotions, are men who are suffering from *too much father*. They are men who, like myself, are walled in by the negative senex, and who are struggling desperately, like Pirsig's narrator and Steven Spielberg's Peter Pan, to recover the spark of youth and the flow of creativity. In the current discourses on men's lives, there should be less emphasis upon the Absent Father of my childhood, or the Idealised Father of the spirit world, and more upon the Devouring Father of my present psychological world. It is this internal negative senex who kills creativity, as in my dream of the grey-suited murderers of youthful spontaneity. It is this largely unconscious part of ourselves that eats up men's creative impulses, and that turns us into soulless parodies of a powder-dry and repressive senex archetype. Men want to blame all sorts of things – feminism, the law courts, television, dull routine at work, absent fathers, chronic fatigue, and numerous other things – for our loss of creative energy, spontaneity and spirit. But we must see that we are our own worst enemy. The power-drive within us, the internal authoritarian, the man-eating monster at the end of the beanstalk, all these figures and images that constrict and bind are descriptive of the archetypal complex that gets bound up with our ego and that alienate us from the sources of creativity.

It could well be that some of the modern emphasis upon the brutal and rejecting 'Absent Father', upon the father who apparently *rejected me as a boy*, is a fantasy-projection of what men are suffering at the moment. Namely, our internal father, our dominant and controlling image of masculinity, does not include or befriend our vulnerable, creative puer. This 'memory' of how father rejected me as a boy, has to be seen through for its metaphorical resonances about the *present* state of my adult psyche. Like all collective symbols, this one of the cruel and rejecting father stubbornly resists being psychologised and prefers to remain in the literal and historical domain. It would hurt too much, and would be too personally confronting, to have to 'own' this image for ourselves. But when I see middle-aged, dried-out, senex-ridden men cry at weekend retreats because their fathers did not love them enough, I see not just human pain but a symbolic statement that has yet to be seen through. At that moment, we men are wholly identified with the suffering and threatened internal puer who will not be embraced by the stern senex who continues to govern our psychological lives. What remains scandalously 'absent' is an internal settler of limits who is capable of tolerating change, uncertainty, and creativity.

7

UNPROFESSIONAL WORK

Embracing the anima

I'm certainly no authority on the feminine, and I don't pretend to be whole. I'm simply a man on a long journey toward recovering the sacred feminine in my life.

Tom Absher[1]

ANIMA AS UNFINISHED BUSINESS

While the archetypal father and son battle it out for possession of a man's soul, a new, third entity arises from the depths of the psyche. This new figure is the anima or archetypal feminine, and it is she who offers a reconciling possibility, a 'third way' between the rigidity of the father and the flightiness of the son. This third way, however, is not easy to follow. Although it has become almost a cliché today to say that the anima can save a man from his masculine one-sidedness, the actual integration of the anima is still a rare achievement which represents a 'master-piece' of psychological work.[2] In discussing the anima, I realise that I am approaching a subject that is intrinsically difficult and slippery, and I am made to feel strangely 'unprofessional' as soon as I enter this territory. Having made that admission, I am also aware that men, virtually by definition, cannot become 'expert' in the field of the anima; it is the one area where we remain eternal beginners, muddlers, forever the amateur. According to Jung, the anima 'sums up everything that a man can never get the better of and never finishes coping with'.[3]

ANIMA AND MOTHER

In my early twenties, when I read a lot of Jung, I felt that I knew exactly what the anima was. 'Anima' was a man's feminine side, the

171

side that compensated his conscious masculinity. But in my early twenties, I don't believe I *had* any conscious masculinity, so in some ways any talk or knowledge about anima was hopelessly premature. My experience of 'the feminine' was largely governed by the mother archetype, and the anima, as a discrete psychic entity, was wholly subsumed by the mother. According to some analytical psychologists, it is not until the masculine self is firmly developed that the anima archetype can emerge properly. If we can believe Erich Neumann, the young man who is immersed in the feminine and identified with the mother is not related to the anima at all, but can only 'win' her after the liberating dragon fight with the primordial parental figures.[4] Neumann tends to construct the anima as a distinctly separate entity from the primordial or elementary feminine, an entity that has to be won through heroic masculinist effort. Jungian populariser Robert Johnson is even more adamant about this distinction between mother and anima: 'Confusing the mother and the anima is a very serious problem, and the ambiguity of the anima in a man's life allows him many mistakes in this area'.[5]

Jung, however, does not appear to be as categorical or as systematic as his followers. For Jung, the mother, the primal feminine, and Eros, are all forms of the general experience of the anima, so that Jung could say, for instance, that 'the growing youth must be able to free himself from the anima fascination of his mother'.[6] Nevertheless, Jung and Neumann agree that the mature experience of the feminine is distinctly different from youthful or immature experience, and whether or not the feminine itself actually undergoes structural change as consciousness develops, the mature man's experience of this archetype is so different that it is 'as if' the feminine itself had gone through some dramatic change. My own experience of the feminine at 20, and again at 40, could easily persuade me to recognise structural difference, but I fully understand that any differences may originate wholly from changes within the perceiving subject. It is another of the psyche's mysterious paradoxes: the feminine is the same, and is not the same, at different stages in a man's life.

In my own situation, the task of coming to grips with the father on the one hand, and the puer on the other, presented me with enough creative tension to go on with, so that the stirrings of the anima were not greeted with much enthusiasm. I already had enough on my plate, and wouldn't she politely go away until I had achieved a greater sense of balance and equilibrium in myself? Jung says that 'It is normal for a man to resist his anima, because she represents . . . all those tendencies and contents hitherto excluded from conscious life'.[7] I guess I did not appreciate enough that the battle fought between father and son *produces*, or, as Jung might say, *constellates* the anima as the reconciling figure and potential answer to that internal crisis. Anima brings with her the possibility of a new kind of wholeness or psychic equilibrium, but this is far from a complacent wholeness or a static equilibrium. The anima's way is dynamic, challenging, processual, stormy, and full of pitfalls and dangers.

In my first book, I studied the works of an Australian writer who resisted the advances of the anima because he feared that she would devour the ego and wreck his life.[8] In other words, the anima was subsumed by the figure of the devouring mother, and so long as this situation continued psychological development could not take place. Notoriously, creative men sometimes cannot go forward into life because they sense their individuality being eaten up by social convention; nor can they go backwards because they fear that the maternal unconscious will rend and overpower them. Caught between fear of the social order and fear of the unconscious, a neurosis develops in place of real development.[9] Although the feminine unconscious can appear frightening, men must have faith that the positive anima will rise up out of the unconscious and guide them to real transformation. The anima, if allowed into psychic reality, comes to bring a genuine healing and reconciliation, but her healing potions can look at first like poisons, and her wholeness can seem like a terrifying fragmentation to an ego that lacks the courage to accept her challenge.

ANIMA AS FATE AND PERSONAL GUIDE

In one sense, the encounter with anima makes the battle with the tyrannical father look relatively simple. If the father, who 'fixes consciousness in a wrong direction', turns a man into a stiff figure of convention or tradition, anima dissolves that stance and brings about a dramatic rapprochement between the man and his driving life-force, talent, or 'genius'. There are countless terms to talk about this inner essence – guardian angel, guiding star, inner destiny, My Lady Soul, and so on – and all of these terms have, I think quite rightly, a mystical dimension, precisely because a man's encounter with his innermost driving *daimon* is a profoundly spiritual experience. It is an encounter with fate itself, and such an encounter cannot be explained in scientific or material terms. One looks automatically to great visionary literature and to religious documents to find historical parallels and antecedents, and not to the arid textbooks of academic psychology. The anima emerges with enormous power and persuasion, so much so that a man in her grip will readily be able to challenge the authority of the father and to establish a counter-authority in her name.

During my own analysis in America, I watched this process enacted before me in the life and career of James Hillman. Hillman found that being a 'classical Jungian' was not enough for him, that this position cramped his style and obscured his creativity. In the name of anima,[10] Hillman felt impelled to create a 'post-Jungian' identity, to develop depth-psychology toward new insights, to remain open to change and ongoing revelation. Personally, I feel certain that Jung would have condoned this standpoint, since he often stated that depth psychology is a pioneer science, and no-one should presume that we can now rest on our laurels and be content with the present state of knowledge. I think it is wrong to construct Jung as a Devouring Father who would inhibit growth and further development. (However, Jungianism, of course, can play the role of non-creative, fixed, or dogmatic senex.) Jung was anima-inspired, and that condition must necessarily empower those who come after him to 'dream the work onward' in the same spirit of enquiry and creativity. Whether or not we accept the *revisionings* of anima-inspired followers is a separate question, but we must always defend, I think, the right of those who come after to put forward their own visions.

The emergence of the anima in mature years almost always fore-shadows disruptions in professional identity and in career, because the social role adopted until this critical moment is invariably a product of convention and the 'Law of the Father', which is by defi-nition not synonymous with individual talent. The anima works to loosen one's ties to one's social role, to point out that it is, after all, a role, and not one's true self. The anima can effect this loosening by detachment and reverie, by loss of interest and depression, by creating new persuasions and enthusiasms, or by engendering a sense of humour, playfulness, and irony. However she does it, the anima will create an expectation that one's true self lies elsewhere. What one's 'true' self is, of course, is the leading question here, and one which is impossible to answer in the abstract. Actually, I often

174

feel that the *true self* is nothing other than a dream of the future, or a dream about future possibilities, which in my case always involves an expectation of increased creativity and spirituality. It is a dream that makes us restless and impatient with the present, yet which also, paradoxically, makes the present livable and endurable precisely because we are able to imagine a better future. Anima points ahead, forward in time, always urging us to a larger self, and giving us the libido and interest to embark upon a voyage of self-transformation. 'The Eternal Feminine leads us upward and on.'[11]

THE PROTEST OF THE SOUL: CHANGE OR BUST

In the previous chapter, I outlined my gradual fusion and identification with a father image that worked to alienate me from my creative processes. I lost touch with my own *daimon*, and walked hand in hand with the father of academic tradition and intellectual authority. I think I knew deep down that this pose would not last, that it would give way to something else. My own fate is inextricably tied up with the archetypal feminine, with the return of the anima and mother in a post-patriarchal era, and my life as the son of the patriarch would not last. It was simply a matter of time.

Over a period of some years, several things transpired that all pointed to the same diagnosis. For no apparent reason, I felt desperately unhappy, even though my career was moving ahead in leaps and bounds. At odd moments I felt myself overwhelmed with sadness, and sometimes I would burst into tears and have bouts of trembling. Then I developed heart palpitations and minor spasms that really shocked me. I had too much anxiety, the doctor said, and had developed an 'executive stress' disorder. I should go for walks and try not to work so hard. Then I realised that my creativity had dried up. Although in the 1970s I had been a musician (drummer/percussionist), I had not played any music for years. Nor was I even listening to music. And although I fancied myself to be a writer, I had not written or published anything for what seemed like ages. I was most active in committees, organisation, administration, teaching, and other areas involving the imposition of senex order and control. I had everything so much 'under control' that I was starting to lose control altogether. This is the pathetic and even humorous side of the negative senex: it worries away at controlling the small and the minute, but meanwhile huge chunks of psyche start protesting against this narrow order, creating havoc while the ego is still obsessed with the details. I felt like an ageing, nutty professor, polishing my footnotes while the entire house of personality was tumbling down due to violent reactions at the foundational level.

I went to Delphi, Greece, looking for a new orientation, and all I felt was my own deep despair. While in Greece, I dreamed of a suicidal anima-figure:

> I am in the back seat of a car with my estranged lover or partner. We are quarrelling continually as we are driven to an official function by a well-groomed, professional-looking man and woman. I tell my partner that she must not behave in this way; she is embarrassing me and disturbing our hosts. Suddenly my partner screams, 'I've had enough!'. She gets out of the car, which is blocked in a traffic jam, and runs across to the other side of the street, where traffic is moving freely. She lies down upon the road, arms above her head, legs outstretched, as if upon a sacrificial altar. 'Oh no,' I scream, 'she is trying to kill herself.' In an instant, our smooth and capable host pulls the car out of the congested lane and drives across to the opposite side, so that his car protects her from being hit by oncoming vehicles.

My psychic traffic toward official places with well-groomed people is 'blocked', relationship with the feminine is bad and getting worse, and the situation moves rapidly toward a crisis. This is my own 'midlife' crisis, instigated by a rebellious and protesting anima. The anima deserts the scene, runs to the opposite side of the two-way street, and is prepared to sacrifice herself to the outward-bound traffic. This means that I experience a 'loss of soul' on my professional way, and the anima clearly runs in the opposite direction, away from my professionalism, toward the unconscious, where the traffic is moving freely. She seems prepared to sacrifice herself to this contrary or 'counter' movement. Interestingly, it is not the ego but the persona-figure who moves quickly to the anima's support. The ego seems too frazzled and caught up in itself, while the smooth persona mobilises its practical skills and comes quickly to the rescue. This suggests that my professional style could in fact be employed in service of the anima and the 'contrary' movement of the soul. Noticing that the life-principle had deserted the forward journey, the male persona is prepared to move in the opposite direction, in support and defence of the soul.

176

This proved to be a prophetic dream. Upon returning home after overseas excursions, I realised I had no alternative but to back the soul in its protest and rebellion. I could no longer support my former professional attitude, which was engendering chaos, anxiety, and sterility. I did not 'give up' my career; that would have been too literal a response, or an 'acting out' of my internal confusion, but I simply transformed it. I got out of my blocked lane and went across the divide in service of soul. I focused my mind and energy upon the longings of the heart, which had been muffled during my phase as a conventional intellectual. My heart took off on spiritual and transformative themes, and I began writing in a way that I had not experienced for at least ten years. I gathered together these writings, mostly on Aboriginal spirituality, Hillman's 'anima mundi' psychology, and environmentalism, and my book *Edge of the Sacred* was born.[12] This book, as many reviewers noted, was a 'cry of the heart', a passionate plea for transformation in Western consciousness, and an attempt to link up my own personal spiritual crisis with the larger critical issues facing my own national culture. To my surprise, the book was a national best-seller, and the first print-run sold out in six months. If we have the courage to follow the way suggested by the psyche, our efforts to serve the soul may be recognised by the community.

The dream indicates that sacrifice is the way of the future. First, the ego's forward movement must be sacrificed to attend to the desperate soul. Second, the anima shows through her remarkable prostration that sacrificial rituals must be followed. He who has his life will lose it, and he who loses his life for the soul's sake will find it. For an intellectual such as myself, embracing the anima demands the sacrifice of a certain kind of attachment to the rational intellect. This does not mean that I must 'lose my mind' and turn anti-intellectual, as many participants in the 'expressive' men's movement seem to believe. We are not called to drop the mind and go bananas over the 'body'. In his work on the anima, Hillman says that 'the *sacrificium intellectus* in analytical psychology today sometimes becomes perverted from its authentic meaning – dedicating intellect to the Gods – to abandoning the burden of it for tender-mindedness and fuzz'.[13] *Sacrificium intellectus* does not mean getting rid of the intellect to become mushy; it means dedicating one's intellectual energies and skills to the service of the transpersonal and supra-rational world.

For me, the cost of this sacrifice was felt almost immediately

177

in professional terms. Some people saw me as a religious crank, which is part of the human legacy of any conversion experience, and part of the cost of stepping outside the cult of rationality into the service and care of the soul. One cannot properly explain to others why one has 'converted' to a religious point of view, and any attempt to do so results in misunderstanding and bitter division. One simply has to say that one feels called to serve the soul, and leave it at that, hoping that others will not see this announcement as foolish, pretentious, or ridiculously overblown. Two hundred years ago, I would have become a fool for Christ, but today, in the era of the uprising feminine dimension of God, I have become a fool for anima.

MEETING THE SACRED FEMININE: THE GAIN AND THE LOSS

I am impatient for that loss
By which the spirit gains.
James McAuley[14]

Soon after this I had what Jung would call a 'big dream', and I think its resonance and meaning will be felt in my life for many years to come.

I am attending an intellectual conference beside the sea, but I want to leave this place to board a flight to a major city. Upon the plane, I am seated near the front, and I have an excellent view of the surroundings through the pilot's window. We take off, but the plane flies very low, hardly rising above the surface of the landscape. In fact, it keeps flying in circles just above the ground, and at certain points it actually flies beneath some of the unusual landscape formations. I become irritated when I realise that we are flying in large circles, and I wonder when we will actually get to our destination.

The pilot turns around to face the passengers, and he asks us, very seriously, 'Am I flying with believers?' An unknown woman beside me says yes, and I follow her lead with the same affirmation. The pilot then hands this woman a precious token or medallion. Suddenly a holy sanctuary appears just before us. It is shimmering, oval-shaped, with a holy woman seated at the centre, upon a raised throne. The priestess has long hair, wears a long, loose white gown, and is surrounded by sculptured forms and religious iconography. She motions to us to come forward, and the woman beside me hands her the medallion, which she clasps gratefully in her hands.

Then it appears that the plane has crashed. I stand on the sandy beach, looking across the sea at some of the floating wreckage. At first I think I am dead, but it becomes clear that all have survived the crash, since the low-flying plane had hardly any distance to fall. The survivors begin to gather together, searching in the mess for their personal possessions. After some period of disorientation, we begin to hug and greet each other, offering mutual protection and support.

Ever since the incest dream which appeared in Chapter 3, my psychic energy, supported by a father-loving anima, has wanted to move skyward. Hillman was puzzled by this ascensionist impulse, because according to his own theories, anima or soul moves downward toward the depths and 'vales', whereas masculine spirit aspires to the 'peaks'.[15] In one session, Hillman got me to crouch down on the floor, and I was to imagine the skyward energies moving along the spine and then rocketing into space. Was this yoga, Sufism, or Kundalini? The important thing, he said, is that the energy should be allowed to go where it wants to go, only the ego must not be carried away by this spiritual flight. I could see a lot of sense in this. The eagle dreams of Chapter 6 revealed that the relentless upward movement was indeed dangerous, and should be defended against.

Hillman writes that low-flying in dreams is 'part of anima phenomenology'.[16] A flight that does not soar upwards, but hovers near the things of the earth, is not governed by puer, Zeus, or Icarus, but by anima. So this dream has me aboard a different kind of flight, and it is not one that the ego likes or is familiar with. All the figures on the plane, the pilot, the unknown female passenger, and the holy woman, appear to belong to a phenomenology that is new to me. The plane is not only close to the ground, but it actually flies beneath certain natural landscape formations. It will not take the ego where it wants to go. A new kind of anima, not opposed to the earth or ground, but still related to air (intellect, or spirit), has hijacked my life's journey, and I feel as if I am no longer in control.

The pilot demands some firm reassurance. Although I 'believe' in a more transcendent, masculine, goal-oriented journey, I am asked to believe in the new journey. This belief has to be publicly announced and affirmed. The ego must be seen to support the new flight; this is part of the sacrifice it has to make. Presumably, with this admission of faith, a new level of reality becomes discernible. The holy woman and her sacred sanctuary become visible, as it were, out of nowhere. This new sacredness is *relational*: it involves human exchanges, tokens, or sacraments, between the pilot, the passenger, and the divinity. The token or medallion suggests a true symbol (Greek: *sumbolon* = token), whose role is to provide a living, vital connection between the archetypal realm and the real, between the divine and the human. The priestess appears to be a figure of the world-soul, anima mundi, or the spiritual dimension of the created world. She bestows life and wonderment upon us, and in return we give the sacramental token to her.

Jung wrote that an experience of the Self, or divinity, is a devastating loss for the ego.[17] The dream puts this experience in most dramatic terms. The ego feels that it is getting nowhere, and then the entire plane crashes to the ground. It appears that a revelation of the sacred feminine occurs at great personal and physical cost – at least, it does so for the male ego. But it is a revelation that nevertheless puts the ego back upon the earth. The ego is bruised, confused, and disoriented, but it survives. And it has a new sense of purpose, because it has witnessed the anima mundi who infuses all life, who gives meaning to creation, who fills the ordinary with the wonderful glow of the extraordinary. With this return to earth there is a new-found appreciation of community: people hug and greet each other, there is a new warmth and common humanity. When the ego is carried by the winged spirit or mythic eagle to great heights, it is always alone, heroic, self-important. When the anima mundi dumps the ego back to *terra firma*, the 'horizontal' level of community and human engagement is activated.

THE EROTICS OF THE SOUL: DESIRE, SEXUALITY, AND SPIRITUALITY

One can hardly write a short chapter on anima experience without discussing sexuality and desire. It is obvious that anima plays a key role in the onset and experience of the so-called midlife crisis. Notoriously, the arrival of the anima in a man's life is associated with the appearance of the mysterious or desirable 'Unknown Woman' who breaks up marriages, disrupts conventions, and throws a man's life into a mixture of erotic excitement and moral and personal chaos. However, the anima may or may not be linked to an actual human experience of an 'other' woman in a man's life. With or without this external dimension, anima will unsettle and disturb ego consciousness, forcing the man to new states of being and new definitions of self. In some ways, it is easier for men to experience anima externally and in projection upon women, because in this case women act as the convenient carriers for the emotions, passions, energies and feelings that are part of the psychic reality of the anima-complex. If this complex is carried by others, then one is relatively free from the challenges that anima poses to male consciousness.[18]

The more this archetype is projected, the 'freer' the man is to live his life as before, unimpeded by the onslaught of the repressed or the challenge of new and strange emotions. A man's family life and 'external' reality may be in fragments, but the ego preserves basically its former shape and continues as before. Anima therefore threatens both external and internal order, and there are certain 'trade-offs' involved in confining her activity to one or the other plane of reality. However, I am not so dour or puritanical as to believe that men *must* confine this archetypal encounter to the internal plane, even though my own introverted bias would tend to privilege the internal above the external. Anima works on both planes, since for her 'inner' and 'outer' are little more than intellectual fictions or artificial barriers designed to impose masculine order on her unfathomable feminine being.

Because the anima is so wholly 'Other' in a man's psyche, there is a natural tendency for a man at midlife to look beyond, above, or behind his marital partner for the invigorating and libidinous life of the feminine soul. Of course, in many ways, the wife is already the carrier of the man's unconscious anima, but it is precisely because this complex is coming to new consciousness and life that this conventional husband-and-wife pattern is frequently disrupted. The man is plagued by the nagging doubt that his ideal erotic and intellectual partner is to be found outside the marriage, and he finds himself, part-consciously, part-unconsciously, snooping around for the ideal 'soul mate'. If the man is in analytic therapy, he may be told to tone down the search for the unknown woman in the outer sphere, especially if this involves ignoring or abusing the woman to whom he is already betrothed. The chronic sense that one's 'true' soul mate is other than one's present partner is very likely to be the legacy of the mother-complex. The son with a mother-complex, said Jung, has a strong tendency toward promiscuity and Don

181

Juanism. The promiscuous son 'unconsciously seeks his mother in every woman he meets'.[19] The mother is always the unattainable lover, the one who is desired but who cannot be secured.

But the spiritual aspect of the desired 'otherness' must also be respected. If I am not content with my partner it is because I am not content with myself. I know that there is 'more' to reality than I am currently seeing or experiencing. In much cinema and popular culture, the pursuit of the soul turns a man away from his wife, toward either another woman or to an emotional or spiritual undertaking that for the time being appears to be a working vessel for soul-making. In my case, writing is a highly erotic occupation, and I often use 'writing' as my excuse for turning away from wife and family in pursuit of some 'higher' experience of Eros and desire. The images and words on the page help me get closer to the invisible, intangible world of soul and meaning that I so much crave. Interestingly, when I feel I have connected with soul through the ritual act of writing, I always find that I return to my wife and family with renewed interest and energy. Writing is my 'yoga', it is what links me to the divine. When I get scratchy, irritable, moody, it is because I have not had my 'fix' of soul-making, and I know I can get unbearable in human company when I feel hollow inside and without soul-substance.

It seems to me that there is a quite specific correlation between the lack of libidinous contact with soul, and the quantum of sexual energy for the so-called unknown woman. We must at all costs maintain our erotic relations with forces greater than ourselves and larger than the personal ego. Monastic orders were developed to foster and maintain this erotic connection with a higher spiritual reality, and for this reason nuns were 'married' to Christ, and monks 'wedded' to the Holy Mother. The knowledge and practice of these mystic weddings and ritual connections will have to be brought out of religious cloisters and esoteric orders, and distributed widely to the general public, since my own belief is that more 'ordinary' people such as myself are going to arrive spontaneously and independently at a recognition of the need for 'higher' or spiritual dimensions of our erotic life. In the course of any life, lust naturally evolves into Eros, and Eros into something closer to *agape*. If this is the case, then we desperately need to have knowledge about how these transformations occur, how to encourage them, and how to protect our human or 'earthly' marriages from the assaults that take place when desire leaves the domestic situation and heads toward idealised 'heavenly' figures.

In a simple though effective way, the Hollywood movie *Hook* shows how this process takes place in ordinary human experience, and how potentially disruptive the spiritual anima is to the earthly marriage.[20] In the film, Peter Pan loses interest in his lovely and enchanting wife Moira. His own blocked consciousness has lost the capacity to see her natural beauty and enchantment, and at this moment the fantasy figure Tinker Bell appears, as the ultimate anima-fantasy of the modern male (Tinker Bell is played by actress Julia Roberts, of *Pretty Woman* fame). Tinker Bell lures Peter away from his messy and depressing life, and with a pinch of fairy-dust, a wish and a deep longing, they are already up and away.

Tinker Bell and the wife Moira form a pair of anima figures, the one leading away from the world, and the other leading back into worldly commitment and adult responsibility. At the end of his quest, when Peter has recovered his *puer aeternus* or 'Pan' nature, and Hook has been overcome, Tinker Bell sadly realises that the game is over and that Peter must now leave Never Land and return to the ordinary human world. Is this how (usually younger) anima-women feel when their middle-aged married lovers finally 'get themselves together' and go back to resurrect their marriages? At the end of the film, Tinker Bell transforms from a miniature fairy to a full-sized human being. As a 'symbol' of Peter's own anima, Tinker Bell is manifesting in her new personhood the change and development in Peter's psyche. The anima is released from the 'spell' of otherworldliness, and now demands a fuller, more mature existence. However, Peter has profoundly changed as well, and any deep change demands sacrifice. He is forced to relinquish his otherworldly anima (Tinker Bell) and his attachment to the infantile *puer aeternus* (the Lost Boys). In this sense, the growth within Tinker Bell herself is more symbolic than literal. Like Captain Hook, Tinker Bell is an imaginal being, not a human being, and we are not permitted to literalise her place in the story.

Tinker Bell's self-transformation, the growth of the anima, actually heralds Peter's renewed erotic interest in his own wife. As Peter and the adult-sized Tinker Bell kiss, Peter can only think of his wife. We are not meant to feel that Tinker Bell has suddenly been jilted, but we are able to celebrate his renewed interest in Moira, the human world, and in his own role as a human father. The moral of this Hollywood fable is that we recover our humanity, and our erotic attachments to our human partners, when we learn to deal with our erotic connections to archetypal figures. In this sense, cultivating a passionate spiritual or imaginal life is the best thing we can do to recover sexual feeling, and to regain the spontaneous flow of earthly Eros.

TOWARD A NEW UNION OF SPIRIT AND NATURE

I experience desire as a spectrum of instinctual and spiritual possibilities. When I was in my twenties, and strongly under the influence of the mother-complex, desire led me into many sexual liaisons and encounters. My dreams at that stage stood in a compensatory relationship to promiscuous sexuality: they often urged me to refrain from sex, to abandon it partially or altogether in favour of spiritual activities. I once dreamed that I was engaging in sexual intercourse, when I suddenly noticed a huge ulcer on my penis, which prevented me from continuing with the sexual act. Upon close examination, the ulcer was a cluster of gold crystals and the sore seemed to have immense beauty and value. Outside the bedroom, a group of nuns engaging in a ritual procession were banging on dust-bin lids and urging me to join them in their pilgrimage toward a sacred shrine. My partner and I quickly got dressed, and we both joined the procession. The central image of this dream, the painful ulcer that nevertheless has great value (gold) and is a precursor to a spiritual journey, reminded me of Jung's famous remark that 'the Gods have become diseases'.[21] In our purely secular age, the psyche sometimes inflicts disease and hardship in order to deepen our lives in the direction of spiritual meaning.

In those early days, the anima seemed to play the role of a *spiritus rector*, anxious to assert the authority of spirit against the indulgences of the instincts. However, twenty years later, under the influence of a powerful father-complex, my psychic energy has seemed in danger of becoming far too 'spiritualised', so that the opposite kind of one-sidedness has asserted itself. We have already seen how a new kind of anima has emerged; the 'low-flying' anima who refuses spiritual elevation (and the ego's trip), and who brings the spirit back to earth with a miraculous bang. Her wisdom is incarnational, bodily, erotic, and communal. In some ways, I feel the psyche urging me toward a post-patriarchal, non-transcendentalist 'creation spirituality'. Although many leaders of Christianity feel sceptical and even hostile toward Matthew Fox's creation spirituality, my own hunch is that Fox may well be the pioneer of a future religious vision, one that equally validates the body and the spirit, nature and pneuma, the World Mother and the Heavenly Father.[22] Christianity itself must come 'down to earth'; it must be redeemed from its own transcendentalist denial of the feminine, the earthly and the sexual. The Heavenly Father can only be revived today through the agency of the archetypal feminine. The 'descent' into body and matter must begin, not to regress to pre-Christian paganism, but to move onward to a post-patriarchal world where spirit and nature are experienced in a new, transformative wholeness.

In reflecting on how to conclude this chapter, I had the following dream which seems to comment, somewhat humorously and ironically, on many of the themes I have been developing in these pages.

The British monarchy has decided that the divorced Princess Diana is to have an 'official' Australian husband and consort, and I am chosen for that role. The monarchy believes that this will strengthen the ties between Britain and Australia. Whenever the Princess comes down to Australia, I am to accompany her on her many official visits and at all formal occasions. We engage in what seems like endless pomp and ceremony, all in stiff, regal attire. The only thing I dislike is that there is no personal contact with Diana herself. As soon as the ceremonies are over, she typically scuttles off with her British officials, and I never get to be with her.

After a dinner party, I am asked about my role as Australian consort, and I protest bitterly that I do not get any personal time with the Princess. Prince Charles is beside me on this occasion, and he snorts with obvious disapproval. He indicates that I am damn lucky to be this close to royalty, and that I should be more grateful of the honour already bestowed upon me by the monarchy. Apparently, the Princess soon learns of my complaints. At our next gathering, she approaches me after the ceremony, accompanied by a second Princess, a tall, gracious woman wearing a jewelled crown. I am standing with my Australian wife and daughter, and my parents and others are talking with us. Diana and the second Princess approach me, and Diana says: 'Do you want to sleep with me, or her?' Her second reference, made clear by a gesture, is to the other, unknown Princess. I flush with embarrassment, and, looking at my wife and family beside me, I stutter, 'No'. This is a lie, but I find the situation too confronting. Diana walks away with her official party, and I am left with my Australian family, all of us looking at each other in speechless astonishment.

Here we see the ego's relationship with an exalted anima figure in a slightly different light. In the earlier dream, the ego encountered an unknown woman and a holy priestess in a plane (pun intended) above the ground. Now we find a different kind of exaltedness in the figure of a royal princess who has come 'down to earth' in Australia, which is itself the land 'down under'. The dreams keep emphasising that an incarnational process is underway, that spirit is coming down to earth, and that the dangerous gulf between spirit and nature can only be bridged by the archetypal feminine as 'mediatrix',[23] the figure who unites the opposites.

This dream emphasises formality and a good deal of rigidity in the ego–anima relationship. My professional ego, that part of me that daily performs in public, giving speeches and lectures at formal occasions, constantly draws on a spiritualised or intellectual anima for insight and knowledge. Most of my lectures are about imagination, literature, myth, archetypes, and I could not speak with authority on these matters except through the agency of anima. But this relationship is now somewhat conventional, pat, even routine. We turn up to public occasions together, put on our performances, and then go our separate ways. I feel the occasional stimulus of anima during 'animated' moments of my lectures, but I frequently fail to develop any relationship with her outside these events. The whole affair is very cerebral, abstract, icy, and a bit remote.

This relationship now requires more passion and excitement. The ego calls for a more 'intimate' relationship, but this is bound to upset the status quo, the current formal arrangements, the tidy but often routine and sterile events. To 'sleep with' the royal anima suggests to me that Eros and spirit must be brought into a closer relationship. The brash and almost brazen proposition put by this over-formalised soul-figure suggests that she too wants a different relationship, with more heat and passion. Her somewhat sassy suggestion that sex is available with either of the princesses is what Hillman might call 'an archetypal correction to her own sentimentality'.[24] By this proposition, the anima breaks the mould in which I had cast her. She smashes the sexless pedestal upon which she has been placed and trapped. This is an internal feminist campaign: this woman wants to re-experience her libidinal nature. The story of Lady Chatterley, over-sophisticated, stiff and formal, with an unattended erotic life, is here recast at an intrapsychic level.

Interestingly, the ego is made aware that it does not 'belong' to the royal family; it is not grandly archetypal, but it has been appointed to act as consort to a royal figure. This symbolism makes clear a time-honoured religious theme: the ego is not exalted or divine, but acts in an *instrumental* relationship to divine forces. The ego is from a lesser world, and it must not forget its ordinary humanness and servile role. In case the ego has any 'inflated' tendencies, the Prince Charles figure acts as a conservative influence who reminds the ego that it is not a member of the royal family, and that it should not look for increased intimacy. Of course, Charles, as the original royal husband, is also the ego's jealous rival, who will do all he can to prevent the 'formal' relationship from blossoming. In this sense, Charles is an internalised figure of convention and sexual prohibition, a disapproving puritanical superego who will use his 'higher' status to block any eroticised developments.

The ego is unable to acknowledge publicly its erotic longings for the exalted anima. In a flush of embarrassment it says no to her proposition. Behind this inability we could perhaps see the rigid superego figure, with its emphasis on decorum, right behaviour, and manners. There is also fear of shaking the established arrangement; the ego both wants and does not want the present situation to change. And there is a public 'shaming' here: the anima puts the proposition before the earthly wife, child, and the wider family circle. This is critical to the ego's rhetorical rejection. In our secular culture, men are not expected to have a relationship with the divine or archetypal world, let alone develop a passionate or sexualised romance with the sacred feminine. Sexuality is supposed to be 'contained' within the social institution of marriage. 'Sexuality' here can stand for all sorts of things: passionate involvement, energy, fervour, interest. In cultures not governed by shame or guilt, I think it is much easier for men to develop spontaneous and eroticised bondings to spiritual, cultural, or royal figures and realities. We are conditioned to believe that we can have only one focus of erotic attention, and that if our energies move elsewhere we are fickle and unfaithful. This dream shows that a man has several 'wives' and potential 'lovers', and that the earthly marriage is complemented by an unearthly or exalted marriage with an archetypal figure. But the embarrassment is not just to do with sexual infidelity: our secularism makes us embarrassed to be erotically involved with spiritual realities.

The artist Michael Leunig has said that 'in a moment of embarrassment there's a truth present. The embarrassing moments are when control is imperfect, when other people see that there's some big force'.[25] This broader cultural perspective is very helpful. Today we are strangely made to feel guilty about our spiritual lives, because we are not supported by cultural expectations to have eroticised feelings for the archetypal realm. When other people see that 'there's some big force', that we are having a relationship with something huge and archetypal, there is embarrassment all round (the dream has everyone looking at each other in speechless amazement), because our ordinary conditioning has not prepared us for this dimension of experience. We are not expected to mate with spirits, souls, Goddesses, Princesses, or angelic beings. A man's longing for spiritual life is a 'big force' which has been left off the secular agenda and omitted from social reality.

The sexualised longing for the anima must be brought back into public awareness. If it is not, this longing will always take place covertly, secretly, and be acted out in various ways. If our culture were more sexualised, professional men would not feel so burdened by erotic attractions for clients, students, secretaries, and others. What we need to solve the problem of sexual harassment in the workplace in not more prohibitions and punishments, but a new general receptivity to Eros and desire. The cure must be homeopathic: like cures like, or a release of Eros cures the repressed abuses of Eros. I believe this dream is asking me to be more erotic and spontaneous in my life and career. The 'spirit' that inspires our work cannot afford to be remote, aloof, and dully routine. Sometimes we have to take risks, sometimes we have to let others see there is 'some big force' to which we are bound. Sometimes men have to acknowledge that irrational factors hold sway over us. When we can admit these risks and epiphanies without feeling ashamed, then we have cured ourselves, and we have also started to cure our culture of its secular rigidity and puritanical obsessiveness. Desire must be released from its entrapment in conventions, and our longing allowed to reach out to that archetypal world which also longs to be embraced by us.

8

CONCLUSION
Revolution in the soul

We are living in what the Greeks called the *kairos*, the right moment, for a 'metamorphosis of the gods', of the fundamental principles and symbols.

Jung[1]

RECOGNISING THE FORCES THAT BIND

In this book I have been exploring ways in which men can achieve increased social-political and psychospiritual liberation. I have used my own life and experience to illustrate ways in which liberation is lost or compromised, and ways in which liberation can be recovered or renegotiated. By 'liberation' I do not mean shooting down everything that gets in the ego's path. On the contrary, the greatest liberation of all arises when we are able to shed the demands of the ego and its tyrannical hold upon the energies of personality. Liberation, for me, means first seeing and locating the forces that bind us in both psyche and society, and developing a fuller awareness of these forces so that we might achieve a modicum of independence from them. I am too steeped in the history of culture and in the psychology of the unconscious to subscribe to a utopian dream of 'total' freedom. The best we can aim for is a pattern of life where due recognition is given to psychic and social determinisms, and where consciousness works to develop its own separate authority, even as it respects the authority of the traditions that bind and constrict it. In archetypal terms, the two big obstacles to a liberated consciousness can be categorised as *paternal* and *maternal domination*. Our psychosocial lives are lived in relationship to, and in reaction against, the primal figures of the father and mother archetypes. Acknowledging the power and might of these figures,

189

without falling victim to them in unconscious domination, is the real challenge facing men today.

With regard to paternal domination, we have to become acquainted with university-style, profeminist liberational discourses. These discourses understand the insidious nature of the patriarchy, how it insinuates itself in social and psychological experience, and how men quickly become enlisted in, and devoured by, the supremacist project of the tyrannical father. Profeminist discourse recognises that, despite recent talk about the 'end' of patriarchy, social-political patriarchy is still alive and well, and the negative senex may even be undergoing an injection of new life now that it knows it is being constructed as 'politically incorrect'. Profeminist discourse sees through the smiling, kindly patriarch who seductively invites the son to become 'initiated' into the patrilineal community. It recognises that, in exchange for social acceptance and gender certainty, the son sacrifices much of his individuality and becomes absorbed into an unconscious social and political ideology. This ideology is hegemonic, coercive, and constructed in opposition to women and the feminine. If the son wants to be politically creative in today's world, he must first become conscious of patriarchy as a psychosocial reality, and then struggle in personal and political ways to oppose its dominance.

One danger of the university-style discourses is that they tend to demonise all styles of masculinity, not just the patriarchal-hegemonic masculinity that is rightly under attack. There is a corresponding tendency to idealise the maternal and the feminine, and a general unwillingness to see how men can rid themselves of paternal domination, only to succumb to domination by the mother. The 'devouring' nature of the maternal archetype is not recognised, since this side is blocked by systematic idealisation. Hence, the need for men to develop enough masculine potential to 'oppose' the dragon mother is not respected, and the strengthening of the masculine against the might of the primal feminine is viewed as so much stupid masculine heroics and negative social programming. There is a marked tendency to fall into an unresolved Oedipal cycle, where the son 'kills' the father's authority and uncritically adopts the mother's view of the world. When Oedipus governs our erstwhile 'liberation', we become embroiled in a politics of guilt, crippled by doubt and self-loathing, and deprived of the phallic-creative energy needed to bring about change. The son never grows up; his criticisms are puerile and extremist, and he lacks the ability to embrace or affirm. The radical academic discourses fail to realise that, without the father, the son can never reach masculine maturity. Today's universities provide us with many examples of the 'mother-devoured' intellectual: hypercritical, pedantic, effeminate, jargon-ridden, ineffectual, unable to communicate with 'ordinary' men, and with a semi-incoherent rage against conventional society.

The popular 'Jungian' discourses recognise full well that masculinity must be developed so that it can oppose the mother-complex. The mythopoetic men's movement recognises that Oedipus cannot be our model for the future, and that archetypal masculinity must be embraced, not killed. It understands that the father holds the key to the son's masculine development. The danger here is the easy slide into idealisation of the father and paternal domination. This movement does not distinguish clearly enough between the old and the new, between patriarchal and post-patriarchal styles of masculinity. The tyrannical, killing side of the negative father is obliterated in a vaguely romantic, idealising haze. These men have effectively 'killed' the mother and 'married' the father. By returning like prodigal sons to the social father, formerly 'soft' or mother-complexed men fail to see that the 'initiation' that the father offers comes at a great price. As these men submit themselves to a belated initiation, they are sacrificing their individuality in favour of the institution of patriarchy. Patriarchy does not tolerate difference, it despises creative individuality, and the difficult state of standing outside the mainstream symbolic system is constructed merely as an 'uninitiated' condition. The emotional sentimentality of this movement makes it impossible to view with clarity and criticism the actual psychodynamics at work.

What the father-loving men's movement lacks is a keen awareness that we serve the spirit of the father best by challenging and criticising his established traditions. If the father's traditions are to maintain integrity and not be allowed to lapse into parody or corruption, they must be updated, reconstructed, and revived. The archetypal son actually personifies the creative life of the archetypal father, and if that life is not put to good use, the father has been neglected and betrayed. 'Ironically, the perfection the senex seeks is reflected in his antagonist and son'.[2] The father–son relationship is therefore full of amazing complexity and paradox. The son's duty is to change the father, even as the father's role is to tame and mature the son. If the creative son fails to stir the social stew, it sets hard and cannot be served up to the wider community. If the puer submits entirely to the powerful senex, there has not been any spiritual regeneration in psyche, family, or society. The father knows, deep down, that the son who submits without a fight is a son who has failed his archetypal mission.

The sentimental impulse that emphasises 'unity' with the father has also betrayed the feminine spirit of the time. If patriarchy is being gradually disrupted, it is because the rejected and excluded feminine forces are awakening to a new life, and demand to be heard. Any movement which blandly 'seals over' the cracks and fault-lines that are appearing in the fabric of patriarchy must therefore be construed as historically backward and regressive. The uprising feminine spirit must be allowed to create havoc within the comfort-zones of patriarchy. This perspective is best understood by radical academic discourses, although here the argument is confined largely to women's political experience, due to the materialistic and extraverted bias of mainstream academic enquiry. The reactivation of the feminine impacts upon men and women's experience, and pointing out this 'universal' or archetypal dimension must not blind us to the fact that it is traditionally women who have suffered most as a result of the repression and denigration of the feminine. Materialistic commentators will habitually misread any attempt to emphasise the transgendered nature of this repression as a ploy to avoid the direct challenge of political feminism.

If individual men feel impelled to develop their masculinity they must realise that they perform this task in a cultural context that is moving in the reverse direction. Here I would remind James Hillman of the contradictions involved in his participation in Robert Bly's masculinity-generating men's movement. I would also remind this movement what its own 'leading psychologist' said before he was drawn into the cult of Iron John. In 1972, in *The Myth of Analysis*, Hillman wrote:

> We are cured when we are no longer only masculine in psyche, no matter whether we are male or female in biology. . . . *The end of analysis coincides with the acceptance of femininity.*[3]

Robert Bly has said that James Hillman 'is the most lively and original psychologist we have had in America since William James',[4] and, based on the above statement, we can certainly agree with him. Hillman was right on target in the 1970s, brilliantly alert to the progressive spirit of the time, and able to speak for and on behalf of this feminine spirit with eloquence and poise. But what happened after that? I am only able to speculate that the brilliant puer became assimilated to a new-age version of the senex, as promoted by Robert Bly. Hillman has also suffered personal and professional disappointments, which seem to have had the effect of generating a wave of protective conservatism.

THE IDEA OF CHANGE IN A MATERIALIST PARADIGM

The hope of the future lies in the capacity of ordinary men to change, and in a hegemonic-masculinist culture 'change' means the capacity of men to accept the feminine archetypal principle within women, society, and themselves. It is not impossible for academic and intellectual men like myself to change, since we live and work in a critical environment where collective norms and prevailing stereotypes are frequently assigned a negative value. (But the counter-establishment stereotypes within our ranks are often promoted without criticism.) However, in the so-called real world it is still far too easy for men to conform to patriarchal stereotypes in an uncritical and unthinking way. Moreover, men are vigorously encouraged to conform by virtue of a set of social rewards that Bob Connell calls the 'patriarchal dividend'.[5] Patriarchy has been a self-serving and self-perpetuating system, and it is difficult to stop what tradition and social structure have mobilised and upheld.

In the radical profeminist discourses, we find both an optimistic view that argues that change is possible because 'patriarchy' is merely a social construct that can be undone by progress, and a markedly pessimistic view that says men will not change because the patriarchal dividend and its attendant privileges are too attractive to those who gain from these privileges. In both cases, a lack of respect for the archetypal dimension of masculinity and patriarchy blinds these discourses to certain awarenesses that can only be gleaned from depth psychology.

Some of the radical optimism is shallow because it does not see the archetypal nuclei that underpin the traditional images of masculinity. A brave new discourse, supported by social construc-tivism, is able to announce that patriarchal masculinity, 'does not really exist in the sense that we are led to think it exists'. Masculinity 'exists as ideology; it exists as scripted behavior'; it is a mere construct that we can readily deconstruct.[6] According to this view, our inherited concepts of masculinity are the result of nurture, not nature, and progressive social engineers can set to work to

193

reprogramme society in a new and liberating way. We can only support this view if we forget the lessons of history and the psychology of the unconscious. Social stereotypes do not emerge out of thin air; they represent an amalgam of nurture and nature, culture and psyche, time and eternity. The way in which masculinity is socially reproduced is of course a product of ideology, but this ideology has archetypal foundations that are ignored at our own peril. At the basis of patriarchy stands Chronos-Saturn, the devouring father – and who are we to say that he 'does not really exist'? He is not a person, not a material reality, but he has effect and impact that makes him more 'real' than reality itself. A positivist social science that is blind to archetypal process will not be able to support us in our work of liberation, and I guess that is partly why its influence is largely confined to the academic sphere.

If change is simply a matter of deconstructing what has been constructed, then why hasn't a lot of change occurred, given that more of us are becoming educated and enlightened? When sweeping reform does not eventuate, many sociologists and radical thinkers become depressed and pessimistic. They typically assume that men won't change because it is not in their interests to change.[7] As Kenneth Clatterbaugh puts it, feminist scholars see men as having 'too much to lose to be reliable allies in the struggle against patriarchy'.[8] If men are viewed as conditioned pieces within a set patriarchal system, there is virtually no hope for us, because we will never voluntarily renounce our supremacist position or hegemonic power. The point is taken, but the argument hinges on the thoroughly materialistic premise that men are simply parts of a social process. Fortunately, men are more than mere cogs in a social machine. We also have psyches or souls, are moved by archetypal forces, and belong to the collective psyche. To my materialistic colleagues I can only say, as Hamlet said to his fellow student:

> There are more things in heaven and earth, Horatio,
> Than are dreamt of in your philosophy.[9]

MEN, FATE, AND THE FEMININE SPIRIT

We participate in a psychic environment in which the feminine archetypal principle is demanding, and bringing about, real and substantial change. There is a radical 'feminism' at work on the inside of the Western psyche, and this has been constellated as a compensatory response to the patriarchal excesses of consciousness. When internal psychic reality can no longer support the masculine persona, when the spirit of the time opposes the patriarchal stereo-types, no man is safe from the 'houndings' of feminism, because it is right inside his own being. When the feminine soul can no longer stand the destructive charade that passes for 'progress', 'science', 'knowledge', 'heroism', then we will certainly have change, either with or without the cooperation of men. Jung quotes Cleanthes: 'The Fates lead the willing, but drag the unwilling'.[10]

If men do not change, we will be wounded, handicapped, or maimed by the soul. Jung said that 'the Gods have become diseases', not because they are diseases, but because in our materi-alist culture they have no way to express themselves other than as agents of pathology and as 'irritants' of change. If the feminine archetypal principle is not consciously admitted into masculinity, it will be unconsciously, and usually negatively, admitted. Hence, rather than 'integrate' the feminine, men will become strangely effeminate, moody, and irritable, and the rationalistic male consciousness will be invaded by 'irrational' psychic contents. Jung speaks about a man becoming like 'an inferior woman', when no attempt is made to assimilate or integrate the anima complex.[11] If the feminine is not admitted into psyche it may simply invade the body: as impotence, weakness, exhaustion, tiredness, or 'burnout'.

Gloria Steinem has said that men must overcome their fear of the feminine: 'they have nothing to lose but their coronaries'.[12] I take this advice very seriously. The feminine soul will, and often does, attack the feeling heart of the manly man. The men who finally admit that they must change have often arrived at this aware-ness through some kind of trauma or failure. Men sometimes have to suffer a nervous breakdown, unbearable stress, chronic fatigue, a broken marriage, the first heart attack, or a debilitating disease before they think about 'reconstructing' their lives. Only a big shock will awaken some men from the shallowness of their patriarchal role, and urge them to embark on a search in which the soul is redeemed.

> Now that my ladder's gone
> I must lie down where all the ladders start
> In the foul rag and bone shop of the heart.[13]

Only when the symbolic 'ladder' has been removed, when we can no longer go on or upwards to patriarchal heights, are we forced to deal with the wholly unglamorous life of the feeling heart.

When the persona has been rent asunder, men are exposed to the psychic life which is opposed to (or at least 'compensatory' to) the directions and values of their conventional masculinity. However, it is by no means the case that all men who fall into the psychic pit emerge renewed and reborn. In recent years, I have personally witnessed several colleagues and friends who have fallen into the pit and never returned to life. In my own country, the suicide rate for mature and adolescent males is soaring, and this would suggest to me that the foul rag and bone shop is sometimes too much to bear. Men fall into the deep unconscious and see only desolation, darkness, and despair. According to Jung, the emotionality of the anima 'might explain the very much greater number of suicides among men'.[14] But it could also be the case that, as argued in Chapter 4, men instinctively sense that an old 'self' has to die, and lacking any rituals to contain this psychic death, the desire for change becomes a tragic and literal death of the human being.

If the soul of man is on the rampage, we have to deal with a dramatic internal feminism that protests against internal patriarchal oppression. In this sense, the negative and fearful response that some men develop toward women and especially to 'feminism' can be interpreted as a Freudian 'reaction formation' to what is happening on the inside. Men are being pursued by an angry and denied anima-complex, and this internal drama is often conveniently projected upon women. Men with phobic responses to women seem to find their way into the men's liberation movement, where they ignite and stir up these same archetypal fantasies in other men. Some men cannot tolerate the idea that significant forces beyond their control are threatening to redefine their lives and behavioural patterns, so this danger is defensively projected outside and literalised as an external threat. Men can go to great lengths to counter what they perceive as the lethal threat posed by 'angry' wives and 'hounding' feminisms, but these fantasies urgently need to be seen through for the tell-tale symptomatic expressions that they are.

Our culture is experiencing what could be called a *frustration of archetypal intent*.[15] The psyche pushes the feminine into our lives, and men keep failing to achieve any satisfactory integration. Adler's notion of the 'masculine protest' may also be theoretically useful.[16] Adler felt that a showy 'masculine protest', a tough and strong resistance from a psychic content under threat, can be kept up for a limited time, but eventually the protesting content collapses in exhaustion because the machismo is not only artificial, but it actually depletes the entire psychic economy upon which it is based. Jung felt the same way about the repression of archetypal intent: if the psyche wants change, this command is frustrated at our peril. Men fail to see that what they style as the 'enemy' of their masculinity wants to transform them, not destroy them. The rising feminine in our time is looked upon as a devouring maw, not as the creative and inspired archetypal partner of masculine consciousness. The male conundrum is that the creative feminine is forced into an adversarial role by our continued resistance, so we never allow the feminine to transform us.

THE BOY WITH HIS DRAGON, THE MAN WITH SOUL

This leads us to a final reflection about the kind of masculinity that keeps blocking the soul's advances. Freud and Jung knew that masculine identity is an ongoing struggle and a site of endless psychological conflict. The young male ego relates to the feminine as mother, and, although the primal parent is first experienced as nurturing and supportive, she is soon felt to be a dangerous threat to consciousness and phallic security. The heroic ego rises up to oppose the maternal dragon, or in clinical terms it defeats the mother-complex. After this developmental crisis, the ego is always on guard against the feminine, sensing that it is about to undermine or destroy it. The male ego, caught in the heroic stance, thenceforth strives to 'overcome' the feminine in inner and outer worlds. The cry of the boyish Western hero is 'away from the feminine'. As so many writers have commented, modern man is 'in flight from woman', since woman appears to embody the suffocating maternal matrix from which he must flee.[17] The feminine has castrating teeth, the womb is a *vagina dentata*, and the boy-hero has to get the hell out of there.

When boyishness dominates a culture, 'real men' are represented as men who have conquered the feminine and divested themselves of feminine influence. 'True' masculinity is that which defeats, slays, controls, overwhelms, and outwits the feminine. This operates internally as a suppression of the unconscious, of feeling, emotion, intuition, body-awareness, Eros, connection-making, beauty, and aesthetics, and externally as the suppression and domination of women, gay men, and all those who fail to demonstrate or express hegemonic masculine prowess. The feminine is then linked with weakness, not because the feminine is weak, but because boyish consciousness feels weakened and vulnerable before the feminine. The patriarchal idea that the feminine is weak is a defensive strategy designed to protect men from the overwhelming power of the feminine. The feminine is devalued because it is feared that masculinity will be disintegrated (in Freud's language, 'castrated') when it comes into contact with it. In pubertal boys, at the stage where male-bonding is paramount and where confirmation and support is sought from male peers and fathers, girls and women are avoided almost as if they possessed some magical power that might destroy a budding masculinity and drag identity back into the matrix. Boys sometimes fear that association with girls and women will render them weak and 'effeminate'.

We can strive to educate boys to feel otherwise, but for nascent masculinity the feminine is all-mother and it makes the ego feel insecure and inadequate. There is no possibility of an equal relationship, because the mother-image dwarfs the masculine as her 'son'. We are not dealing merely with 'sexist' conditioning, but with an archetypal predisposition that cannot be corrected by a moral attitude that preaches against prejudice and misogyny. Unless the inward psychological dynamics are properly understood the male fear of the feminine will continue as before, only surrounded in a haze of impenetrable guilt and 'explained away' by reductive polit-ical argument. Men urgently require psychological insight into the psychodynamics of their masculine journey, so that the 'dragon' can be realised as an inner figure, and not projected upon women or the social feminine.

In the myths of mature masculinity, the feminine (as anima) stops opposing consciousness and starts supporting and comple-menting it. This is the meaning behind the motifs of the 'slaying of the dragon' and the 'marrying of the maiden'. Hegemonic masculinity appears to have forgotten these foundation myths of our culture. Patriarchy does not trust the feminine to be creative and supportive; it always imagines that it will undermine its authority, which is another way of saying that patriarchal masculinity is a structurally infantile and deficient form of masculinity. Western masculinist culture still does not know the anima or soul. So long as the feminine remains 'mother', the male ego remains 'son' and 'infant'. If the male ego shows genuine maturity, the teeth will fall out of the mythical womb, and adult intercourse and partnership will be achieved. An American porn artist spreads her legs during her performances, and asks the men in the audience to closely examine her genitals: 'Look guys', she says, 'no teeth!'. What continues to be resisted in the West, but forced upon us by the psyche, is a necessary partnership with the creative feminine power.

LEADERSHIP FROM UNCONVENTIONAL MEN

My own youthful identification with the feminine, outlined in Chapter 3, was fitting for a mother's son who had yet to touch the dynamic power of his own repressed masculinity. Identification with the feminine gave me the kind of 'feminist' outlook that academic gender studies would applaud, but which depth psychology would recognise as stunted masculine development caused by a mother-complex. My later immersion in masculine archetypal contents, described in Chapters 5 and 6, was a compensatory reaction to the long-standing fusion with archetypal femininity, a fusion fostered by years of university-style feminism.

As a young man growing up in outback Australia, I was frequently made aware that my presence and 'feminine' demeanour constituted an emotional 'affront' to the macho boys and men around me. I was pushed around in the schoolyard by youths who felt threatened by my otherness, and for several years I expected to be bashed or chased by more conventional boys. 'Pretty boy', 'poetry boy', 'cissy', were the frequent taunts at recess or after school. When I began to write this book on men's experience, I could easily have fallen into the trap of writing a Cissy's Revenge – an antimasculinist diatribe against conventional men. But I could not seek revenge in this way, because so much of my analysis and self-analysis brought up the buried masculine elements – phallic pride, aggression, anger, ambition, drive – that had previously been swallowed by the mother-complex. Although conventional males experience an early 'attack' of testosterone at about 12 or 13, I would have my own backlog of masculinity to contend with from about the age of 32. The grown-up cissy would repeat in more sophisticated and indirect ways (such as professional ambition), the typical masculine agenda that we expect to see played out in the schoolyard.

When my belated masculinity got too full of itself, it was subsequently checked and balanced by a newly rising feminine principle. This was no longer the mother-complex, but the awesome challenge of the anima or soul. I now see that I had not betrayed the feminine by focusing on masculine energies, but I had simply made a kind of detour around it. It seems to me that the feminine spirit supports the development of the masculine, if only so that 'she' can secure for herself a more mature and viable partner. 'The anima cannot live without the ego and seeks it passionately'.[18] If the rising feminine in our time has a salvational intent and a mission of world-redemption, then she pursues her goals best by weaning men away from the inertia of the primal mother toward a life of activity and service in support of the anima.

At this time in history, where traditional masculinity is threatened with collapse and where ordinary men are thrown back upon themselves without any psychological knowledge or resources, it is certainly time for the 'feminine' men to step forward and to show the way out of the crisis. Cissies pushed around in the schoolyard are very often the grown-up therapists and inspired lecturers who guide ordinary men to a more rich and rewarding life. The secret is to lead masculinity onward to new, post-patriarchal definitions, and the best ones to conduct this development are the feminine men, the gays, and the misfits who were never in the first place beneficiaries of the patriarchal dividend.

NOTES

References to the writings of C. G. Jung will be indicated by the essay or chapter, followed by *CW* (*Collected Works*), the volume number, and paragraph number. All references are to *The Collected Works of C. G. Jung*, translated by R. F. C. Hull, edited by H. Read, M. Fordham, G. Adler, and William McGuire, and published in England by Routledge, London, and in America by Princeton University Press, Bollingen Series XX, 1953–1992. There are 20 volumes in the collected works, plus four supplementary volumes.

Epigraphs

1 Shere Hite, *Women and Love*, London: Penguin, 1987, p. 685.
2 Alix Pirani, *The Absent Father: Crisis and Creativity*, London: Arkana, 1989, p. xiii.
3 James Hillman, 'On Psychological Femininity', in *The Myth of Analysis* (1972), NY: Harper & Row, 1978, p. 292.
4 Tom Absher, *Men and the Goddess*, Rochester, VT: Park Street Press, 1990, p. xiii.

POLEMICAL INTRODUCTION

1 This Jungian tradition would include the works of Erich Neumann, Edward C. Whitmont, Ann Ulanov, Marion Woodman, Naomi Goldenberg, Demaris Wehr, Carole Douglas, Carol Schreier Rupprecht, and many other writers on 'the rising feminine' too numerous to mention.
2 The best and most lively source for the classic Greek myths is still C. Kerenyi, *The Gods of the Greeks* (1951), London: Thames and Hudson, 1976. For Chronos-Saturn, see Kerenyi, Chapter 2.
3 Robert Bly, *Iron John: A Book About Men*, Reading, Mass.: Addison-Wesley, 1990.

4 R. W. Connell, *Masculinities*, Berkeley, Cal.: University of California Press, 1995; and Sydney: Allen & Unwin, 1995, p. 13.
5 See especially Andrew Samuels, *The Political Psyche*, London: Routledge, 1993; *The Plural Psyche*, London: Routledge, 1989; *The Father: Contemporary Jungian Perspectives*, New York University Press, 1986; and *Jung and the Post-Jungians*, London: Routledge, 1985.
6 See especially James Hillman, *The Myth of Analysis* (1972), NY: Harper & Row, 1978; *Re-Visioning Psychology* (1975), NY: Harper Perennial, 1992; and *The Dream and the Underworld*, NY: Harper & Row, 1979.
7 Peter Tatham, *The Makings of Maleness*, London: Karnac Books, 1992; Peter O'Connor, *The Inner Man*, Sydney: Pan Macmillan, 1993; James Wyly, *The Phallic Quest*, Toronto: Inner City Books, 1989; James Hollis, *Under Saturn's Shadow*, Toronto: Inner City Books, 1994; William Doty, *Myths of Masculinity*, NY: Crossroad, 1993; Robert H. Hopcke, *Jung, Jungians, and Homosexuality*, Boston: Shambhala, 1989.
8 See Anthony Elliott, *Psychoanalytic Theory*, Oxford: Blackwell, 1994.
9 Robert Moore and Douglas Gillette, *King, Warrior, Magician, Lover*, San Francisco, Cal.: HarperCollins, 1990, pp. 7–9.
10 This is the title of Chapter 4 of Robert Bly's *Iron John*, and virtually an article of faith in the mythopoetic men's movement.
11 Moore and Gillette, op. cit., p. 10.
12 See Chapter 2 of this book for an examination of the idealised father in the men's movement.
13 Such handbooks and manuals include *The King Within*, *The Warrior Within*, *The Magician Within*, etc., all by Robert Moore and Douglas Gillette, and published by Avon Books, New York.
14 Guy Corneau, *Absent Fathers, Lost Sons*, Boston: Shambhala, 1991; and Alfred Collins, *Fatherson: A Self Psychology of the Archetypal Masculine*, Wilmette, Ill.: Chiron, 1994.
15 Gregory Max Vogt, *Return to Father*, Dallas: Spring Publications, 1991.
16 Robert Bly, 'What Men Really Want', an interview with Keith Thompson, originally published in *New Age Journal*, May 1982, and reworked as the opening chapter of *Iron John*. The original interview format is preserved in Keith Thompson (ed.) *Views From the Male World*, London: HarperCollins, 1992, pp. 16–23.
17 For references to academic profeminist men's studies, see references to Chapter 2.
18 Kerenyi, op. cit., p. 23.
19 William Blake, 'Proverbs of Hell', in *The Marriage of Heaven and Hell* (1793), in Geoffrey Keynes (ed.) *The Complete Writings of William Blake*, Oxford University Press, 1976, p. 151.
20 Jung, 'The Self', *Aion* (1951), *CW* 9, ii, para. 47.
21 Robert Johnson, *He: Understanding Masculine Psychology* (1974), NY: Harper & Row, 1977, p. 7.

22 Robert Johnson, *She: Understanding Feminine Psychology* (1976), NY: Harper & Row, 1977; *The Psychology of Romantic Love*, London: Routledge & Kegan Paul, 1984.
23 Lyn Segal, *Slow Motion: Changing Masculinities, Changing Men*, London: Virago, 1990; Susan Faludi, *Backlash: The Undeclared War Against Women*, NY: Crown, 1991.
24 Segal, op. cit., p. xii. This is not Lynne Segal's view, but her characterisation of a certain pessimistic tradition of writing.
25 Segal, op. cit., p. xiii.
26 An interesting article on the revisioning of 'inner' and 'outer' in Samuels and Hillman is Dolores E. Brien, 'Challenging the Boundaries: James Hillman and Andrew Samuels', *The Round Table Review* (Pennsylvania), Vol. 3, No. 2., December 1995, pp. 1–11.
27 James Hillman, *We've Had a Hundred Years of Psychotherapy and the World is Getting Worse*, San Francisco, Cal.: HarperCollins, 1993.
28 Warren Farrell, *The Myth of Male Power*, NY: Random House, 1994.
29 The words of Australian feminist, Eva Cox, in a debate with Warren Farrell on Australian Broadcasting Corporation television, October 1993.
30 Kenneth Clatterbaugh's *Contemporary Perspectives on Masculinity*, Boulder, Col.: Westview Press, 1990.
31 Jung, *Psychological Types* (1921), *CW* 6, para. 119.

1 ARCHETYPES, GODS, MEN AND WOMEN

1 Jung, *Mysterium Coniunctionis* (1955–1956), *CW* 14, para. 503.
2 Kenneth Clatterbaugh, *Contemporary Perspectives on Masculinity*, Boulder, Col.: Westview Press, 1990, p. 101.
3 Clarissa Pinkola Estes, *Women Who Run With the Wolves: Contacting the Power of the Wild Woman*, London: Rider, 1992, p. 21.
4 Jung, 'The Relations between the Ego and the Unconscious' (1928), *CW* 7, para. 224.
5 Jung, 'Identification with the Collective Psyche' (1928), *CW* 7, para. 260.
6 Ibid.
7 Jung, 'We must constantly bear in mind that what we mean by 'archetype' is in itself irrepresentable, but has effects which make visualizations of it possible, namely, the archetypal images and ideas', in 'On the Nature of the Psyche' (1947–1954), *CW* 8, para. 417.
8 Jean Shinoda Bolen, *Goddesses in Everywoman*, NY: Harper Colophon, 1985, pp. 22–23.
9 Jean Shinoda Bolen, *Gods in Everyman*, NY: Harper Colophon, 1989.
10 James Hillman, 'Anima I', *Spring 1973* (New York), p. 111; reprinted in James Hillman *Anima: An Anatomy of a Personified Notion*, Dallas, Tex.: Spring Publications, 1985, p. 53.
11 Patricia Berry, 'The Dogma of Gender', in *Echo's Subtle Body*, Dallas, Tex.: Spring Publications, 1982.

12 David Wilde, 'A Reply to Andrew Samuels', *Harvest* (London), Vol. 35, 1990, p. 198.

13 Mary Daly, *Outercourse*, San Francisco, Cal.: HarperCollins, 1992, p. 203f.

14 The 1991 National Women and Drugs Conference at the University of Melbourne; conference proceedings published as *Changing the Story*, Lisa Frank (ed.), Melbourne: Addiction Research Institute, 1991.

15 See Linda Leonard, *The Wounded Woman*, Athens, Ohio: Swallow Press, 1982.

16 Jung, 'Women in Europe' (1927), *CW* 10, para. 254.

17 Jung, 'The Syzygy: Anima and Animus' (1951), *CW* 9, ii, para. 29.

18 James Hillman, *The Myth of Analysis* (1972), NY: Harper & Row, 1978, p. 50.

19 Jung, 'Woman in Europe' (1927), *CW* 10, para. 243.

20 Anthony Storr, *Jung*, London: Fontana/Collins, 1973, p. 48.

21 Wilde, op. cit., p. 196.

22 Andrew Samuels, 'Beyond the Feminine Principle: a Post-Jungian Viewpoint', *Harvest*, Vol. 34, 1988, p. 67.

23 Jung, op. cit., para. 29.

24 Ibid.

25 See Marie-Louise von Franz, 'The Process of Individuation', in C.G. Jung (ed.) *Man and His Symbols*, NY: Doubleday, 1964; and M. Esther Harding, *The Way of All Women* (1933), NY: G. P. Putnam's Sons, 1970; Esther Harding, *Women's Mysteries*, NY: Harper & Row, 1976; Barbara Hannah, *Striving Towards Wholeness*, NY: G. P. Putnam's Sons, 1971; Emma Jung, *Animus and Anima* (1957), Dallas: Spring Publications, 1981; Jolande Jacobi, *The Way of Individuation*, London: Hodder & Stoughton, 1967.

26 Mary Daly, *Gyn/Ecology: The Metaethics of Radical Feminism*, Boston: Beacon Press, 1978, p. 280.

27 Naomi Goldenberg, *The Changing of the Gods*, Boston: Beacon Press, 1979; and Berry, op. cit..

28 Anna Belford Ulanov, *Receiving Woman: Studies in the Psychology and Theology of the Feminine*, Philadelphia, Penn.: Westminster Press, 1981, pp. 73–74.

29 D. H. Lawrence, *Selected Essays* (1929), ed. Richard Aldington, Harmondsworth: Penguin, 1968, p. 19.

30 Even the anti-Jungian scholar Bob Connell has to admit that this masculine and feminine polarity was 'a progressive position in the 1920s', *Masculinities*, Berkeley, Cal.: University of California Press, 1995; and Sydney: Allen & Unwin, 1995, p. 13.

31 Jung, 'Woman in Europe' (1927), *CW* 10, para. 243.

32 See Chapter 2 for my ideas about how ongoing creativity must relate to established tradition.

33 Daly, *Gyn/Ecology*, op. cit.

34 Gareth Hill, *Masculine and Feminine*, Boston: Shambhala, 1992, p. xiv.

35 John Beebe, in his 'Introduction' to Jung, *Aspects of the Masculine*, Princeton, NJ: Princeton University Press, 1989, p. xv.

36 Hill, op. cit., p. 31.

37 Eugene Monick, *Castration and Male Rage*, Toronto: Inner City Books, 1991, pp. 11–12.

38 Richard Noll, *The Jung Cult: Origins of a Charismatic Movement*, Princeton, NJ: Princeton University Press, 1994.

39 Andrew Samuels, *The Political Psyche*, London: Routledge, 1993, p. 188.

40 Andrew Samuels, *The Plural Psyche*, London: Routledge, 1989, p. 100.

41 Connell, op. cit., pp. 13–14.

2 THE FATHER'S ABSENCE AND DEVOURING PRESENCE

1 James Hillman, 'The "Negative" Senex and a Renaissance Solution', *Spring 1975* (New York), p. 83.

2 On the motif of the sick king in fairytales, see Marie-Louise von Franz, *An Introduction to the Interpretation of Fairytales* (1970), Dallas: Spring Publications, 1978.

3 See Marion Woodman, *Conscious Femininity*, Toronto: Inner City, 1993.

4 W. B. Yeats, 'The Second Coming' (1920), in T. Webb (ed.) *W. B. Yeats, Selected Poetry*, London: Penguin, 1991, p. 124.

5 James Hollis, in an untitled review of Guy Corneau's *Absent Fathers, Lost Sons*, in *Quadrant* (NY), Vol. 25, No. 1, 1992, p. 134.

6 Sam Osherson, *Finding our Fathers*, NY: Fawcett Columbine, 1986.

7 See Alexander Mitscherlich, *Society Without the Father*, London: Tavistock, 1969.

8 James Hollis, op. cit.

9 James Hillman, 'The Great Mother, Her Son, Her Hero, and the Puer' (1973), in Patricia Berry (ed.), *Fathers and Mothers*, Second Edition, Dallas: Spring Publications, 1990, p. 167.

10 'Kronos, Rhea and Zeus', in C. Kerenyi, *The Gods of the Greeks* (1951), London: Thames and Hudson, 1976, pp. 22–23.

11 F. Guirand, 'Greek Mythology', in *New Larousse Encyclopedia of Mythology* (1959), London: Hamlyn, 1978, p. 91.

12 Kerenyi, op. cit., p. 23.

13 Michael Kaufman (ed.) *Beyond Patriarchy*, Toronto: Oxford University Press, 1987; Rowena Chapman and Jonathan Rutherford (eds) *Male Order: Unwrapping Masculinity*, London: Lawrence and Wishart, 1988; Jonathan Stoltenberg (ed.) *Refusing to Be a Man*, NY: Meridian, 1990; Harry Brod (ed.) *The Making of Masculinities: The New Men's Studies*, London: Allen & Unwin, 1987.

14 Francis Baumli (ed.) *Men Freeing Men: Exploding the Myth of the Traditional Male*, Jersey City, NJ: New Atlantis, 1985.

15 'The Construction of Masculinity and the Triad of Men's Violence', in Kaufman, op. cit., p. 13.

16 Guirand, op. cit., in *New Larousse Encyclopedia of Mythology*, p. 193.

17 Bob Connell, Tim Corrigan, and John Lee, 'Toward a New Sociology of Masculinity', in Harry Brod (ed.), op. cit., p. 64.
18 Sigmund Freud, *The Ego and the Id* (1923), in Anna Freud (ed.) *The Essentials of Psychoanalysis*, London: Penguin, 1991, p. 455f.
19 Jung, *Symbols of Transformation* (1912–1952), *CW* 5, Chapters 6 and 7.
20 This phrase is from Lyn Segal, *Slow Motion: Changing Masculinities, Changing Men*, London: Virago, 1990, p. 60.
21 Hillman, 'The "Negative" Senex and a Renaissance Solution', p. 83.
22 Susan Faludi, *Backlash: The Undeclared War Against Women*, NY: Crown, 1991.
23 Alfred Collins, *Fatherson: A Self Psychology of the Archetypal*, Wilmette, Ill.: Chiron, 1994, p. 9.
24 Guy Corneau, *Absent Fathers, Lost Sons*, Boston: Shambhala, 1991, p. 9.
25 Gregory Max Vogt, *Like Father, Like Son*, NY: Plenum, 1991; Corneau, op. cit.; John Lee, *At My Father's Wedding*, NY: Bantam, 1991; and Gregory Max Vogt, *Return to Father*, Dallas: Spring Publications, 1991.
26 Corneau, op. cit., p. 10.
27 Ibid., p. 9.
28 Jung, 'The Phenomenology of the Spirit in Fairytales' (1945/1948), *CW* 9, i, para. 414.
29 Alfred Collins, op. cit, p. 12.
30 Andrew Samuels, *Jung and the Post-Jungians*, London: Routledge, 1985, p. 28.
31 Robert Moore and Douglas Gillette, *King, Warrior, Magician, Lover*, San Francisco, Cal.: HarperCollins, 1990.
32 Hillman, 'The "Negative" Senex and a Renaissance Solution', p. 82.
33 James Hillman, 'Oedipus Revisited' (1987), in James Hillman and Karl Kerenyi, *Oedipus Variations: Studies in Literature and Psychoanalysis*, Dallas: Spring Publications, 1991, p. 116.
34 Ibid.
35 Hillman, 'The Great Mother and the Puer', p. 173.
36 Friedrich Nietzsche in *The Joyful Wisdom* (1887), quoted in R. J. Hollingdale (ed.) *Nietzsche: Thus Spoke Zarathustra*, Harmondsworth: Penguin, 1969, p. 14.
37 Andrew Samuels, *The Political Psyche*, London: Routledge, 1993, p. 192.
38 Hillman, 'The Great Mother and the Puer', p. 80.
39 Shakespeare, *Hamlet* (1603), T. J. B. Spencer (ed.) London: Penguin, 1980; Act 1, Scene 4, line 90.
40 Jung, *Aion* (1951), *CW* 9, part 2, para. 301.
41 See Anthony Stevens, 'The Frustration of Archetypal Intent', in *Archetypes: A Natural History of the Self*, London: Routledge & Kegan Paul, 1982.
42 This is the theme of Robert Johnson's book, *Transformation:*

Understanding the Three Levels of Masculine Consciousness, San Francisco, Cal.: HarperCollins, 1991.

43 For Freud on *Hamlet*, see his *The Interpretation of Dreams* (1900), Harmondsworth: Penguin, 1976, p. 366f. Also see Ernest Jones, 'Hamlet and Oedipus' (1949), in John Jump (ed.) *Shakespeare: Hamlet*, Casebook Series, London: Macmillan, 1968.

3 CONTEMPORARY DILEMMAS OF FEMININE MEN

1 Alix Pirani, *The Absent Father: Crisis and Creativity*, London: Arkana, 1989, p. xii.
2 Jung, 'Psychological Aspects of the Mother Archetype' (1939–1954), *CW* 9, i, para. 159.
3 Ibid.
4 Sigmund Freud, *The Ego and the Id* (1923), in Anna Freud (ed.), *The Essentials of Psychoanalysis*, London: Penguin, 1991, p. 455.
5 Jung, *CW* 9, i, para. 159.
6 Jung, *CW* 5, para. 419f.
7 James Hillman, 'The Great Mother, Her Son, Her Hero and the Puer' (1973), in Patricia Berry (ed.), *Fathers and Mothers*, Second Edition, Dallas: Spring Publications, 1990, p. 169.
8 Ibid., p. 170.
9 Ibid., p. 171.
10 Ibid., pp. 171–172.
11 Jung, *CW* 16, para. 181.
12 Jung, 'Marriage as a Psychological Relationship' (1925), *CW* 17, para. 326.
13 Erich Neumann, 'The Two Characters of the Feminine', in *The Great Mother* (1955), Princeton, NJ: Princeton University Press, 1972; and Gareth Hill, *Masculine and Feminine*, Boston: Shambhala, 1992.
14 See Jung, 'The Mother Complex of the Son', in 'Psychological Aspects of the Mother Archetype' (1939–1954), *CW* 9, i, para. 164.
15 Hillman, 'The Great Mother and the Puer', p. 175.
16 Ibid., p. 173.
17 Ibid., pp. 178–179.
18 Marie-Louise von Franz, *Puer Aeternus: A Psychological Study of the Adult Struggle with the Paradise of Childhood* (1970), Second Edition, Santa Monica: Sigo Press, 1981, p. 5.
19 Marie-Louise von Franz, 'Über religiöse Hintergrunde des Puer-Aeternus-Problems', in A. Guggenbuhl-Craig (ed.) *The Archetype*, Basel: Karger, 1964.
20 See David J. Tacey, *Patrick White: Fiction and the Unconscious*, Melbourne: Oxford University Press, 1988.
21 Russell A. Lockhart, *Psyche Speaks*, Wilmette, Ill.: Chiron, 1987, pp. 4–5.
22 Andrew Samuels, 'Introduction', in Samuels (ed.) *The Father*, New York University Press, 1986, p. 3.

23 Robert Bly, *Iron John: A Book About Men*, New York: Addison-Wesley, 1990. In England this text was published in 1991 by Element Books, Shaftesbury, Dorset.
24 Robert Bly, 'What Men Really Want' (interviewed by Keith Thompson), first appeared in *New Age Journal* (May 1982), pp. 30–51. It was reprinted, among other places, in Franklin Abbott (ed.) *New Men, New Minds*, Freedom, Cal.: Crossing Press, 1987, pp. 166–181.
25 David Tacey, 'Attacking Patriarchy, Redeeming Masculinity', *The San Francisco Jung Institute Library Journal*, Vol. 10, No. 1, March 1991, pp. 25–41.
26 Eugene Monick, *Phallos: Sacred Image of the Masculine*, Toronto: Inner City Books, 1987, p. 9.
27 Thompson, in Abbott (ed.) *New Men, New Minds*, p. 167. In this chapter I will quote from the earlier Bly–Thompson interview-essay, rather than from the newer version of the essay in Chapter 1 of *Iron John*, because in the more recent book Thompson has been edited out, and his critical presence in the interview provides a vital counterfoil to Bly's effusive idealisations.
28 Bly, in *New Men, New Minds*, p. 167.
29 Thompson, in *New Men, New Minds*, p. 175.
30 Bly, in *New Men, New Minds*, p. 168.
31 'Iron Hans', in *The Complete Grimm's Fairy Tales*, NY: Pantheon, 1972.
32 Bly, in *New Men, New Minds*, p. 168.
33 Bly, in *New Men, New Minds*, p. 180.
34 Jung, 'Wotan' (1936) and 'After the Catastrophe' (1945), in *CW* 10.
35 Christopher X. Burant, 'Of Wild Men and Warriors', *Changing Men*, No. 19, Spring Summer 1988, p. 7.
36 Barbara Ehrenreich, in R. Todd Erkel, 'The Birth of a Movement', *The Family Therapy Networker*, May/June 1990, p. 32.
37 Robert Bly, in a letter to David Tacey, 3 June 1991.
38 Bly to Tacey, 19 August 1991.
39 See H. W. Koch, *The Hitler Youth*, London: Macdonald and Jane's, 1975.
40 These prerequisites for fascism accord with Theodore Adorno's observations in his *The Authoritarian Personality*, NY: John Wiley, 1964.
41 Bly to Tacey, 19 August 1991.
42 Hillman, 'The Great Mother and the Puer', p. 193.
43 Ibid. p. 170.
44 Robert Bly, *The Sibling Society*, NY: Addison-Wesley, 1996.
45 Ibid., p. 185.
46 Ibid., p. 232.
47 Christopher Lasch, *The Culture of Narcissism*, NY: Norton, 1978; Robert Hughes, *Culture of Complaint*, NY: Oxford University Press, 1993.
48 Hillmann, 'The Great Mother and the Puer', p. 170.
49 James Hillman, 'The Feeling Function', in Marie-Louise von Franz

and James Hillman, *Lectures on Jung's Typology* (1971), Zurich: Spring Publications, 1975, p. 116.

50 In the fairytale that so interests Bly, Iron John literally hoists the king's son upon his shoulders and carries him away.

51 Hillman, *Lectures on Jung's Typology*, p. 116.

52 Jung, *Symbols of Transformation* (1912), *CW* 5, para. 553.

53 Hillman, 'The Great Mother and the Puer', pp. 169 and 194.

54 Alix Pirani, *The Absent Father: Crisis and Creativity*, p. xii.

55 Hillman, 'The Great Mother and the Puer', p. 183.

56 Ibid., p. 172.

4 RITES AND WRONGS OF PASSAGE

1 Jung, 'Woman in Europe' (1927), *CW* 10, para. 269.

2 Joseph Henderson, *Thresholds of Initiation*, Middletown, Conn.: Wesleyan University Press, 1967. See also Joseph Henderson, 'Ancient Myths and Modern Man', in C. G. Jung (ed.) *Man and His Symbols*, NY: Doubleday, 1964, pp. 105–157.

3 Jean La Fontaine, *Initiation*, Manchester: Manchester University Press, 1986.

4 Sigmund Freud, *The Ego and the Id* (1923), in Anna Freud (ed.), *The Essentials of Psychoanalysis*, London: Penguin., 1991, p. 455.

5 Ray Raphael, *The Men From the Boys: Rites of Passage in Male America*, Lincoln: University of Nebraska Press, 1988, p. x.

6 See Mircea Eliade, *Rites and Symbols of Initiation: The Mysteries of Birth and Rebirth* (1956), NY: Harper & Row, 1975.

7 See Joanne Greenberg, *Rites of Passage*, NY: Holt, Rinehart, and Winston, 1972.

8 Bruno Bettelheim makes this same point, but gives it a reductively Freudian reading, in his work *Symbolic Wounds: Puberty Rites and the Envious Male*, Glencoe, Ill.: Free Press, 1954.

9 Howard R., quoted in Raphael, op. cit., p. xi.

10 See Robert Bly, *Iron John: A Book About Men*, New York: Addison-Wesley, 1990.

11 See David Tacey, *Edge of the Sacred: Transformation in Australia*, Melbourne: HarperCollins, 1995.

12 Margaret Mead, 'Adolescence in Primitive and in Modern Society', in E. E. Maccoby *et al.* (eds) *Readings in Social Psychology*, NY: Holt & Company, 1958, p. 349.

13 Jung, 'The Psychology of the Child Archetype' (1940), *CW* 9, i, para. 271.

14 Andrew Samuels, *The Political Psyche*, London: Routledge, 1993, p. 191.

15 Mircea Eliade, *Myths, Dreams and Mysteries: The Encounter Between Contemporary Faiths and Archaic Realities* (1957), London: Harvill Press, 1960, p. 25.

16 Mircea Eliade, 'Initiation and the Modern World', in *The Quest:*

History and Meaning in Religion (1969), Chicago: University of Chicago Press, 1975, p. 113.

17 James Hillman, 'The Great Mother, Her Son, Her Hero, and the Puer' (1973), in Patricia Berry (ed.), *Fathers and Mothers*, Second Edition, Dallas: Spring Publications, 1990, p. 173.

18 Jung, 'The Psychology of the Transference' (1946), *CW* 16, para. 396.

19 Richard Eckersley, 'Values and Visions: Youth and the Failure of Modern Western Culture', in *Youth Studies Australia*, Autumn 1995, p. 18. See also M. Rutter, C. E. Izard, and P. B. Read (eds) *Depression in Young People: Developmental and Clinical Perspectives*, NY: Guilford, 1986, pp. 3–30.

20 Arnold van Gennep, *The Rites of Passage* (1908), Chicago: University of Chicago Press, 1960.

21 Greenberg, op. cit.

22 See Luigi Zoja, *Drugs, Addiction and Initiation: The Modern Search for Ritual*, Boston: Sigo Press, 1989.

23 Luigi Zoja, 'Archetypal Fantasies Underlying Drug Addiction', in ibid.

24 Joseph Henderson, 'The Archetype of Initiation', in 'Ancient Myths and Modern Man', in C. G. Jung (ed.) *Man and His Symbols*, NY: Doubleday, 1964, pp. 130–131.

25 Van Gennep, op. cit.

26 Bill Gammage, *The Broken Years: Australian Soldiers in the Great War*, Harmondsworth: Penguin, 1975.

27 James Hillman, 'Mars, Arms, Rams, Wars: On the Love of War', in V. Andrews, R. Bosnak, and K. W. Goodwin (eds) *Facing Apocalypse*, Dallas, Tex.: Spring Publications, 1987, pp. 118–136.

28 See Laura Palmer, *Shrapnel in the Heart*, NY: Random House, 1987; Josefina J. Card, *Lives After Vietnam*, Lexington, Mass.: Lexington Books, 1983. A Jungian approach to this subject can be found in James F. Veninga and Harry A. Wilmer (eds) *Vietnam in Remission*, College Station, Tex.: Texas A & M University Press, 1985.

29 See Paul T. Menzel (ed.) *Moral Argument and the War in Vietnam*, Nashville, Tex.: Aurora, 1971; and Arnold R. Isaacs, *Without Honor: Defeat in Vietnam and Cambodia*, Baltimore, Md: Johns Hopkins University Press, 1983.

30 For the American equivalent to this Australian experience, see Jan C. Scruggs and Joel L. Swerdlow (eds) *To Heal a Nation: The Vietnam Veterans Memorial*, NY: Harper and Row, 1985.

31 Steve Dow, 'Long Hours Make Doctors Work as if Drunk', *The Age* (Melbourne), 19 November 1994, p. 3.

32 Andrew Fuller, 'Risk-taking as a Healing Process', in Ian Gawler (ed.) *The Mind–Body Connection*, Melbourne: Gawler Foundation, 1996, pp. 45–54.

33 Tracey Moffit, 'Adolescence Limited and Life Course Persistent Antisocial Behaviour: A Developmental Taxonomy', *Psychological Review* (New Zealand), 1993, Issue 100, pp. 674–701.

34 T. M. Achenbach and C. T. Howell, 'Are American Children's

Problems Getting Worse? A Thirteen-year Comparison', in *Journal of the American Academy of Child and Adolescent Psychiatry*, 1993, No. 32, pp. 1145–1154.

35 Eckersley, op. cit., p. 18.
36 Solon T. Kimball, in his introduction to van Gennep, op. cit., p. xvii.
37 Marie-Louise von Franz, quoted in L. Mahdi, S. Foster, and M. Little (eds) *Betwixt and Between: Patterns of Masculine and Feminine Initiation*, La Salle, Ill.: Open Court, 1987, p. ix.
38 Kimball, op. cit.

5 HOMOEROTIC DESIRE AND THE FATHERING SPIRIT

1 James Hillman, 'Loving', *Inter Views*, NY: Harper & Row, 1983, p. 185.
2 Christine Downing, *Myths and Mysteries of Same-Sex Love*, New York: Continuum, 1989, pp. 31–32.
3 Robert H. Hopcke, *Jung, Jungians, and Homosexuality*, Boston: Shambhala. 1989, p. 25.
4 Hillman, op. cit., p. 185.
5 Reuben Fine, *The Forgotten Man: Understanding the Male Psyche*, NY and London: The Haworth Press, 1987, p. 55.
6 Ibid.
7 Ibid.
8 Sigmund Freud, *The Standard Edition of the Complete Psychological Works*, Vol. 20, London: Hogarth Press, 1959, p. 38.
9 Freud, *Standard Edition*, Vol. 7, London: Hogarth Press, 1953, p. 145n.
10 See Christine Downing, 'The Universality of Homosexual Desire', in Downing, op. cit., pp. 37–41.
11 Downing, op. cit., p. 49.
12 See Christine Downing, 'Freud: The Classic Cases', in Downing, op. cit., pp. 51–67.
13 See David J. Tacey, 'The Politics of Analysis: Psychology, Literary Culture and Australian Innocence', in *Meanjin* (Melbourne), Vol. 49, No. 1, Autumn 1990, pp. 123–133.
14 Freud, quoted in Downing, op. cit., p. 44.
15 See the stories of Lawson, in Colin Roderick (ed.) *Henry Lawson: Short Stories and Sketches 1888–1922*, Sydney: Angus & Robertson, 1972.
16 Humphrey McQueen, *A New Britannia*, Second Edition, Melbourne: Penguin Books, 1986.
17 Miriam Dixson, *The Real Matilda*, Melbourne: Penguin Books, 1984; and Kay Schaffer, *Women and the Bush*, Cambridge: Cambridge University Press.
18 Graeme Turner, *National Fictions*, Sydney: Allen & Unwin, 1981.
19 Freud, quoted in Downing, op. cit., p. 49.
20 For a journalistic discussion of these legal issues, see 'Bigoted One

Day, Prejudiced the Next', in *HQ Magazine* (Sydney), No. 12, November 1990, pp. 46–51.

21 In my use of the term 'phallos', I am indebted to Eugene Monick, *Phallos*, Toronto: Inner City Books, 1989.

22 Gilbert H. Herdt (ed.) *Ritualized Homosexuality in Melanesia*, Berkeley, Cal.: University of California Press, 1984.

23 For instance, Kinsey found in his mid-century report into male sexual behaviour that a great many males (far more than had been thought) had had homosexual encounters during adolescence; see A. Kinsey *et al.*, *Sexual Behavior in the Human Male*, Philadelphia, Penn.: Saunders, 1948.

24 See Gilbert H. Herdt, *Guardians of the Flutes: Idioms of Masculinity*, NY: McGraw-Hill, 1989.

25 Bruno Bettelheim, *Symbolic Wounds: Puberty Rites and the Envious Male*, Glencoe, Ill.: Free Press, 1954, p. 109f

26 Mircea Eliade, *Rites and Symbols of Initiation: The Mysteries of Birth and Rebirth* (1956), NY: Harper, 1975, p. 3.

27 Camille Paglia, 'Homosexuality at the Fin De Siècle', in *Sex, Art, and American Culture*, London and NY: Viking, 1992, p. 24.

28 Hillman, op. cit., p. 185.

29 Adolf Guggenbuhl-Craig, 'The Destructive Fear of Homosexuality', in *Power in the Helping Professions*, Dallas, Tex.: Spring Publications, 1971, p. 70.

30 Ibid., pp. 70–71.

31 Robert Stein, *Incest and Human Love*, Baltimore, Md.: Penguin, 1974.

32 This is the view of Joseph Henderson, who claims that the desire for intrapsychic union is rarely achieved in active homosexuality. See his *Thresholds of Initiation*, Middletown, Conn.: Wesleyan University Press, 1967, p. 45.

33 Jung, 'On the Psychology of the Unconscious' (1917–1943), *CW* 7, para. 173.

34 Eugene Monick, op. cit., p. 114.

35 Victor Turner, 'Betwixt and Between', in L. Mahdi, S. Foster, and M. Little, *Betwixt and Between, Patterns of Masculine and Feminine Initiation*, La Salle, Ill.: Open Court, 1987.

6 STRUGGLING WITH THE INTERNAL TYRANT

1 James Hillman, 'The "Negative" Senex and a Renaissance Solution', *Spring 1975* (New York), p. 82.

2 Edward F. Edinger, *Ego and Archetype* (1972), Baltimore, Md: Penguin, 1974, p. 132.

3 Erich Neumann, *The Origins and History of Consciousness* (1949), Princeton, NJ: Princeton University Press, 1973, p. 186.

4 Ibid., p. 187.

5 From the Grail Legend according to Chretien de Troyes, quoted in Robert Johnson, *He: Understanding Masculine Psychology* (1974), NY: Harper & Row, 1977, pp. 80–81.

6 See Jung, 'The Phenomenology of the Spirit in Fairytales' (1946–1948), *CW* 9, i, para. 454.

7 Christopher Harding (ed.) *Wingspan: Inside the Men's Movement*, NY: St Martin's Press, 1992.

8 Hillman, op. cit., p. 81.

9 'The Slaying of the Father', in Neumann, op. cit., p. 186.

10 Ibid., p. 187.

11 Murray Stein, 'The Devouring Father', in Patricia Berry (ed.) *Fathers and Mothers*, First Edition, Zurich: Spring Publications, 1973, p. 64.

12 Augusto Vitale, 'The Archetype of Saturn or the Transformation of the Father' (1973), in Patricia Berry (ed.) *Fathers and Mothers*, Second Edition, Dallas, Tex.: Spring Publications, 1990, p. 55.

13 Hillman, op. cit., p. 78.

14 In his 1991 Preface to *Re-Visioning Psychology*, Hillman refers to his unfinished work on the psychology of the *puer aeternus* as 'a prolonged and still incomplete defense of my traits and behaviors', *Re-Visioning Psychology* (1975), NY: Harper Perennial, 1992, p. xiii.

15 Hillman, 'The "Negative" Senex and a Renaissance Solution', p. 78.

16 Hillman, 'Fathers and Sons', in Keith Thompson (ed.) *Views from the Male World*, London: Aquarian/Thorsons, 1992, p. 201.

17 Alfred Collins, *Fatherson, A Self Psychology of the Archetypal*, Wilmette, Ill.: Chiron, 1994, p. 14.

18 *Hook*, 1991; a Columbia Tristar Movie, directed and produced by Steven Spielberg.

19 Dan Kiley, *The Peter Pan Syndrome: Men Who Have Never Grown Up*, London: Corgi/Transworld Publishers, 1983, p. 6.

20 Marie-Louise von Franz, *Puer Aeternus: A Psychological Study of the Adult Struggle with the Paradise of Childhood* (1970), Second Edition, Santa Monica, Cal.: Sigo Press, 1981.

21 Robert M. Pirsig, *Zen and the Art of Motorcycle Maintenance* (1974), London: Corgi Books, 1976. I am indebted to Alfred Collins for his study of this text in his *Fatherson*, p. 14f.

22 Hillman, 'The "Negative" Senex and a Renaissance Solution', p. 92.

23 Robert Bly, *The Sibling Society*, NY: Addison-Wesley, 1996.

7 UNPROFESSIONAL WORK: EMBRACING THE ANIMA

1 Tom Absher, *Men and the Goddess*, Rochester, VT.: Park Street Press, 1990, p. 143.

2 Jung, 'Archetypes of the Collective Unconscious' (1935–1954), *CW* 9, i, para. 61.

3 Jung, 'On the Psychology of the Trickster-Figure' (1954), *CW* 9, i, para. 485.

4 Erich Neumann, *The Origins and History of Consciousness* (1949), Princeton, NJ: Princeton University Press, 1973, p. 39f.

5 Robert Johnson, 'The Mother Mixed with Other Feminine Forms', in *Lying with the Heavenly Woman*, San Francisco, Cal.: HarperCollins, 1994, p. 76.

6 Jung, 'Concerning the Archetypes, with Special Reference to the Anima Concept' (1936–1954), *CW* 9, i, para. 146.

7 Jung, 'Psychology and Religion' (1938–1940), *CW* 11, para. 129.

8 David J. Tacey, *Patrick White: Fiction and the Unconscious*, Melbourne: Oxford University Press, 1988.

9 See Chapter 5, 'The Tightening Knot', in ibid., pp. 121–148.

10 The best introductory text on the anima, which includes hundreds of quotations from Jung's writings, is James Hillman *Anima: An Anatomy of a Personified Notion*, Dallas, Tex.: Spring Publications, 1985.

11 Goethe, the last line of *Faust, Part II* (1831), in *Goethe's Faust*, trans. Charles E. Passage, NY: Bobbs-Merrill, 1965, p. 413.

12 David J. Tacey, *Edge of the Sacred: Transformation in Australia*, Melbourne: HarperCollins, 1995.

13 Hillman, op. cit., p. 3.

14 James McAuley, 'An Art of Poetry' (1954), in Leonie Kramer (ed.), *James McAuley*, Brisbane: University of Queensland Press, 1988, p. 151.

15 James Hillman, 'Peaks and Values', in Hillman (ed.) *Puer Papers*, Dallas, Tex.: Spring Publications, 1979, pp. 54–76.

16 Hillman, *Anima*, p. 25.

17 Jung, 'On the Nature of the Psyche' (1947–1954), *CW* 8, para. 430.

18 Jung, 'On the Psychology of the Trickster-Figure' (1954), *CW* 9, i, para. 485.

19 Jung, 'Psychological Aspects of the Mother Archetype' (1938–1954), *CW* 9, i, para. 162.

20 This continues the discussion of the Spielberg movie *Hook* (1991), which was started in Chapter 6.

21 Jung, 'Commentary on *The Secret of the Golden Flower*' (1929), *CW* 13, para. 54.

22 Matthew Fox, *Creation Spirituality*, San Francisco, Cal.: Harper-Collins, 1991.

23 Jung, *CW* 10, para. 715.

24 Hillman, *Anima*, p. 133.

25 Michael Leunig, in Leunig and Garner, 'A Kind of Reality', *Art Monthly Australia*, No. 56, December–February 1992–1993, p. 4.

8 CONCLUSION

1 Jung, 'The Undiscovered Self (Present and Future)' (1957), *CW* 10, para. 585.

2 Alfred Collins, *Fatherson, A Self Psychology of the Archetypal*, Wilmette, Ill.: Chiron, 1994, p. 12.

3 James Hillman, *The Myth of Analysis* (1972), NY: Harper & Row, 1978, p. 292.

4 Robert Bly, quoted on the cover of James Hillman, *Re-Visioning Psychology* (1975), NY: HarperCollins, 1992.

5 R.W. Connell, *Masculinities*, Berkeley, Cal.: University of California Press, 1995; and Sydney, Allen & Unwin, 1995, p. 79.

6 Michael Kaufman (ed.), *Beyond Patriarchy*, Toronto: Oxford University Press, 1987, p. 13.

7 See A. Hamblin, 'What can one do with a son?' in S. Friedman and E. Sarah (eds) *On the Problem of Men*, London: The Women's Press, 1984, p. 237.

8 Kenneth Clatterbaugh, *Contemporary Perspectives on Masculinity*, Boulder, Col.: Westview Press, 1990, p. 38.

9 Shakespeare, *Hamlet*, Act I, Scene V.

10 Cleanthes, quoted in Jung, 'The Significance of the Father in the Destiny of the Individual' (1909–1949), *CW* 4, para. 693.

11 Jung, 'The Relations between the Ego and the Unconscious' (1928), *CW* 7, para. 309.

12 Gloria Steinem, quoted in Barbara Erenreich, *The Hearts of Men*, New York: Pluto Press, 1983, p. 99.

13 Yeats, 'The Circus Animals' Desertion', in T. Webb (ed.) *W. B. Yeats, Selected Poetry*, London: Penguin, 1991, p. 224.

14 Jung, 'Mind and Earth' (1927–1931), *CW* 10, para. 79.

15 See Anthony Stevens, 'On the Frustration of Archetypal Intent', in *Archetypes: A Natural History of the Self*, London: Routledge & Kegan Paul, 1982, p. 110f.

16 Alfred Adler, *The Individual Psychology of Alfred Adler*, NY: Basic Books, 1964.

17 Wolfgang Lederer, *The Fear of Women*, NY: Harcourt Brace Jovanovich, 1970.

18 Collins, op. cit., p. 13.

INDEX